IMAGES
of America
# CLEBURNE

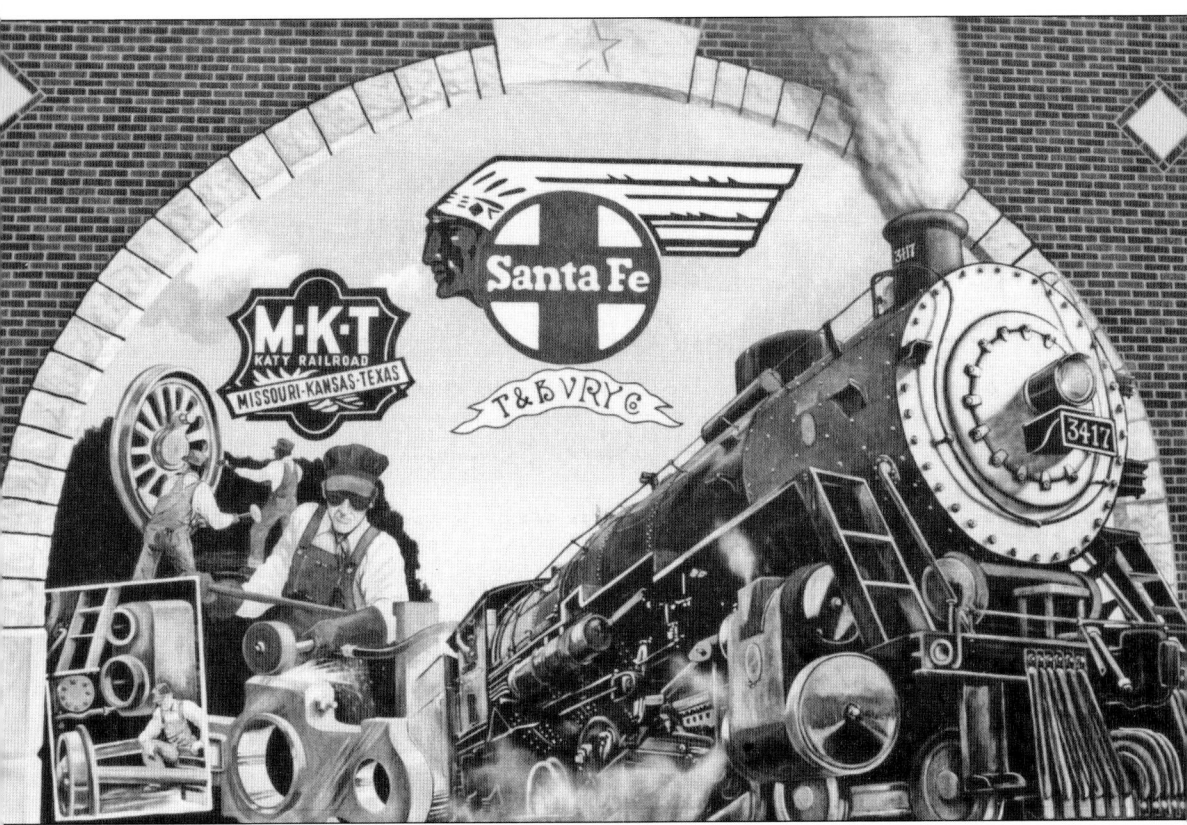

This is a section of the mural facing the Wright building two blocks south of the Johnson County Courthouse. Commissioned by Howard Dudley and painted by Stylle Read, it depicts an important part of Cleburne history, the railroads. Santa Fe Railway arrived in 1881, bringing jobs, money, and families to town for generations. (Courtesy of the author.)

ON THE COVER: This 1934 photograph of the Johnson County Cooperative Gin offers an insight into just how important the cash crop of cotton was. When cotton was king, Cleburne had three gins and a compress. Cotton production increased from 1,212 bales in 1870 to 18,826 bales in 1890. Over 50,000 bales were ginned in 1924. (Courtesy of Dewey C. James.)

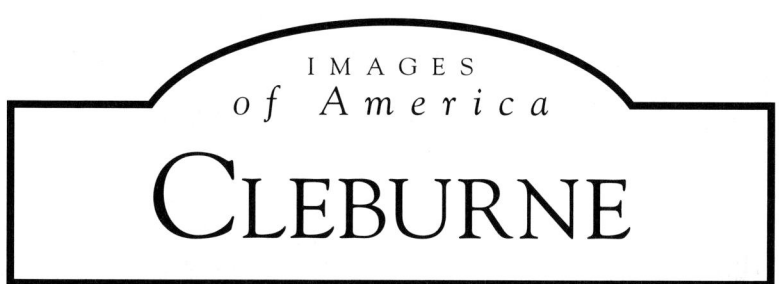

# IMAGES of America
# CLEBURNE

Mollie Gallop Bradbury Mims

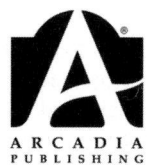

Copyright © 2009 by Mollie Gallop Bradbury Mims
ISBN 978-0-7385-7119-5

Published by Arcadia Publishing
Charleston SC, Chicago IL, Portsmouth NH, San Francisco CA

Printed in the United States of America

Library of Congress Control Number: 2009922899

For all general information contact Arcadia Publishing at:
Telephone 843-853-2070
Fax 843-853-0044
E-mail sales@arcadiapublishing.com
For customer service and orders:
Toll-Free 1-888-313-2665

Visit us on the Internet at www.arcadiapublishing.com

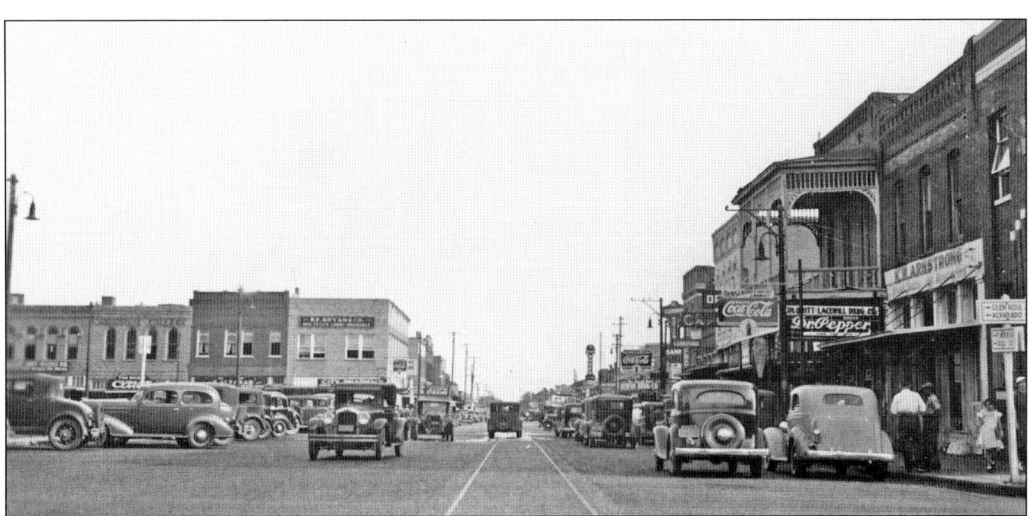

This 1920s photograph was taken looking south on Main Street from the Henderson Street crossing at the northwest corner of the Johnson County Courthouse. Double parked cars and two-way traffic around the courthouse kept the streets busy. (Courtesy of Tommy Altaras.)

# CONTENTS

| | | |
|---|---|---|
| Acknowledgments | | 6 |
| Introduction | | 7 |
| 1. | 1867–1900 | 9 |
| 2. | 1901–1925 | 27 |
| 3. | 1926–1950 | 57 |
| 4. | 1951–1975 | 79 |
| 5. | 1976–2000 | 101 |
| 6. | 2001–2009 | 113 |

# ACKNOWLEDGMENTS

Packed in boxes, glued to the pages of scrapbooks, stored under beds or in closets, and hanging on walls—these are just a few of the places that historic photographs were uncovered and are now printed in the pages of this book.

The majority of images are courtesy of the City of Cleburne's Layland Museum. Over the decades, individuals have donated historic, family, and business photographs to the museum. Now those printed memories are protected and preserved so our history can be researched and shared. The largest photographic collection came to the museum as negatives from the *Cleburne Times-Review*. Without those donations, much of this book would not have been possible.

*Images of America: Cleburne* tells stories of our community using photographs and captions. Several of these images have never been published. Thanks goes to those people who allowed me to scan images from their private collections and to the many people who checked facts and shared stories. A special thanks goes to Sandra Davis Jones, Bob Force, Gary Shaw, Stamm Todd, the *Cleburne Times-Review* staff, and to Jack Carlton for suggesting I write this book.

Members of the Layland Museum staff were encouraging and supportive during each phase of the project. Staff members are Julie Baker, director; Ben Hammons, curator of collections; Bettye Cook, Ed.D., educator; and Dianne Kidd, administrative assistant. Thanks for your preservation efforts and assistance in making this book possible.

Without guidance from Arcadia Publishing and my editor, Kristie Kelly, this project would not have happened.

And to Larry, my husband, thanks for sharing the ups and downs in the process of putting this book together.

To learn more about the history of Cleburne and Johnson County, contact:
Layland Museum
201 North Caddo Street
Cleburne, Texas 76031
817-645-0940
museum@cleburne.net
www.cleburne.net

For local tourist and convention information, contact:
Cleburne Chamber of Commerce
Convention and Visitors Bureau
1511 West Henderson Street
P. O. Box 701
Cleburne, Texas 76033
817-645-2455
info@cleburnechamber.com
www.cleburnechamber.com

# INTRODUCTION

Photographs that represent the highlights of Cleburne's history from its beginning until early 2009 are within these pages. Many photographs were left out of this publication because of space. Other stories were not told because a photograph could not be found. It is not a complete history.

The chapters are arranged by years, focusing on the events and the lifestyle of the residents during those times. It is not a family history book but a book about a community of families. Events of the past will not repeat themselves, but their relevance to our future is undeniable.

The purpose of this introduction is to acquaint the reader with how the county was formed and to give a glimpse into the years before it became Cleburne, Texas, in 1867. Photographs and descriptions in the book include little-known facts or almost-forgotten vignettes that make up our history. Some were major events, while others show the quality of life and the activities available during the decades.

Johnson County was marked off in 1854 from Ellis, Navarro, and Hill Counties. Its population was then 700. The county was named for Middleton T. Johnson, who had served in the Mexican-American War and would later serve in the Civil War.

The first county seat was Wardville, named for Thomas William Ward, the second commissioner of the General Land Office of Texas and a hero of the Texas Revolution. Wardville was located on the West bank of the Nolan River, about 2 miles west of Cleburne. The first courthouse, built by William O'Neal, was a 14-foot-square log structure with one door and a dirt floor.

In 1856, Buchanan was named the county seat because it was found that Wardville had violated the Texas constitutional requirement that a county seat be within 5 miles of the center of the county. The town was named after the recently elected president of the United States, James Buchanan, and was located 5 miles northwest of Cleburne. In 1860, a wooden courthouse was constructed for $500. There were also a school, a jail, a tavern, and several businesses in the town. By this time, the county population had grown to over 4,000.

The western portion of the county was taken away about 1866 to form Hood County, so Buchanan was no longer in the geographical center of the county. The area located near the fresh running springs locally known as Camp Henderson was chosen for the next and final county seat. The land was owned by Nat Henderson and had been used as a rendezvous and campground for the county's Civil War volunteers.

In May 1867, the courthouse, jail, and other buildings were moved from Buchanan to Cleburne. The courthouse was placed on the east side of the square, where the corner of Chambers Street and Caddo Street are today. It was a one-room building with seats in a semicircle and had a raised platform in the center.

A few weeks later, a contract was submitted to fence the public square, then covered in huge oak trees. Lots around the square were selling for $500.

On July 4, 1867, during a picnic, there was a suggestion to give the county seat a more appropriate name. Those who loved and had served with Maj. Gen. Patrick R. Cleburne in the Confederate army and others in attendance that day voted unanimously to change the name from Camp Henderson to Cleburne. In 1881, a section of Ellis County was added to Johnson County, thus completing its current boundaries.

By April 1869, a two-story brick courthouse was completed in the square, but it was deemed inadequate and the court ordered it torn down. The following two courthouses built in Cleburne are pictured and described within the pages of this book.

Open land and natural resources made it easy for the early settlers to choose this Johnson County area. The constant flowing springs of Buffalo Creek lured Native Americans and herds of buffalo before permanent settlers came for the same reason. Although there are no recorded permanent native settlements here, there were tribes who hunted and moved through this area. The springs were also an early-day watering spot for explorers, Confederate soldiers, and settlers. People came many miles to wash, haul needed water, and visit with others. It was an early social gathering place.

Images of early decades show just how rustic it began, with a town full of cowboys, cattle, and saloons. The town square traces its beginning to 1854, when the first house, a log cabin, was built near the constant flowing water. In 1860, livestock was the primary industry, and Indian corn was the largest crop in the area. Buffalo, deer, antelope, wild turkeys, wolves, prairie chickens, quail, and wild horses roamed the prairies.

By the time Cleburne was the official town name, a few settlers had built cabins and opened businesses that catered to Chisholm Trail cowboys and other travelers. Few quality photographs of that era exist.

For many decades, cattle and cotton and crops of various kinds provided jobs and lifestyles. Then Cleburne became nationally known for its progressive Santa Fe Railroad repair and construction shop. Recent growth is attributed to the exploration of the Barnett Shale gas field and the many industries that call Cleburne home.

With growth comes change and challenges. As 2009 unfolded, there were many changes taking place in our town. We even experienced a few minor earthquakes. Cleburne is no longer a rural community. We are diversified in our religions, our professions, and our cultural offerings, but we continue to strive to make this a hometown that is proud to share the past and determined to mold the future in a positive direction.

This book is a tribute to the early settlers who were daring enough to settle in a new area, open businesses, and raise their families on the frontier and to the present-day citizens, who still have the dream to build, mold, and leave their mark in history.

So reader, sit back and enjoy the ride through the pages of Cleburne's history from the eyes of photographers past. As the conductor standing beside the Santa Fe train would holler, "All Aboard!"

# One
# 1867–1900

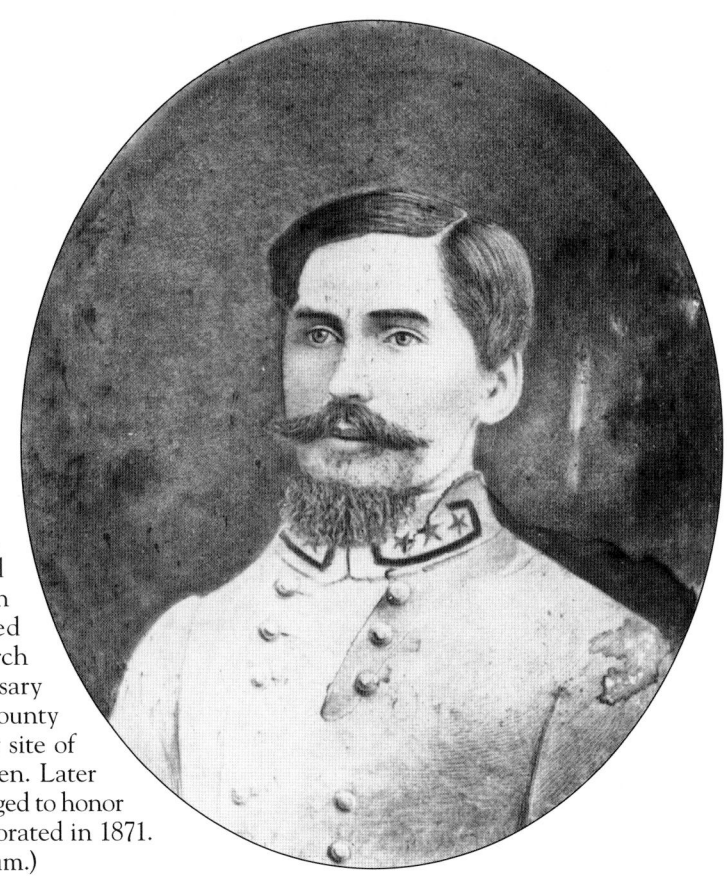

Prior to serving in the Civil War, Maj. Gen. Patrick R. Cleburne was a druggist and attorney. Many local men served with this respected leader from Ireland. In March 1867, when it became necessary to select a centrally located county seat, the Civil War military site of Camp Henderson was chosen. Later that year, the name was changed to honor Cleburne. The town incorporated in 1871. (Courtesy of Layland Museum.)

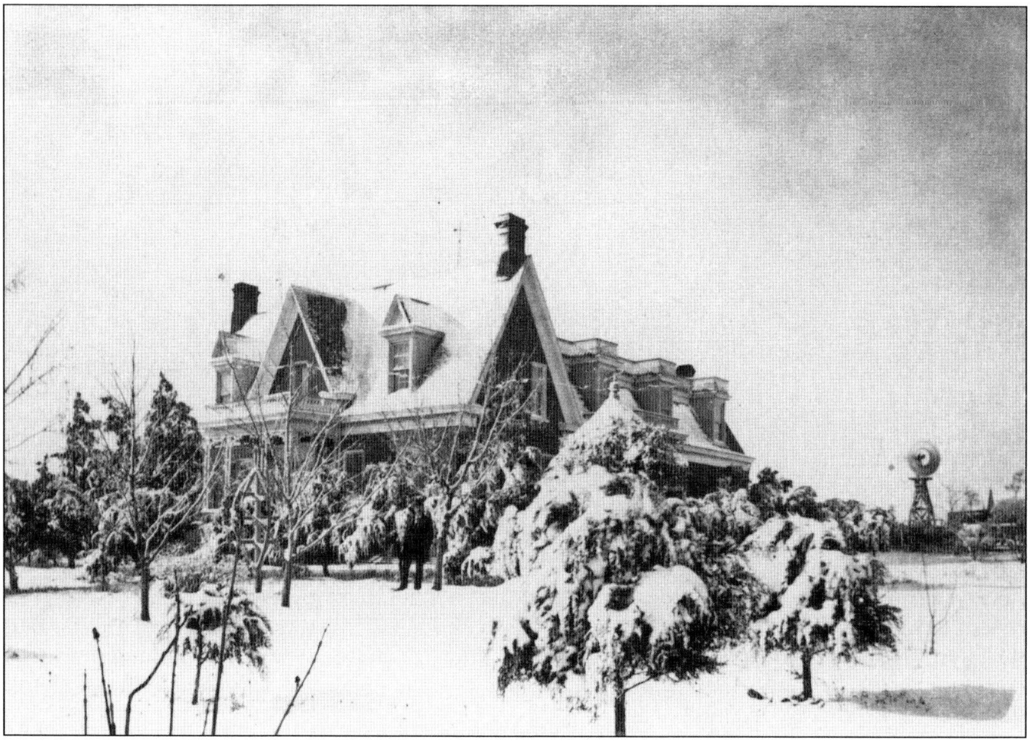

Col. Barzialli Jefferson Chambers was chief surveyor of the Robertson Land district, which included Johnson County. He negotiated the move of the county seat to Camp Henderson after he and Col. W. F. Henderson gave 100 acres to the county. Chambers also gave land for educational and religious purposes and was the 1880 Greenback vice-presidential nominee. The first windmill in the area was on his property near Featherstone Street and Prairie Street. (Courtesy of Layland Museum.)

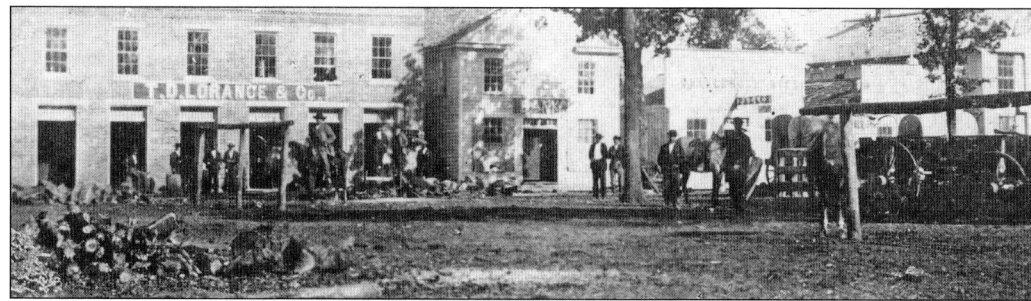
Early Cleburne businesses centered around the square and near Buffalo Creek. A bank, a drugstore, saloons, and general dry good stores provided supplies for early settlers. The wagon yards, a meeting place to buy, sell, trade, or catch up on the latest news, was about a block west of the square. Farmers and travelers could get feed and water for their team and crude overnight accommodations for themselves. (Courtesy of Layland Museum.)

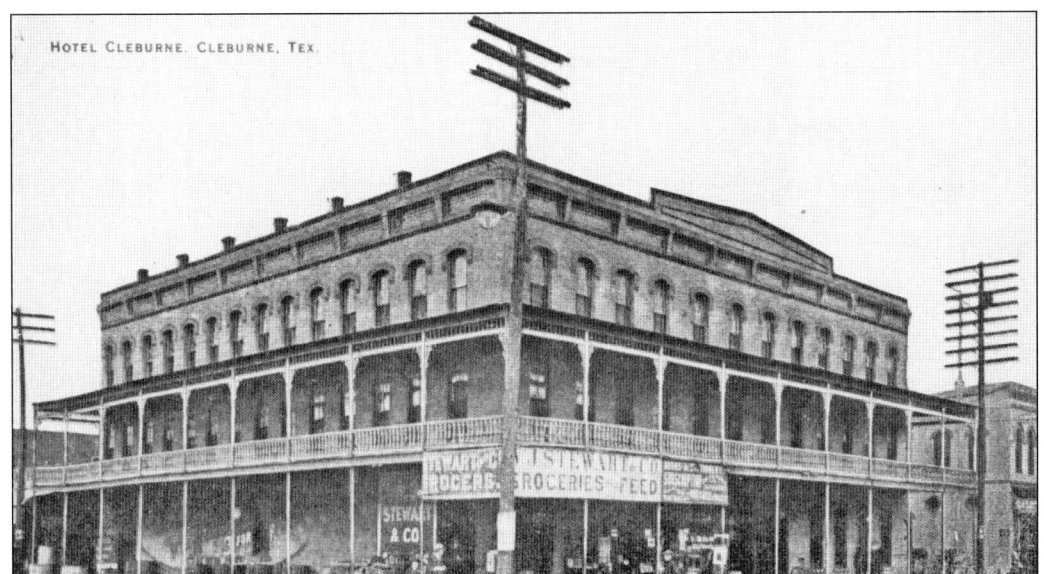

Josephine Wren had the first boardinghouse, called the Cleburne House, on the northwest corner of Main and Henderson Streets. It was a log cabin used for a tavern where no whiskey was sold. By 1906, different owners had enlarged it to three stories with 50 rooms, a restaurant, and a grand lobby. The rate was $2 per day. Today the Cleburne Eye Clinic conducts business there. (Courtesy of Layland Museum.)

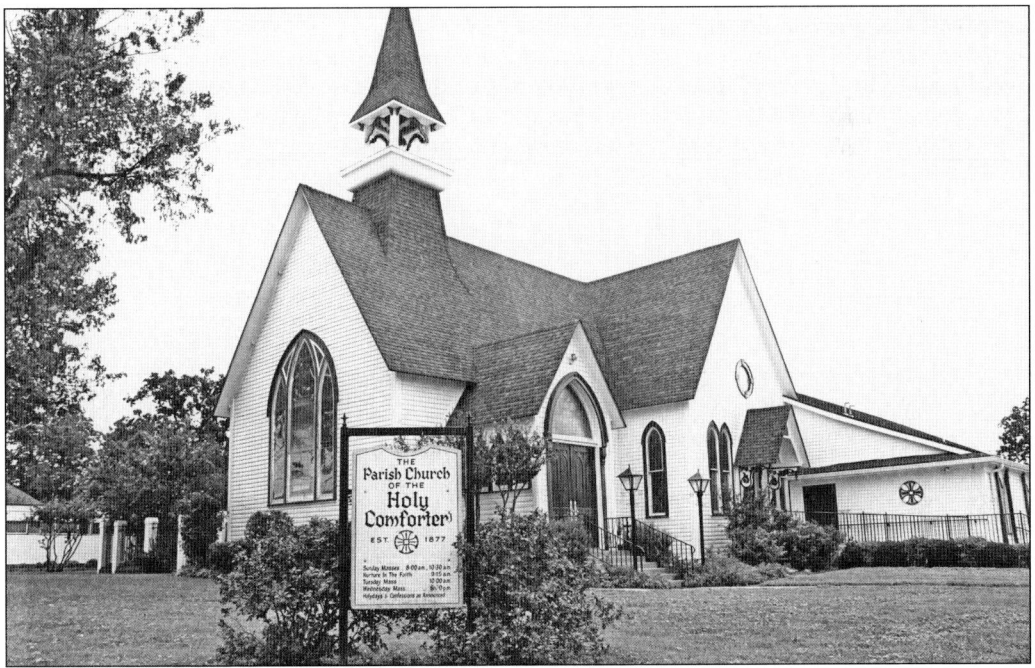

Episcopalians had formed a parish by 1871 and built a small structure where city hall is today. The Church of the Holy Comforter, now at 209 East Wardville Street, was completed in 1893 during the ministry of the Reverend W. W. Patrick. The nave has been in continuous use and is preserved in its original state. The parish hall was added in 1905 and was remodeled in 1985 (Courtesy of the author.)

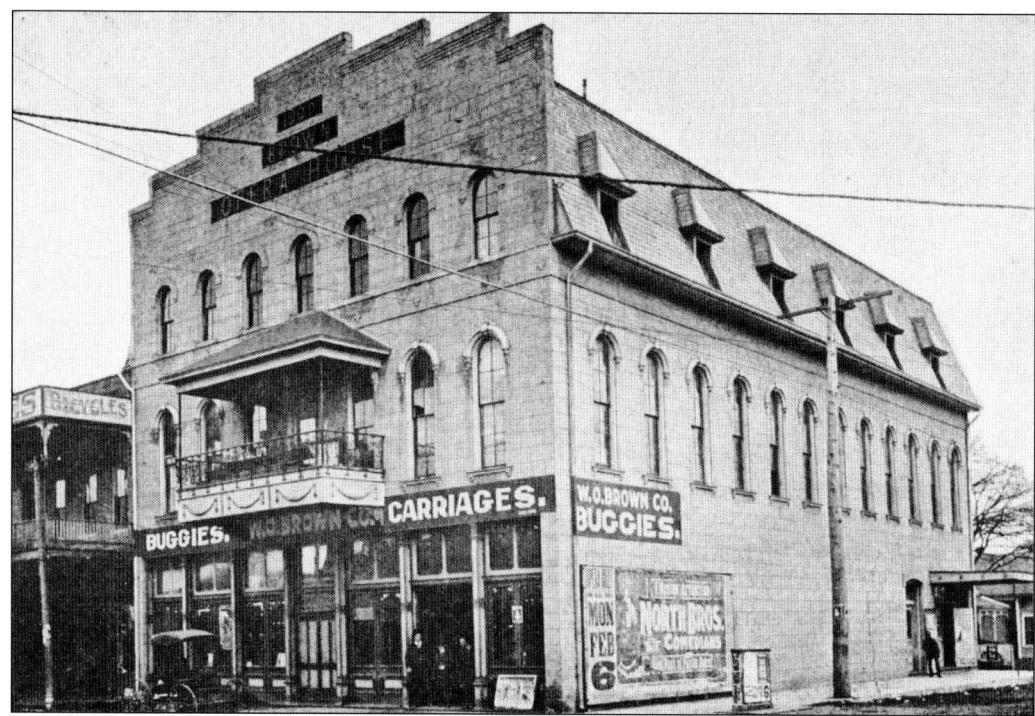

John C. Brown's Opera House, built in 1877, was an impressive, three-story building at the corner of East Chambers and South Anglin Streets. Downstairs was Brown's buggy and carriage business. Upstairs was an auditorium with a stage where productions included live plays and musical performances until it closed in 1911. Friday was Society Night, when well-dressed patrons arrived in carriages for an evening of high-class entertainment. (Courtesy of Layland Museum.)

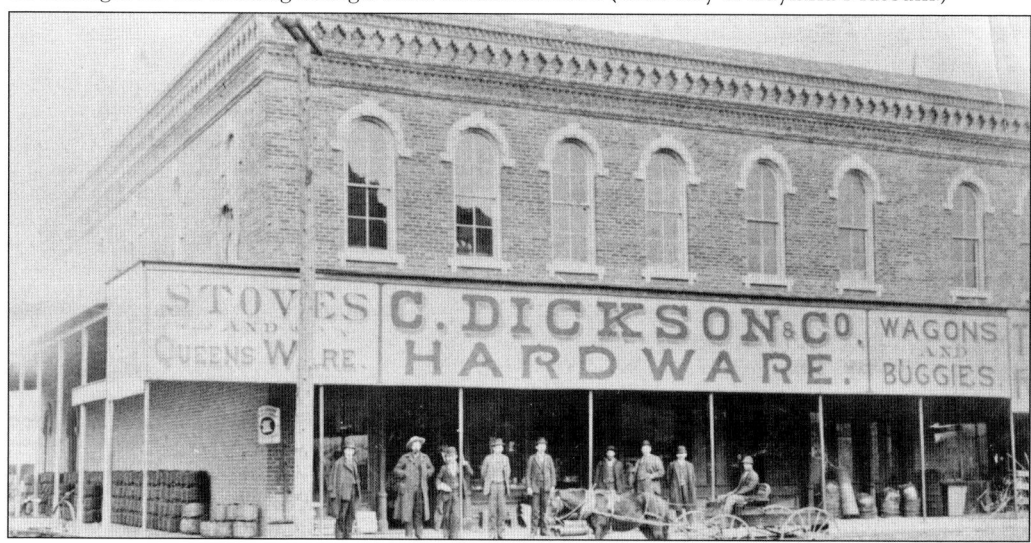

Campbell Dickson took ownership of a hardware store on the corner of Chambers Street and Main Street in 1878 and changed the name to C. Dickson Hardware. The Chambers Hotel was on the second floor. He expanded to the corner of Anglin and East Henderson Streets in 1882, selling hardware, furniture, tinware, stoves, and appliances. Fred Dickson Sr. assumed management in 1911. (Courtesy of Layland Museum.)

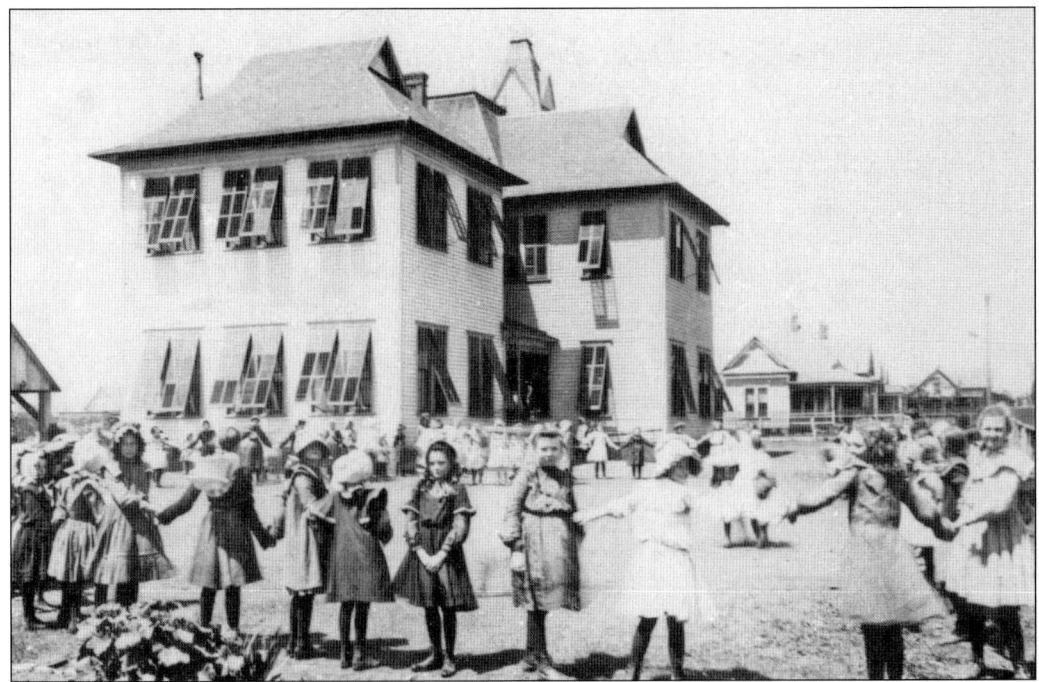

Irving Select School for Young Ladies was opened by Prof. Peyton Irving in 1878. Irving later relocated and built the school pictured. Classrooms were on the first floor and a dormitory on the second. Subjects taught included mechanics, civil government, music, bookkeeping, English, and math and science courses. Irving was also the first county school superintendent. Irving Elementary School was later named in his honor. (Courtesy of Layland Museum.)

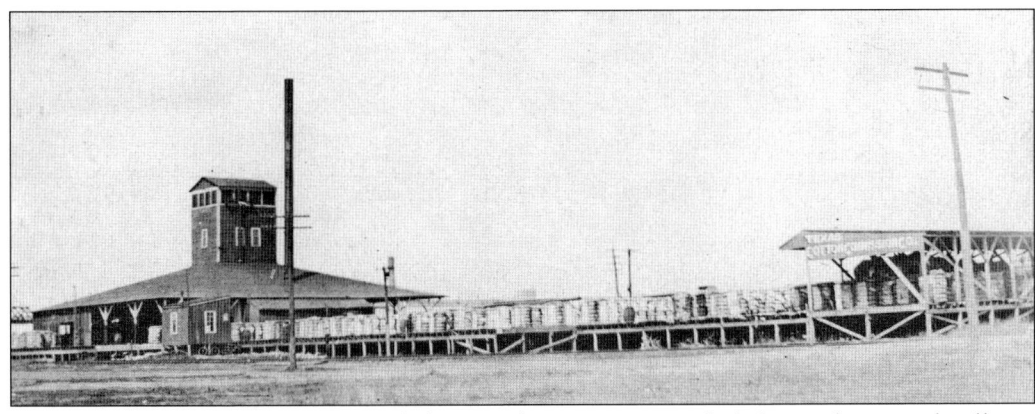

Businesses during the 1880s around the courthouse square included six saloons, a distiller, a shooting gallery, boardinghouses, and many grocery, drug, and general merchandise establishments. The demand for cotton was booming, and the railroad had come to town. The Cleburne Cotton Compress, located near the railroad tracks off North Border Street, hummed with business. (Courtesy of Layland Museum.)

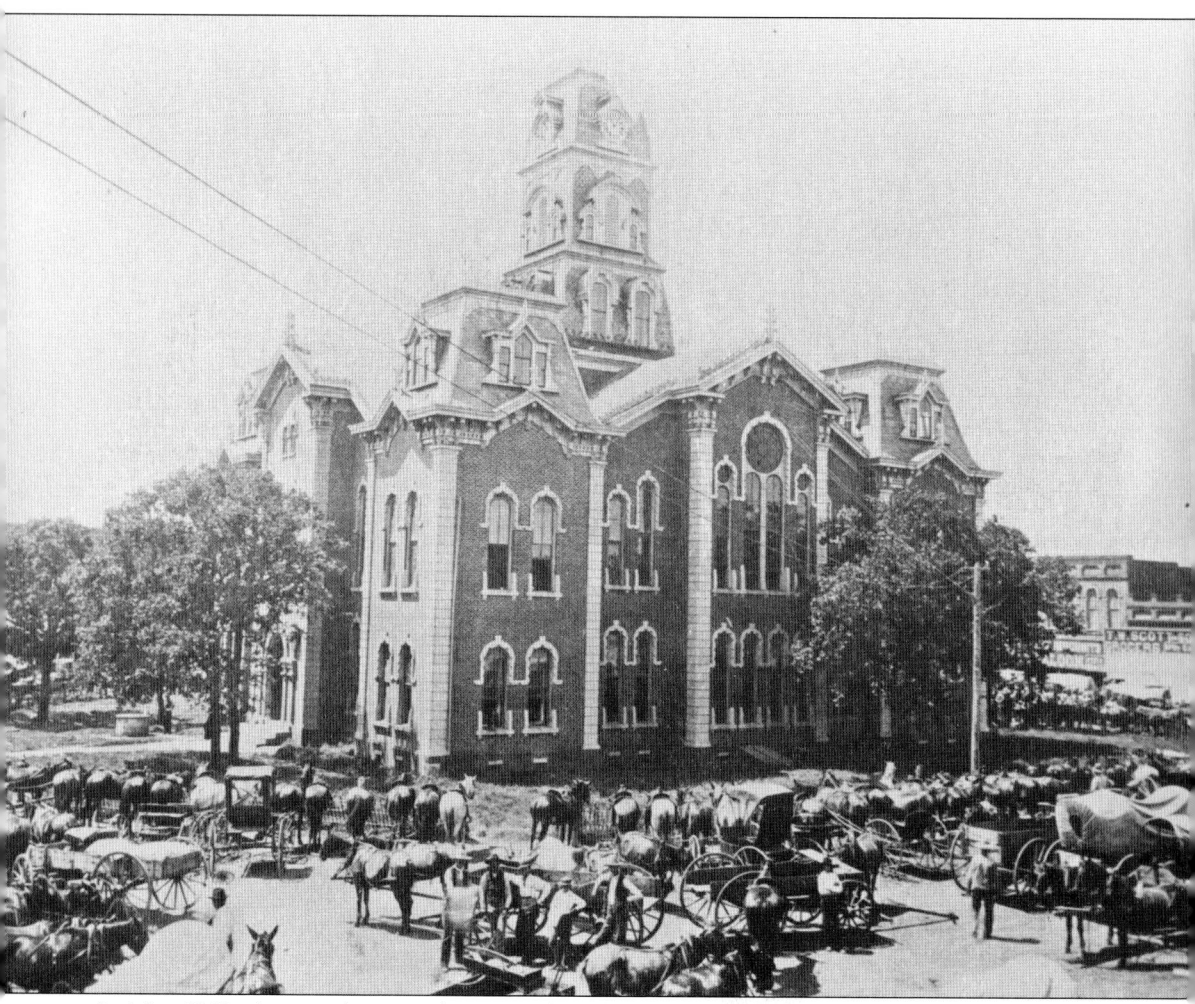

In May 1883, the wooden courthouse, jail, and other buildings were moved to Cleburne from the previous county seat, Buchanan. Soon a survey was done, and lots surrounding the square were sold for $500. More businesses opened—a 10-pin alley, saloons, Morris and Henry Levi's dry goods store, T. W. Scott and Sons Grocers, drugstores, and general merchandise stores. Because the courthouse was determined to be too small, it was torn down, and a new courthouse was completed in 1883 at a cost of $44,685. This Johnson County Courthouse had a bell tower and ornate decorations. It served as a central meeting place to bring wagons and sell goods or perhaps watch a parade. As many as 50 wagons a day were driven into town, where cotton was sold and ginned and other business conducted. On July 4, 1907, a ball was held in the building. The structure burned on April 15, 1912, the same day the *Titanic* sank. (Courtesy of Layland Museum.)

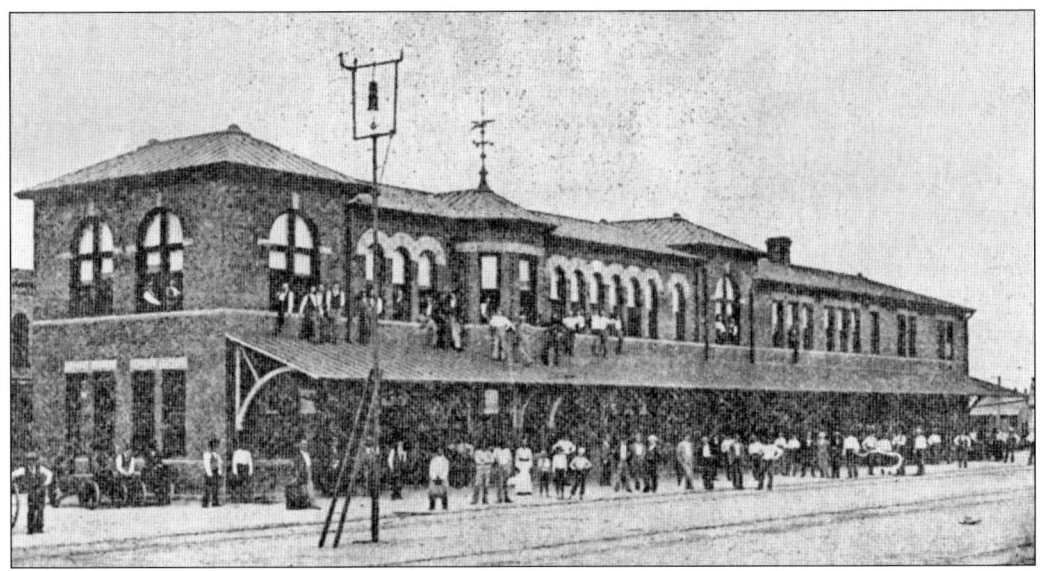

In 1879, the Dallas, Cleburne, and Rio Grande Railway completed a narrow-gauge track to Cleburne from Dallas. The Gulf, Colorado, and Santa Fe Railroad acquired this rail line a year after their initial service to Cleburne in 1881. About 1,000 people witnessed the arrival of the first Santa Fe steam engine, and by 1890, five hundred were employed by the railroad in town. The first passenger train from Galveston came in 1892. Pictured is the second Santa Fe depot, built in 1894. Freight trains hauled needed building material for businesses and homes, forever changing the look and economics of the area. Pictured is the diamond-stacker of 1880, the *Cyrus K. Holiday*, named after the man who founded the system. This engine steamed its way back to Cleburne during the 1954 county centennial. (Above, courtesy of Layland Museum; below, courtesy of Michael Percifield.)

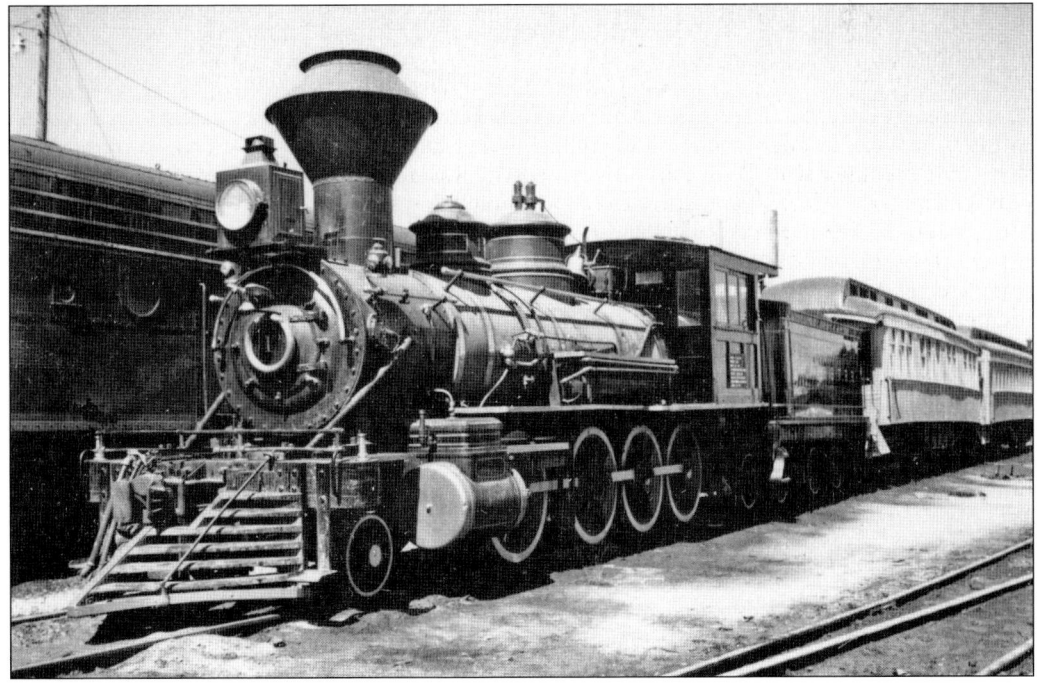

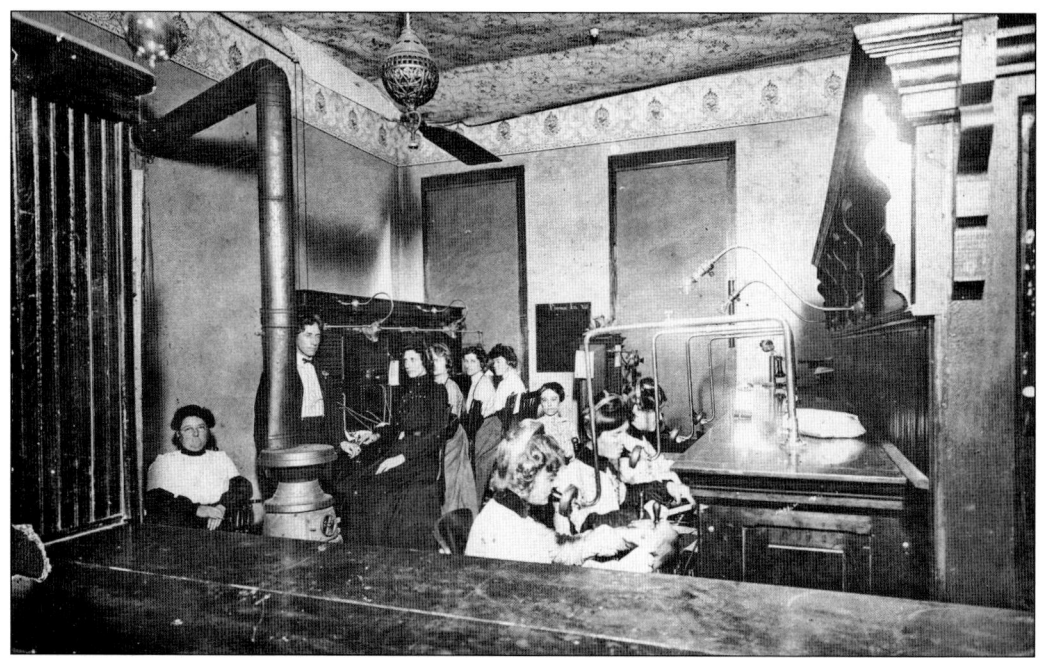

Phone service began in 1882. The company had 42 customers but did not survive. In 1896, J. A. Caldwell opened another exchange, later purchased by Southwestern Telephone and Telegraph Company, at the corner of Henderson and Main Streets. They built the city's first long distance line, to Alvarado, and as pictured, later moved to North Caddo Street above what today is Patrick's Floral. (Courtesy of Layland Museum.)

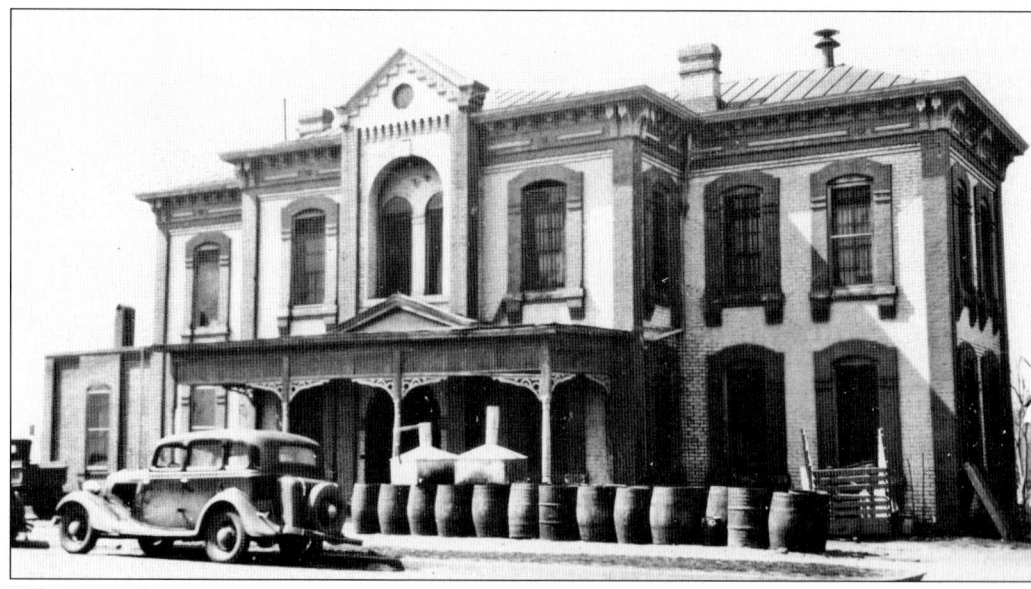

Whiskey stills were common, and so was raiding them. This photograph of the county brick jail built in 1884 shows whiskey barrels and equipment confiscated during a raid years later. Located at 116 South Mill Street for over 50 years, the building cost $26,000 to construct. (Courtesy of Sandra Davis Jones.)

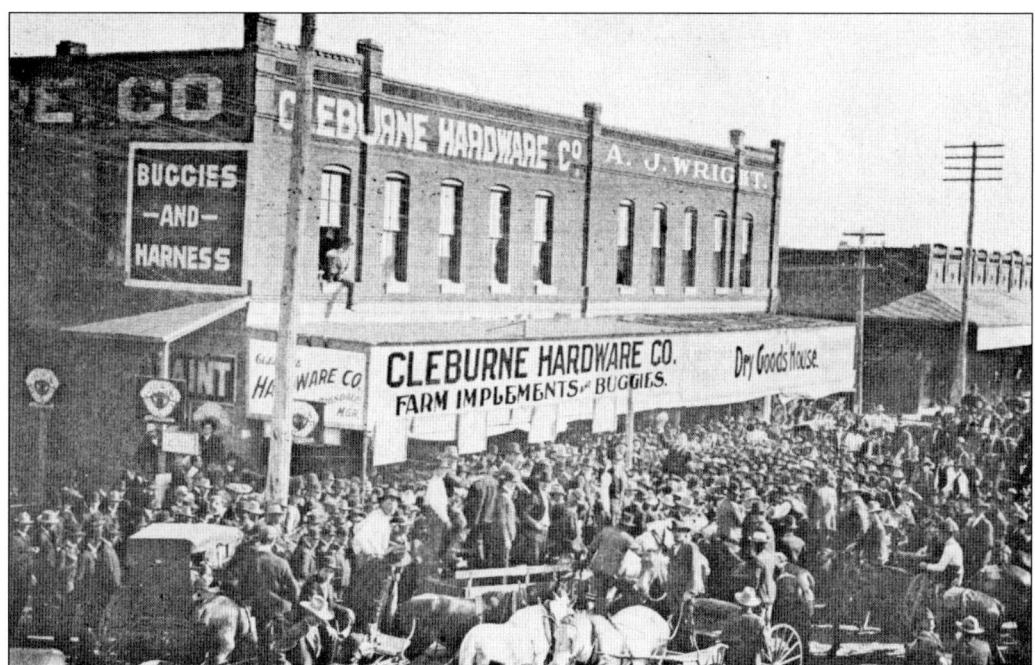

When J. M. Ragsdale opened Cleburne Hardware in 1889 at 111 South Main Street, he sold the first plow in town and carried a full line of hardware and farm implements, oils, paint, wagons, buggies, and cultivators. Someone in this large crowd won a Mitchell Wagon during the drawing. This building has been remodeled and now houses the Plaza Theatre. Pictured is employee Leland Burton (left) with Harold Benson, who along with his wife, Francis, purchased the business in 1973 and moved it to West Henderson Street. They had plenty of parking and carried hardware items plus sporting goods, housewares, plumbing and electrical supplies, and gifts. (Above, courtesy of Layland Museum; below, courtesy of the Benson family.)

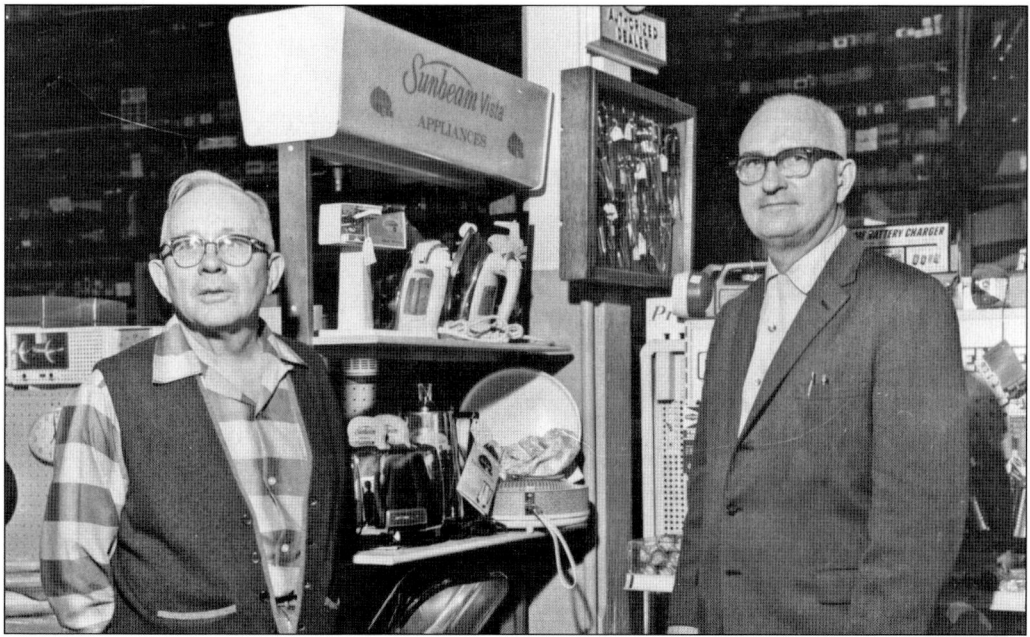

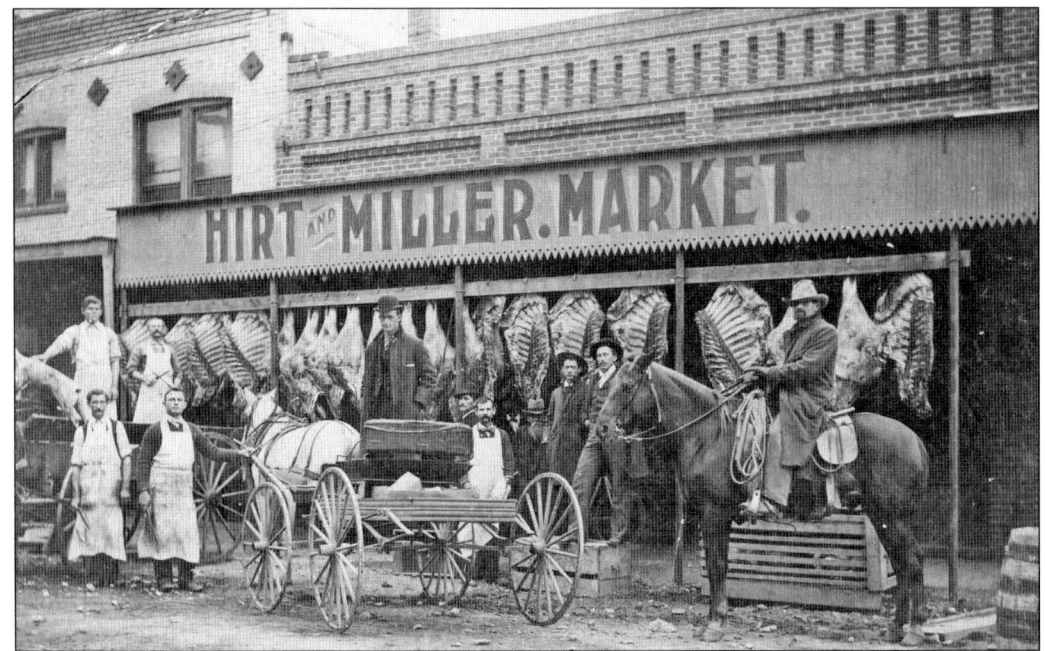

The Hirt and Miller Market was located at 109 North Anglin Street. John W. Hirt, seated on the horse, and John Miller started the business in 1891 and later added a slaughterhouse. Pictured in the center with an apron on is Jim Miller, in the wagon is L. Lee Filgo, and with his hand on the wagon is Dub Collins. (Courtesy of Layland Museum.)

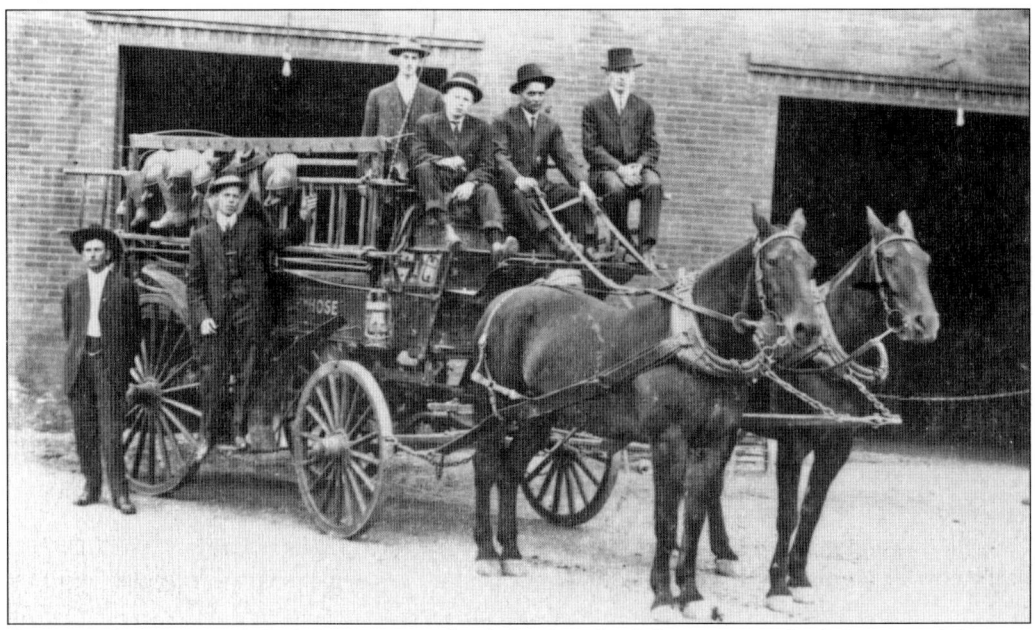

Organized in 1891 with J. A. Lingren as chief, the first firefighting group had three paid drivers, 24 volunteers, a hook and ladder truck, a hose carriage, and three well-trained teams of horses. The drivers received $200 per year. A favorite fire horse, Old Tom, served for 23 years and pulled a street grader when he was not chasing fires. Local officials posed for this c. 1900 photograph. (Courtesy of Layland Museum.)

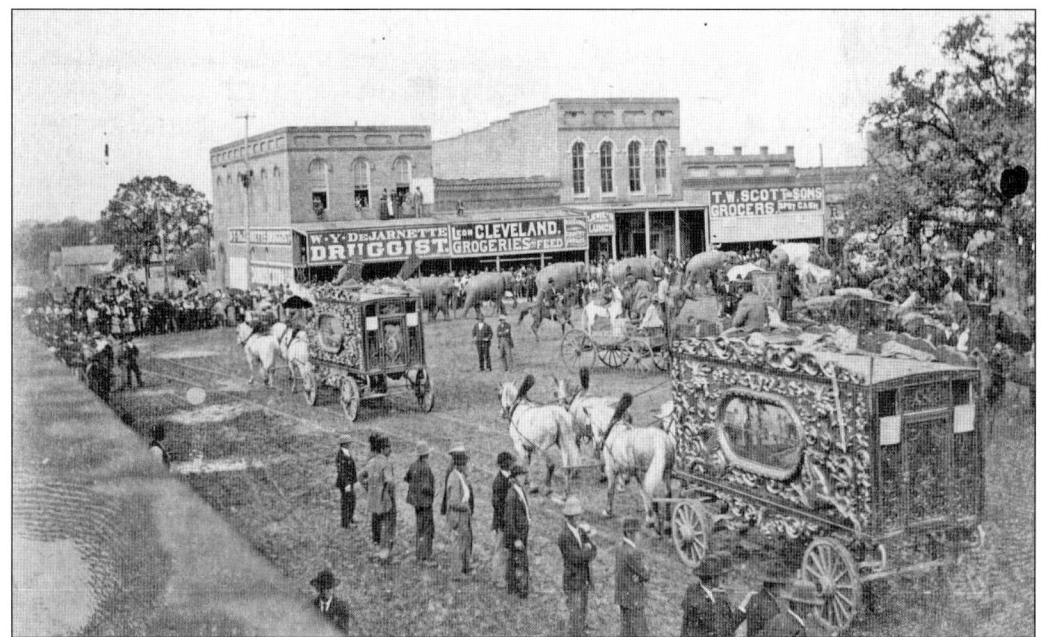

The Ringling Brothers Circus Parade advertised the main event as they paraded wagons and elephants through town at the end of the 19th century. Entertainers with the circus side show included a bearded lady; a tattooed man; a three-legged man; Tom Thumb, who was less than 3 feet tall; Siamese twins; a rubber man; and performers who swallowed swords and ate glass. (Courtesy of Layland Museum.)

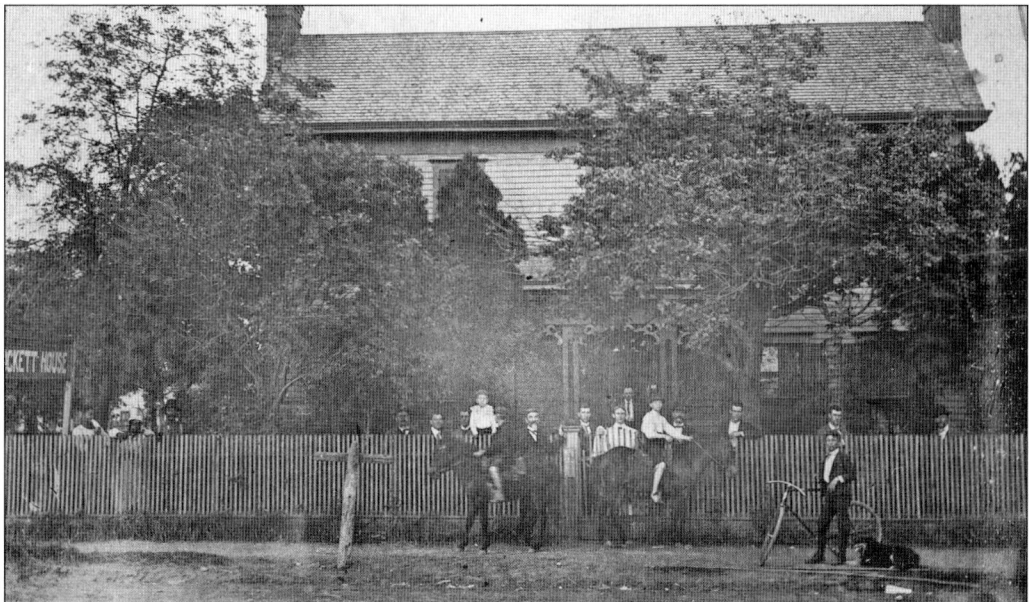

The Lockett House on South Caddo Street was one of the first open for room and board. During the next few years, others followed, including the Haney House, Chaney House, Joplin House, Fry Singer Inn, Hale Rooming House, Capps Rooming House, Gregg Rooming House, Bartlett House, Holland House, Tennessee House, Bishop House, and Crank Rooming House. (Courtesy of Layland Museum.)

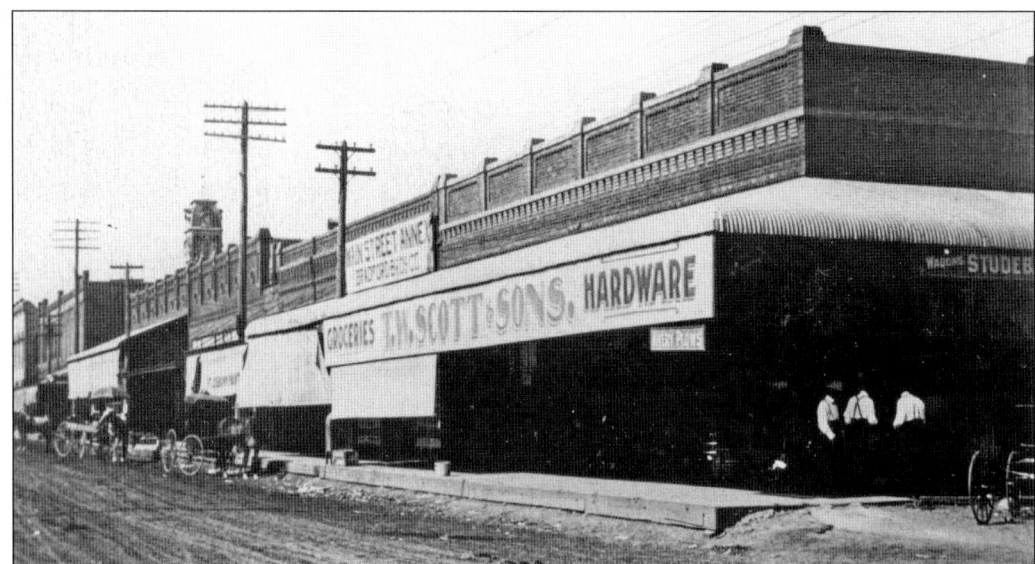

T. W. Scott and Sons Grocery and Hardware store opened first on the west side of the square as Scott's Spot Cash Grocery. It moved to the corner of Harrell and Main Streets in 1904 as pictured. By 1915, an additional brick building was added that reached a city block. The store sold groceries, buggies, wagons, plows, farm implements, coal, and hardware items. A potbellied stove was used for heat. Items arrived and were displayed for sale in barrels, including Arbuckle coffee, sugar, flour, molasses, and cooking oil. Pictured is T. W. Scott in his office during the 1930s. (Above, courtesy of Layland Museum; below, courtesy of Margaret Lee Preston Fraser.)

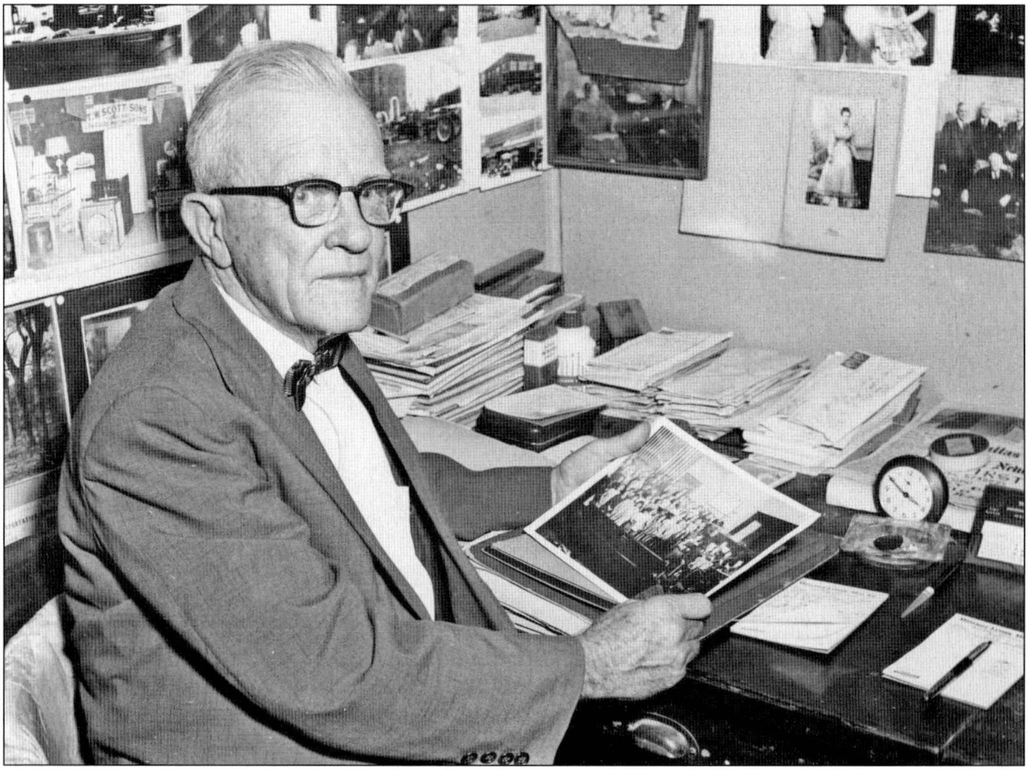

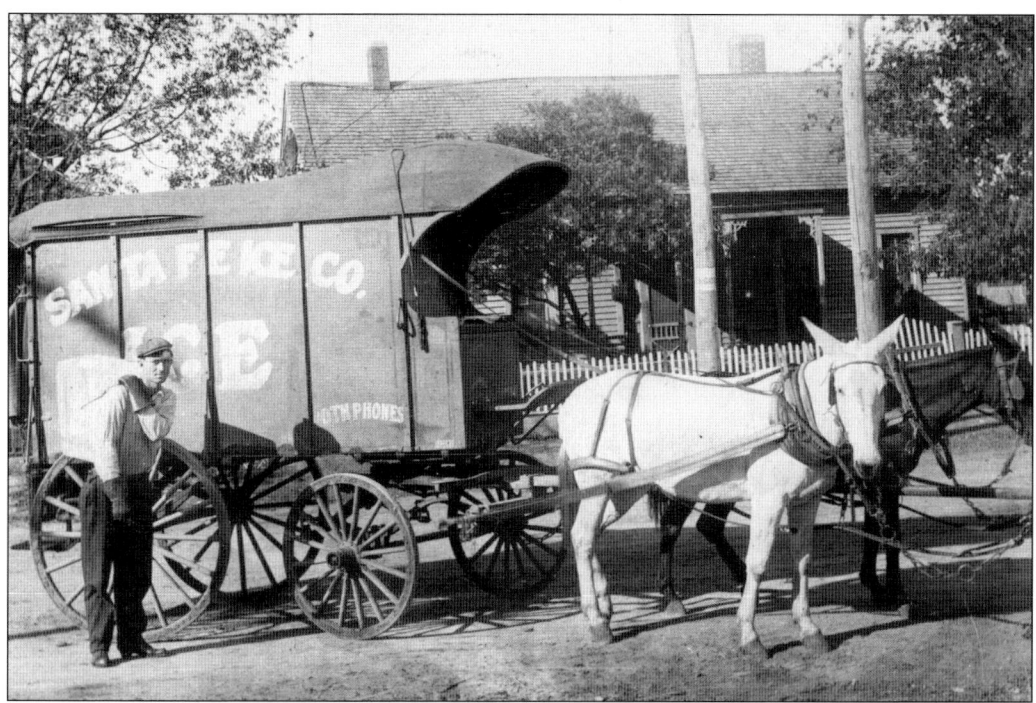

Santa Fe Ice Company had an ice-making capacity of 35 tons per day and delivered daily using one of five wagons. Men carried ice blocks on their backs using a leather strap and cut the ice to order with a saw. Customers would put a card on their door letting the iceman know how much they needed. Cleburne Ice and Cold Storage, located just north of the YMCA and managed by T. J. Flake, provided ice for homes, businesses, and the Santa Fe Railroad. Twenty-five pounds of ice cost 10¢, and 100 pounds cost 40¢. The ice was delivered to homes in one of seven white delivery wagons pulled by mules. (Above, courtesy Sandra Davis Jones; below, courtesy of Layland Museum.)

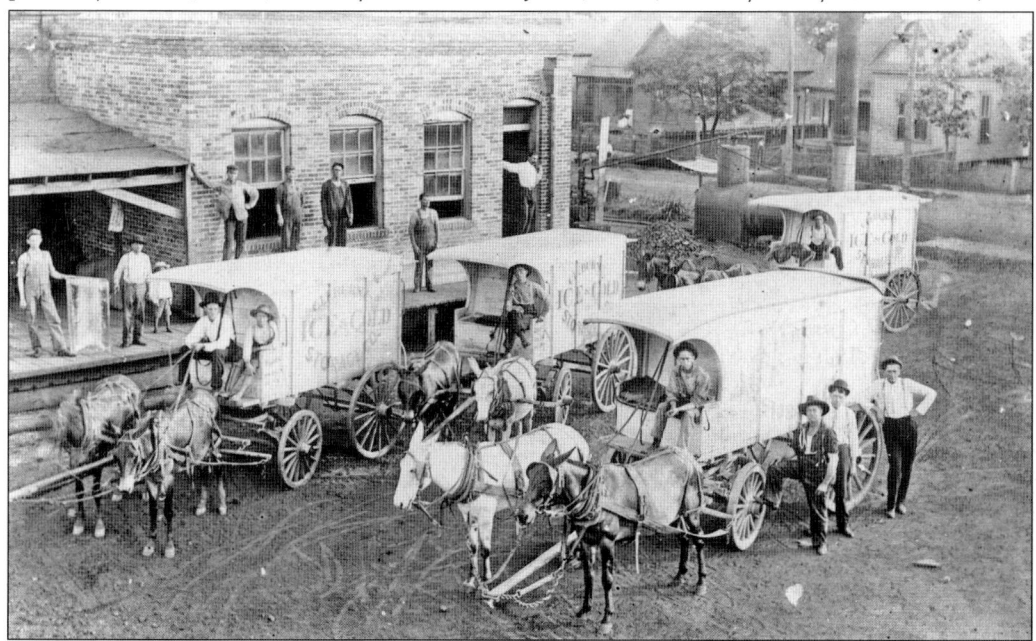

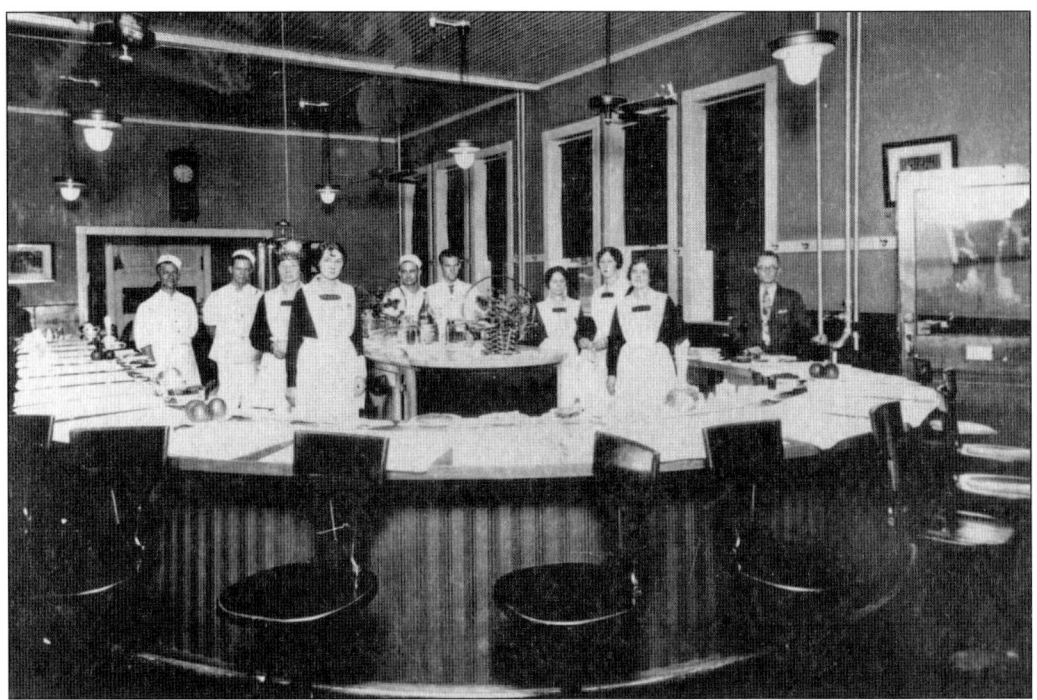

Waitresses, known as Harvey Girls, served fresh, quality food to train crews, passengers, and local folks at the Santa Fe Harvey House on the lower floor of the depot built in 1894. They were required to wear black shoes and a plain black dress with an "Elsie" collar, plus a starched white apron. The young women lived upstairs and could not marry for one year after going to work. Pay began at $17.50 per month plus free room and board. Meals of fresh vegetables and fruit, steaks, chicken, iced drinks, and hot coffee were served on fine china. There was a brass gong outside used to signal when the train was nearing Cleburne. The Allen brothers were cooks, and local baker Zip Plemons made the desserts and bread. The Cleburne Harvey House closed in 1931. (Both, courtesy of Layland Museum.)

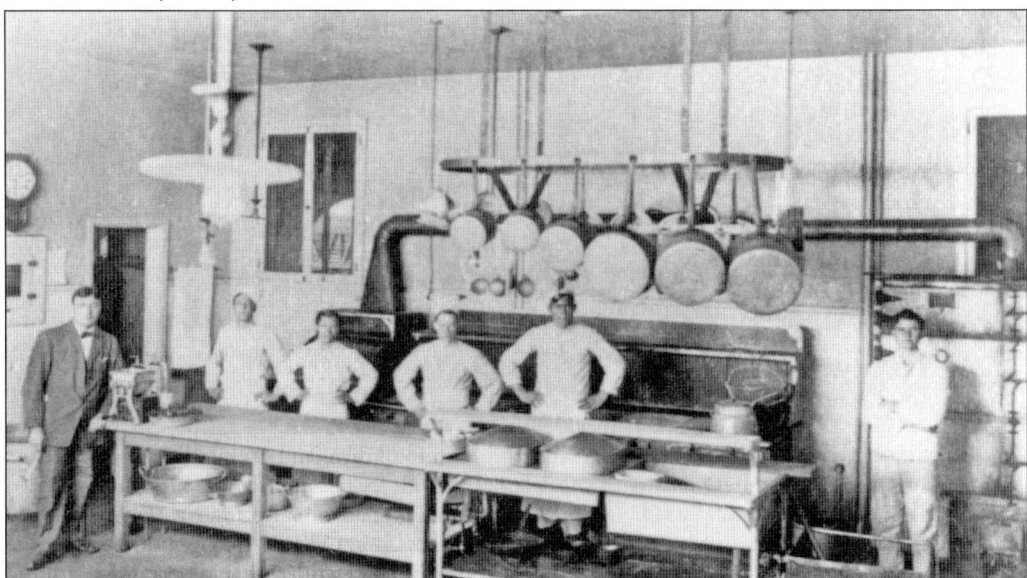

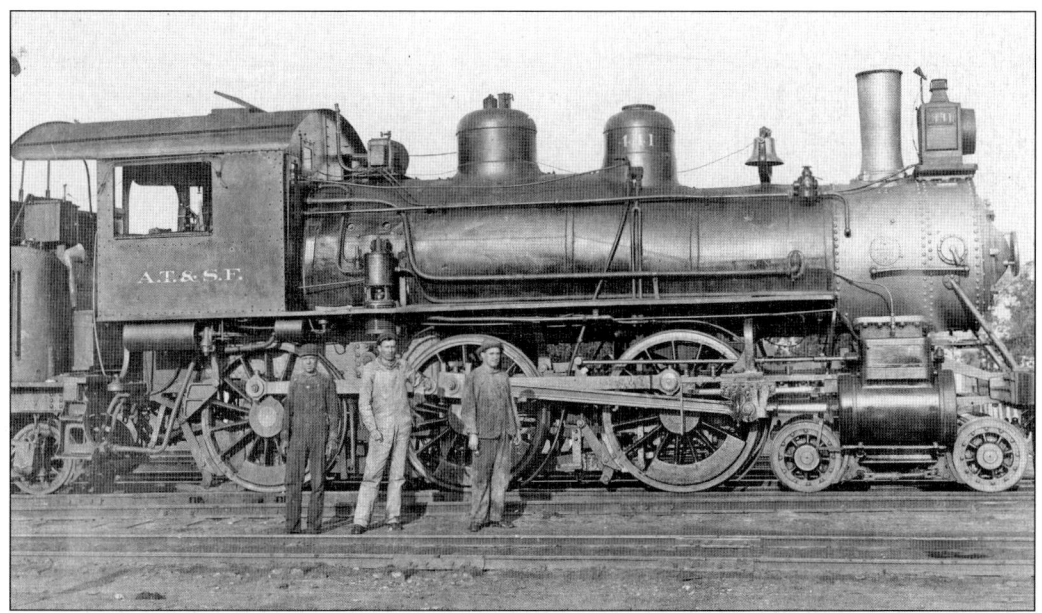

The plentiful supply of soft water needed for steam locomotives was a deciding factor when the Santa Fe Railroad chose to construct a major repair shop in Cleburne. The year was 1897. William Poindexter, T. H. Osborn, Mason Cleveland, William James, H. S. Wilson, and S. E. Moss were instrumental in the persuasion process. The railroad shops included maintenance and construction facilities and a switchyard and brought many new jobs. (Courtesy of Layland Museum.)

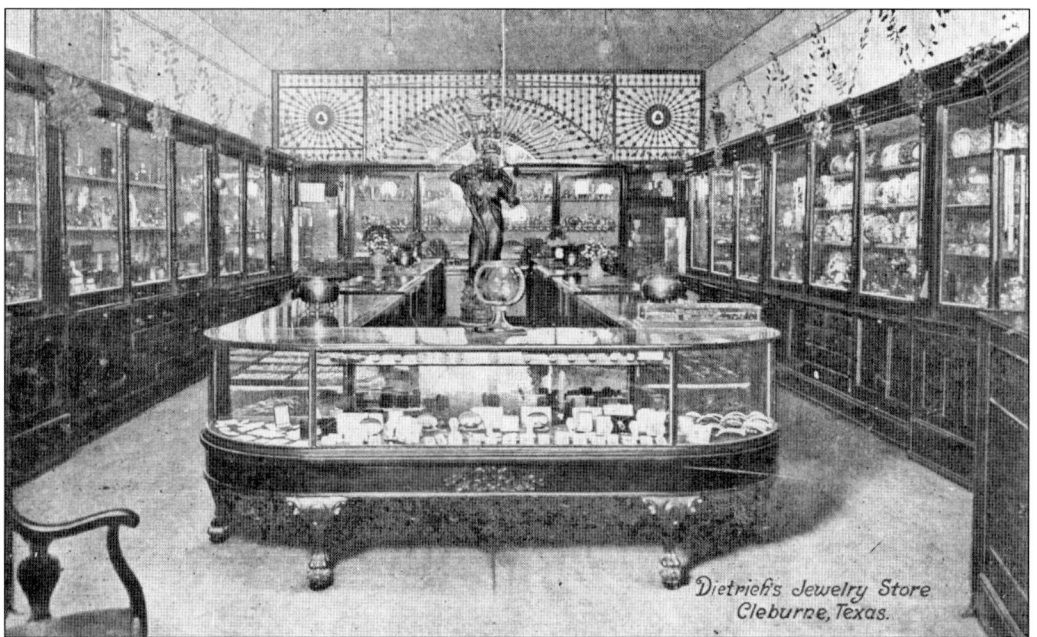

Dietrich Jewelry was on the east side of the square at the end of the 19th century, later moving to 104 East Chambers Street. William Dietrich maintained a optical department and carried clocks, watches, cut glass, hand-painted and imported china, musical items, phonographs, umbrellas, talking machine records, diamonds, and fine jewelry. (Courtesy of J. Gary Shaw collection.)

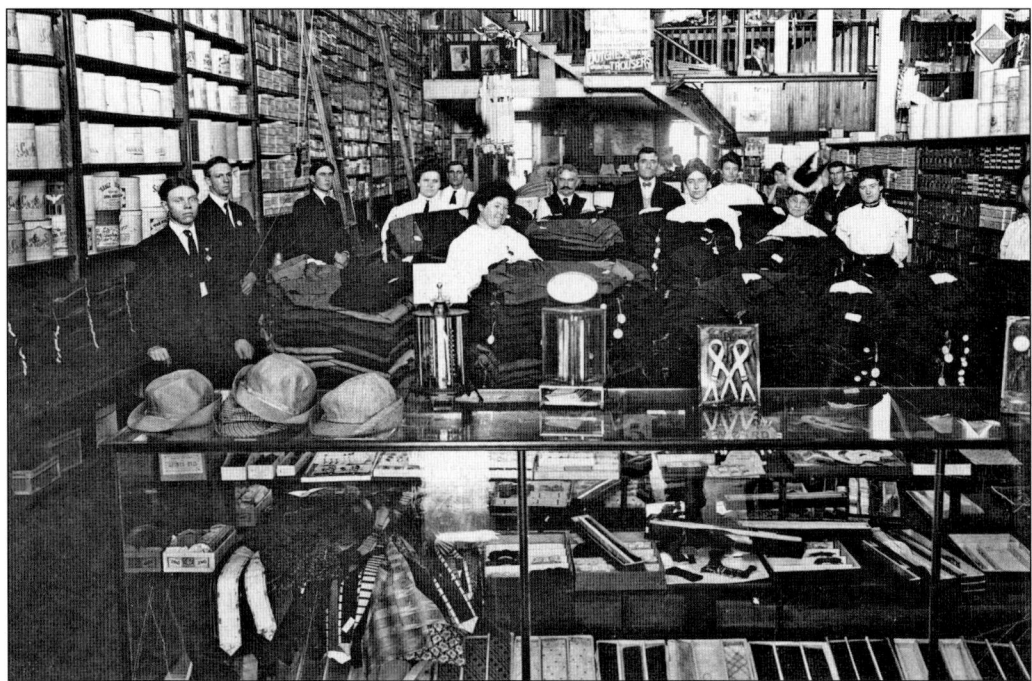

Businessman A. J. Wright was known for constructing brick buildings. The Wrights sold clothing and shoes for the entire family in the 10,000-square-foot building that took up half a city block, reaching from Main Street to Caddo Street. The office was upstairs, and payment for purchases was sent in a basket connected to a wire and a pulley. By 1909, there were 20 clerks. (Courtesy of Layland Museum.)

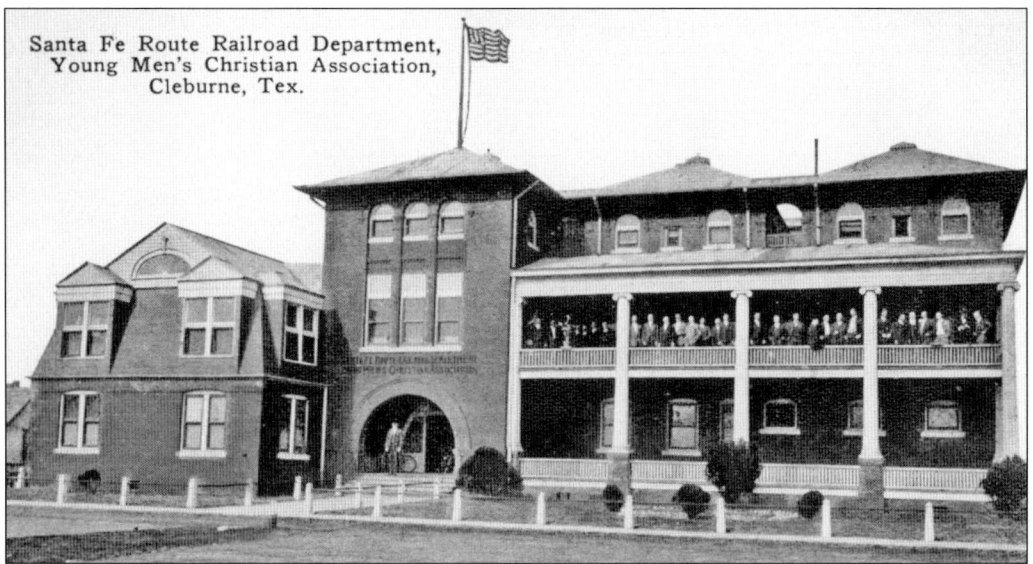

Completed in 1899, the three-story brick YMCA building stood west of the railroad tracks at the corner of Border Street and Willingham Street. Santa Fe Railroad joined forces with the city to construct this facility, which included a library, a parlor with a piano, a bowling alley, a pool, and a gym. Twenty bedrooms on the third floor were used mostly for railroad men on layover. (Courtesy of J. Gary Shaw collection.)

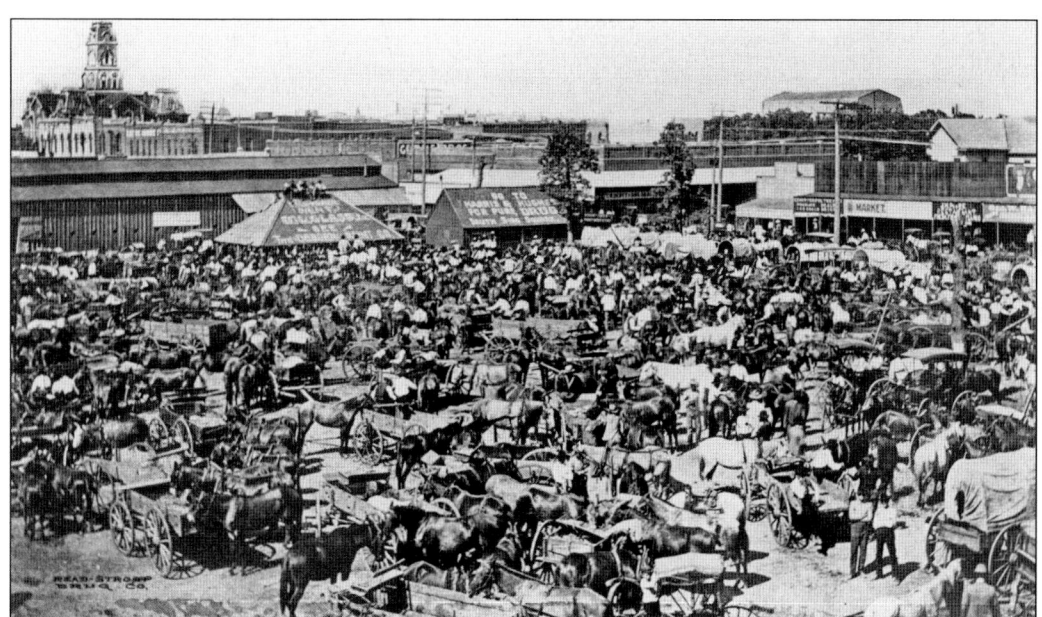

In 1898, Market Square was established on South Main Street to accommodate the growing number of people who came to buy and sell everything from vegetables to horses. This photograph shows the back view of Brown Opera House on the upper right. Occupations at this time included 4 brick makers, 17 grocers, 1 gunsmith, 2 fruit vendors, 1 ginner, 17 farmers, 24 carpenters, 1 well digger, 24 public officials, 20 teamsters, and 7 saddle makers. Across Buffalo Creek west of the market was the Central Public School, which burned in 1916. Because the city could not vote on bonds for a school building, a city hall was constructed in 1887 for the dual purpose of government and educational classes for all grades. Enrollment in 1889 was 948, and teachers were paid $50 a month. (Both, courtesy of Layland Museum.)

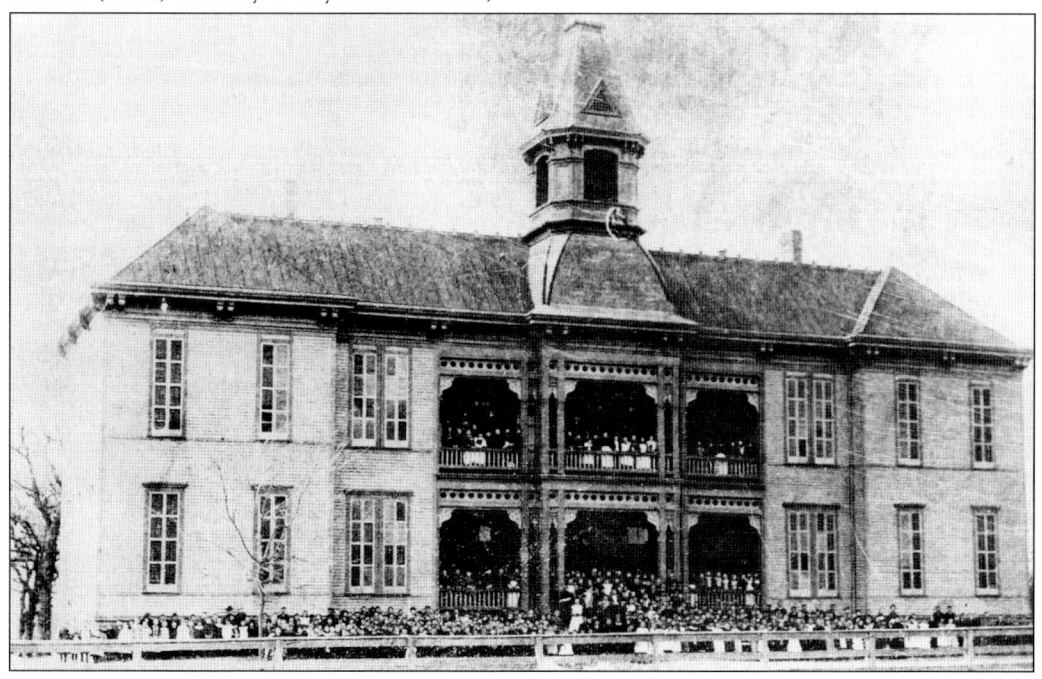

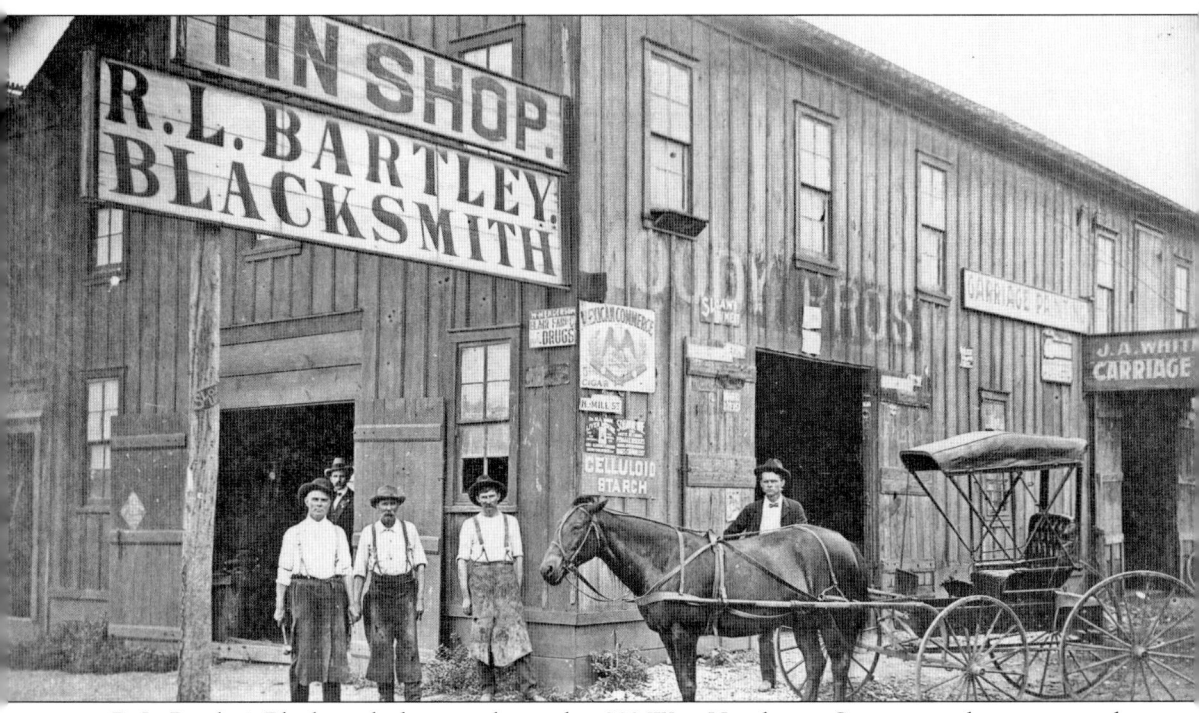

R. L. Bartley's Blacksmith shop was located at 202 West Henderson Street near the wagon yards. He was a professional horseshoer, repaired carriages and wagons, and was an agent for deep well supplies and windmills. By 1911, he had become a farmer, likely due to the advent of the automobile. Other occupations at this time included 2 doctors, 4 dentists, 8 laundresses, 3 photographers, and 15 saloonkeepers. (Courtesy of Layland Museum.)

# Two
# 1901–1925

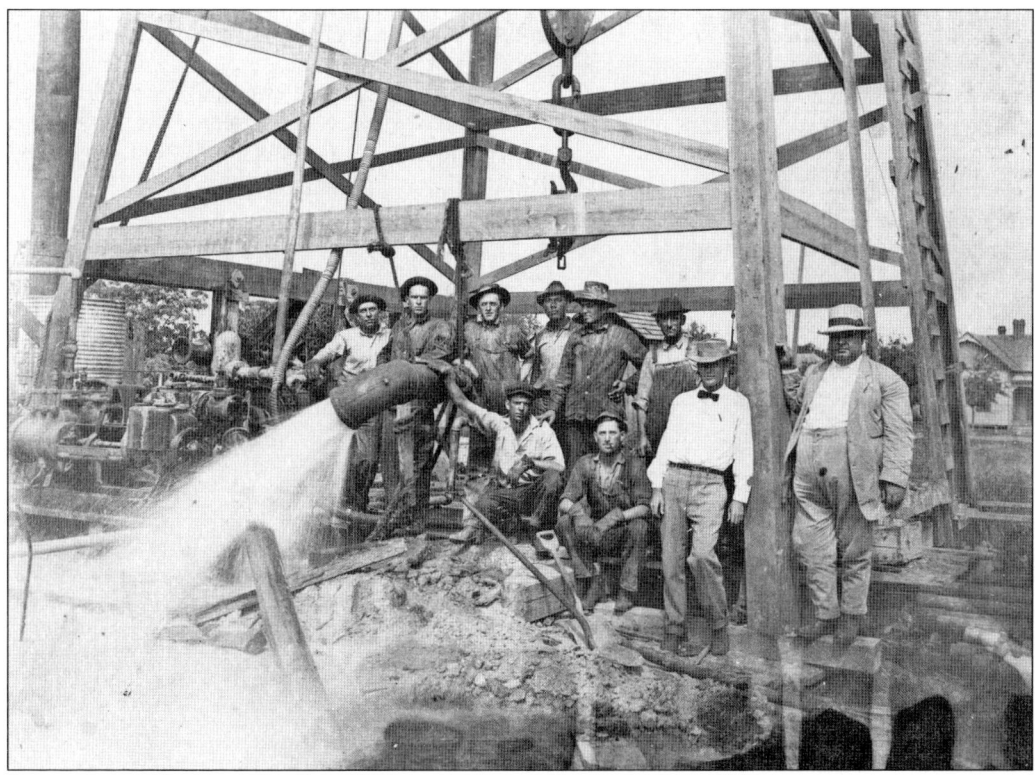

Prior to the waterworks being built, a system of cisterns served the town. At a nickel a bucket, young boys toted water to merchants from a brick-lined pool on West Henderson Street. Water wells like this one, drilled in 1901 by city employees, served as the first tapped city water source. Between 1941 and 1958, seven more wells were drilled. (Courtesy of Layland Museum.)

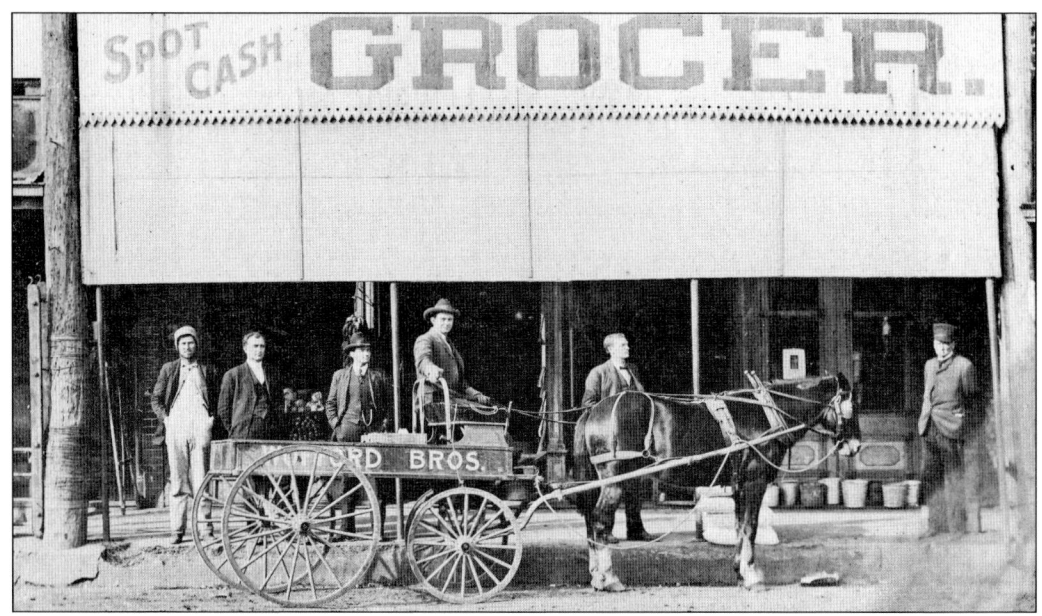

In 1897, James "Jim" Wofford went to work for his uncle, T. W. Scott. Jim established Wofford Brothers Spot Cash Grocer in 1903, and two of his brothers joined him at 7 North Main Street. Jim continued in the business until 1935, when he formed J. J. Wofford and Sons at 13 North Main Street. Assisting in this store were his son, Enoch, and son-in-law, J. W. "Bill" Clarke. (Courtesy of Martha Forrest.)

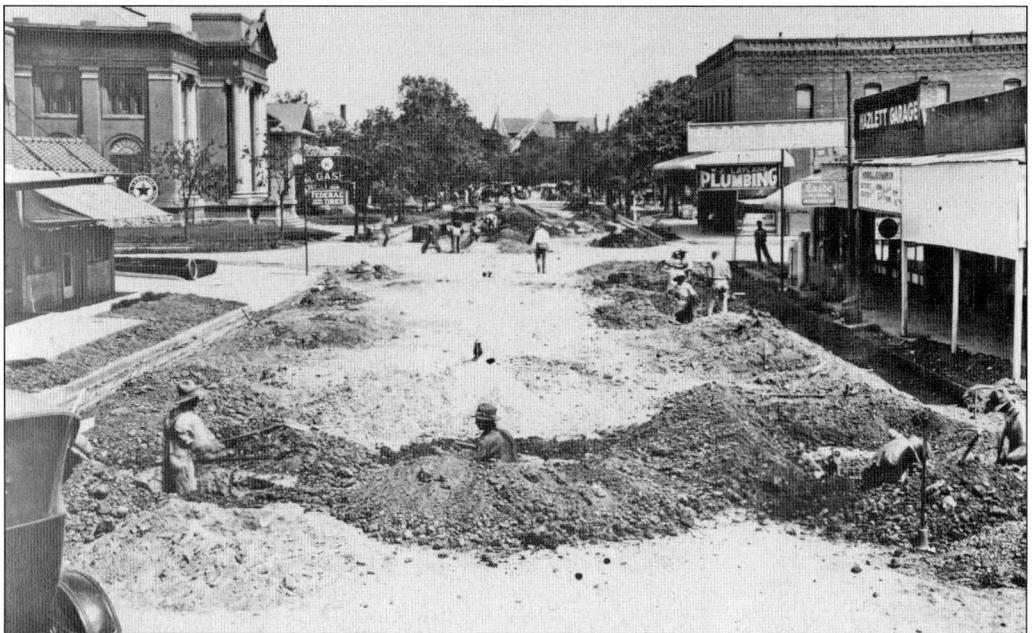

Layland Plumbing, founded by W. J. Layland, installed the first plumbing in Cleburne in 1904. The business is now managed by a fourth-generation family member. Layland donated his world travel collection to the City of Cleburne in 1963 to form a museum upstairs in the Carnegie building. This 1920s photograph shows the paving of Caddo Street, where Layland Plumbing and the museum still thrive. (Courtesy of Layland Museum.)

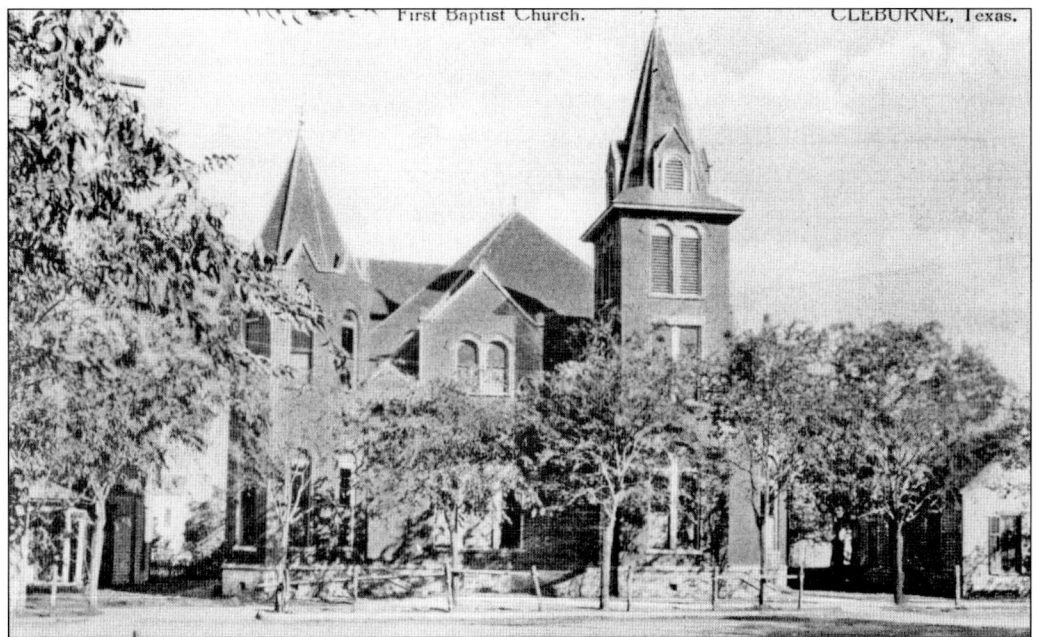

The congregation of First Baptist Church began with 16 members in 1868. Members have helped to organize other Baptist churches in town. The redbrick church was constructed at the beginning of the 20th century, and the educational building was added in 1929. The current worship sanctuary, constructed in May 1941, has a hand-carved sculpture of the Last Supper and stained-glass windows. Main Street Methodist Church was constructed in 1902 at the corner of Main Street and Brown Street and had a towering box spire. The interior sanctuary was gold-leafed and had many stained-glass windows. A pipe organ was installed in 1908. The photograph below shows the church in the 1950s. (Both, courtesy of Layland Museum.)

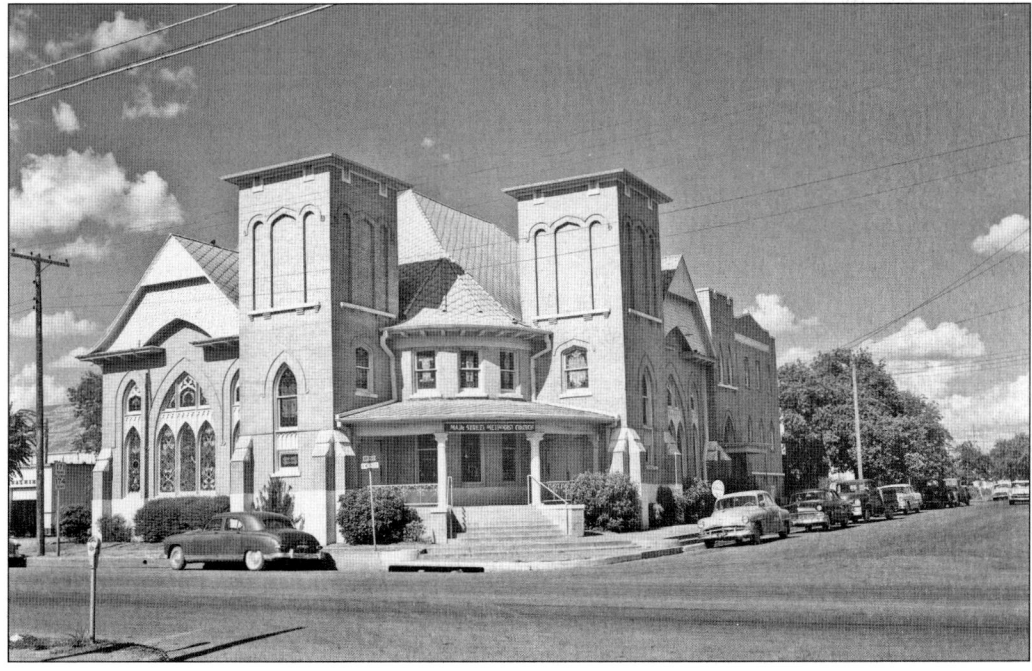

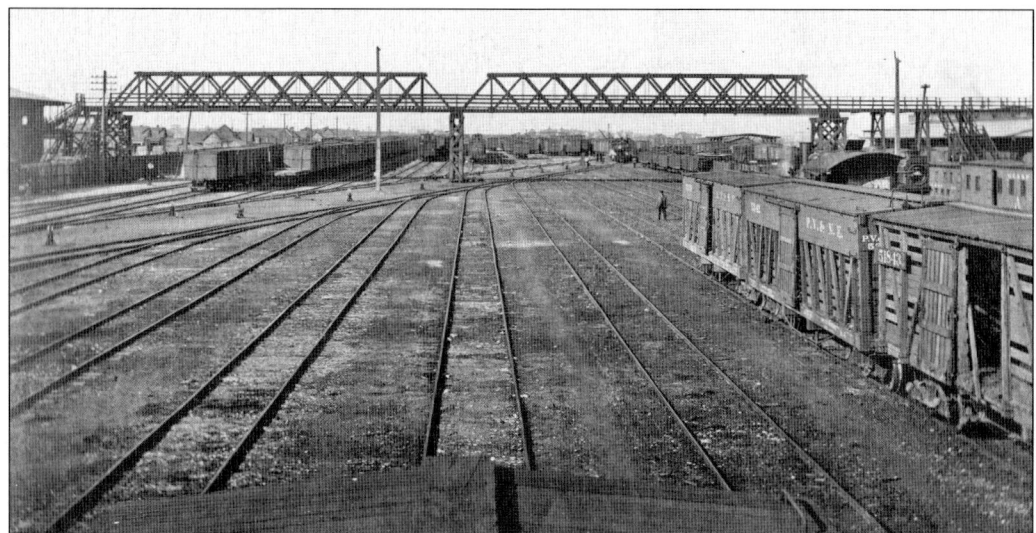

The 1903 viaduct was used for generations of railroad workers for walking over the tracks, allowing safe access to their homes. It was attached to the Master Mechanic Building on the west side of the shops. The railroad ran weekend round-trip excursions to Dallas and the Arbuckle Mountains for $1 and to Galveston for $2. Santa Fe installed electric equipment in 1927. (Courtesy of Layland Museum.)

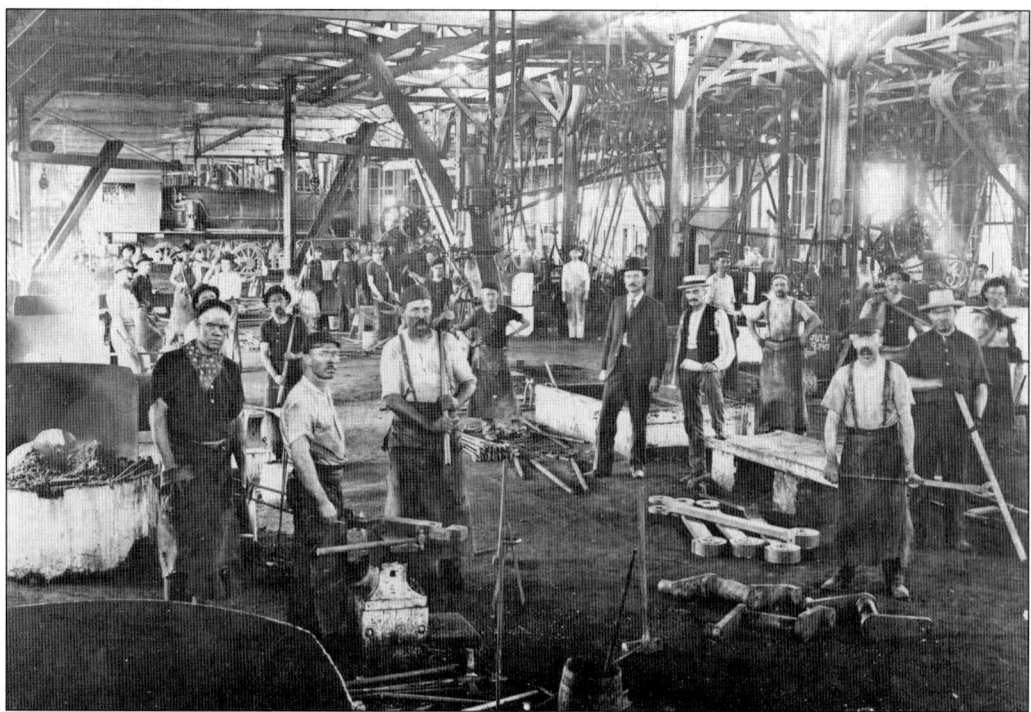

In 1904, there were 1,400 employees in the shops. The following year, they were running 24 trains a day. Blacksmiths at the Gulf, Colorado, and Santa Fe Railway worked in cramped conditions machining specialized pieces, mostly by hand in the early years. Between 1905 and 1915, the shops were reconstructed using bricks, good lighting, and ventilation. Twelve stalls with high ceilings were added to the roundhouse. (Courtesy of Layland Museum.)

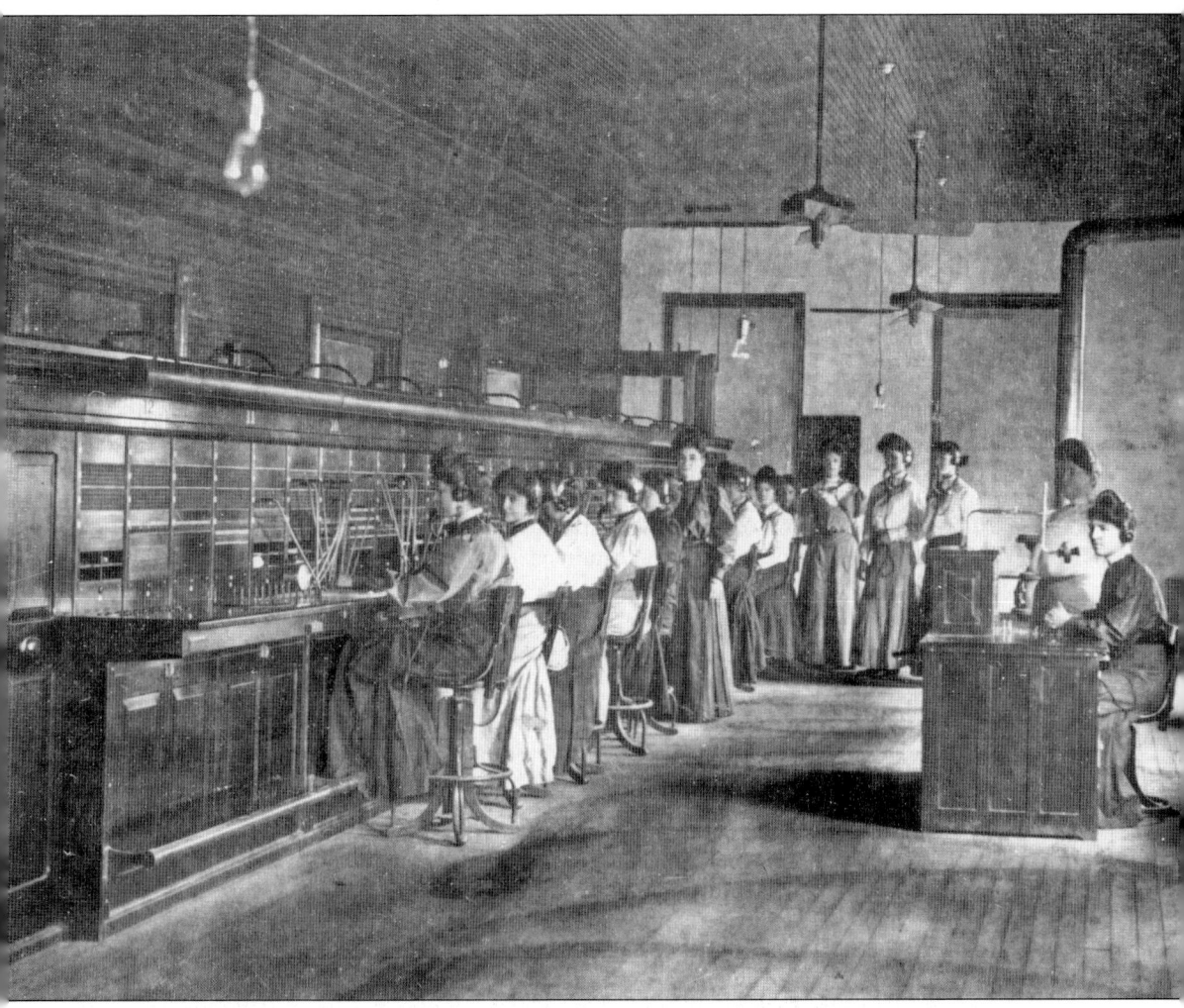

Two telephone companies competed here in the early 1900s. In the second story of Farmers and Merchants Bank, the Cleburne Automatic Telephone Company boasted private lines and "automatic secret service." Prior to this, most lines were party lines. They are credited with being among the first automatic telephone exchanges in Texas. By 1909, the company had 550 customers. It was destroyed by fire in 1912. By 1906, Southwestern Bell Telephone and Telegraph Company was opened in Cleburne and by 1920 had over 2,000 customers. Its name had changed to Southwestern Bell Telephone by 1921. Employees included three switchboard operators, two long distance operators, a manager, a bookkeeper, and a chief operator, plus collectors, ground men, and linemen. In 1951, the 5,000th telephone was installed in Cleburne, and two years later, a new switching center was built at 111 North Robinson Street due to the growth. Rural residents were extended telephone service in 1954. (Courtesy of Layland Museum.)

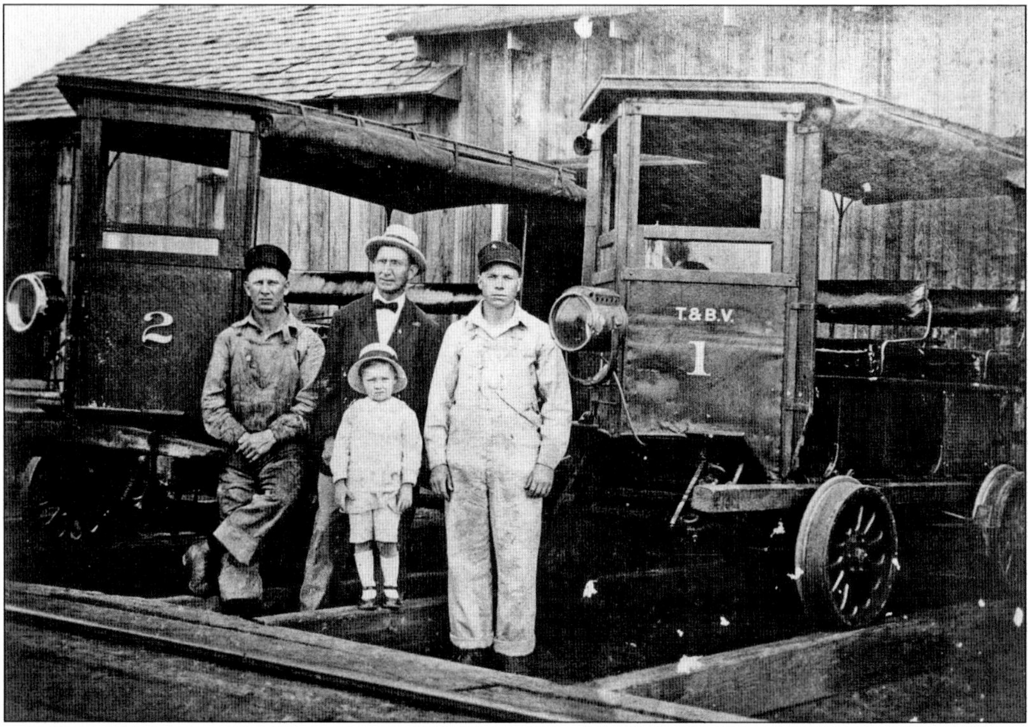

The Trinity and Brazos Valley Railroad (T&BV), commonly known as the "Boll Weevil" after the cotton parasite, operated out of Cleburne from 1904 until the track was abandoned about 1920 after going bankrupt. The railroad was primarily between two rivers, the Trinity and the Brazos. The freight yard and section house, pictured with employees, stood where the large pavilion in Hulen Park is today, facing Hillsboro Street. Portions of the system began to turn insolvent about 1914, and the company went into receivership in 1924. The T&BV depot, located behind the Santa Fe depot, was damaged by fire before being torn down in 1996. (Above, courtesy of Michael Percifield; below, courtesy of Layland Museum.)

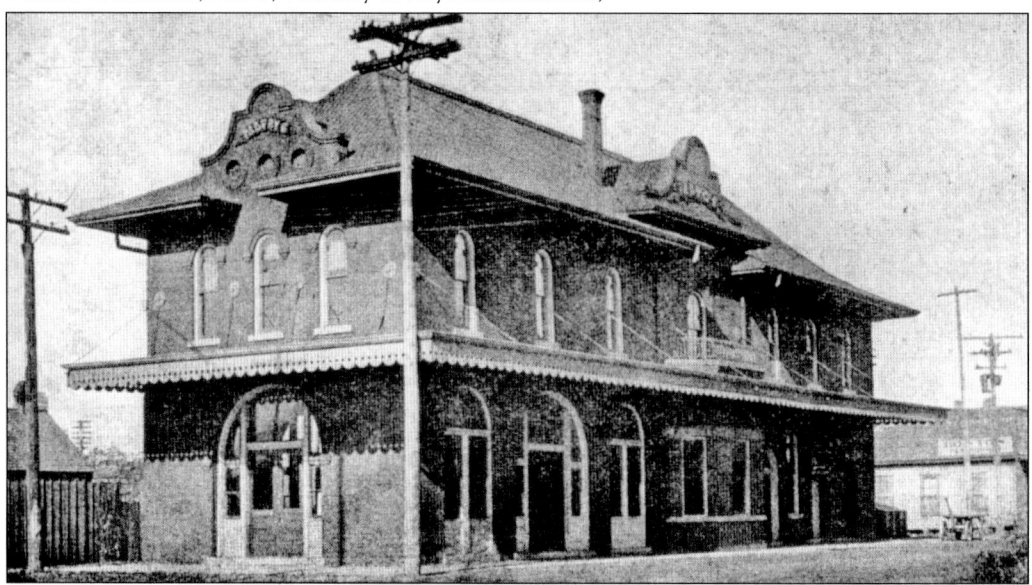

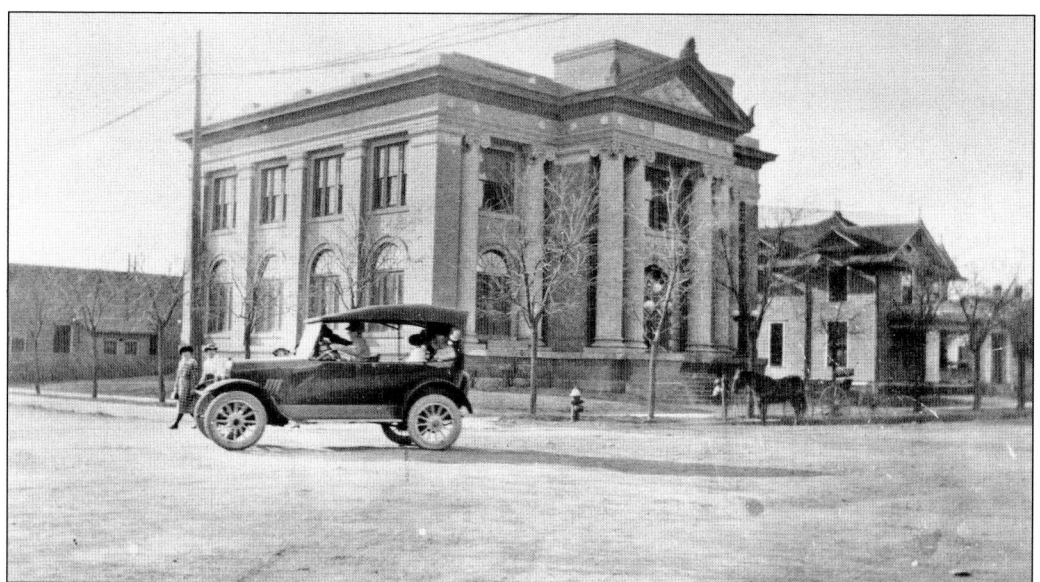

Cleburne Public Library began in 1901 under the direction of a local women's club with funding from benefactor Andrew Carnegie. His gift was matched by local contributions, and this structure was completed in 1905. Featuring details of the Beaux-Arts and classical revival styles and a second floor theater, it housed the library until a new one opened in 1978. (Courtesy of Layland Museum.)

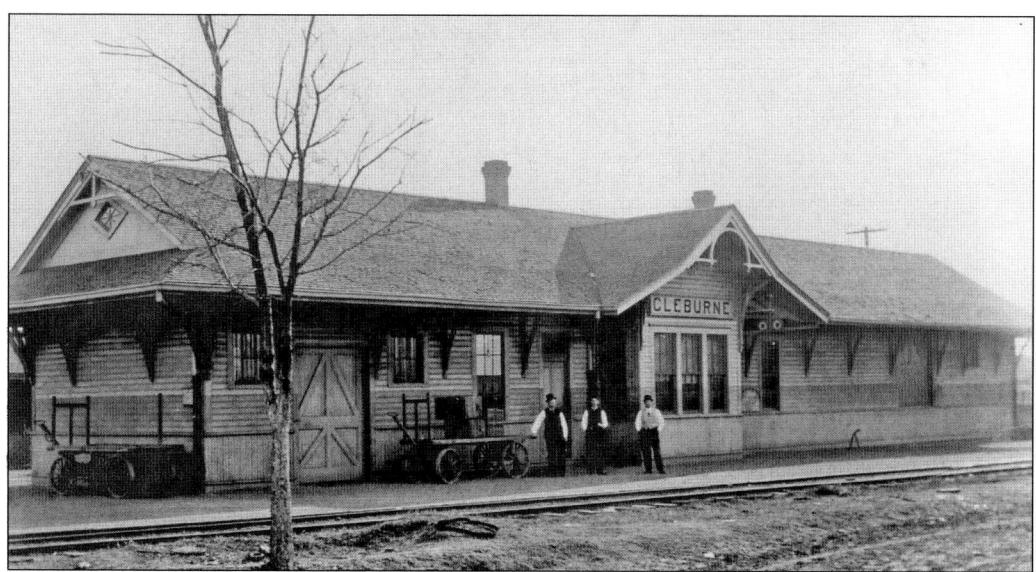

The Missouri, Kansas, and Texas Railroad line, known as the "Katy" Railroad, completed a line from Cleburne to Egan in 1902. Their depot was located on the corner of Front Street and Chambers Street. They did considerable business for several years and had a turntable and freight yard near East Buffalo Creek. This line was sold in 1910. Pictured in the center is station agent John Petro. (Courtesy of Michael Percifield.)

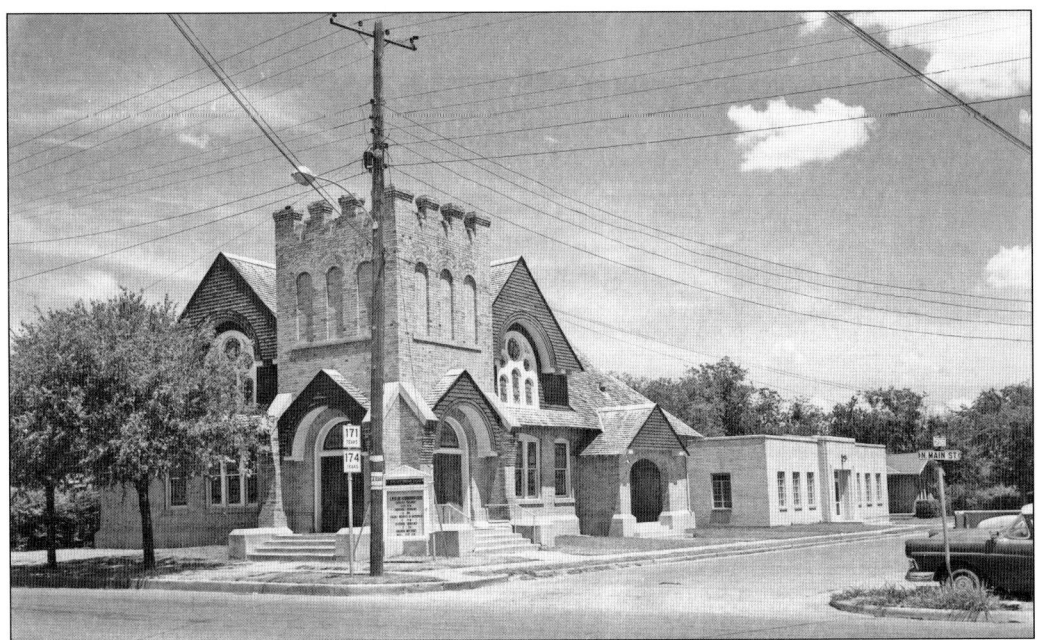

The First Presbyterian Church was organized in 1874. E. J. Zimmerman built the first church at the corner of North Main and Heard Streets in 1904. The membership of this church and those of Anglin Street Presbyterian Church voted to combine and changed their name to the United Presbyterian Church of Cleburne. In 1978, they began meeting in their new sanctuary on Nolan River Road. (Courtesy of Layland Museum.)

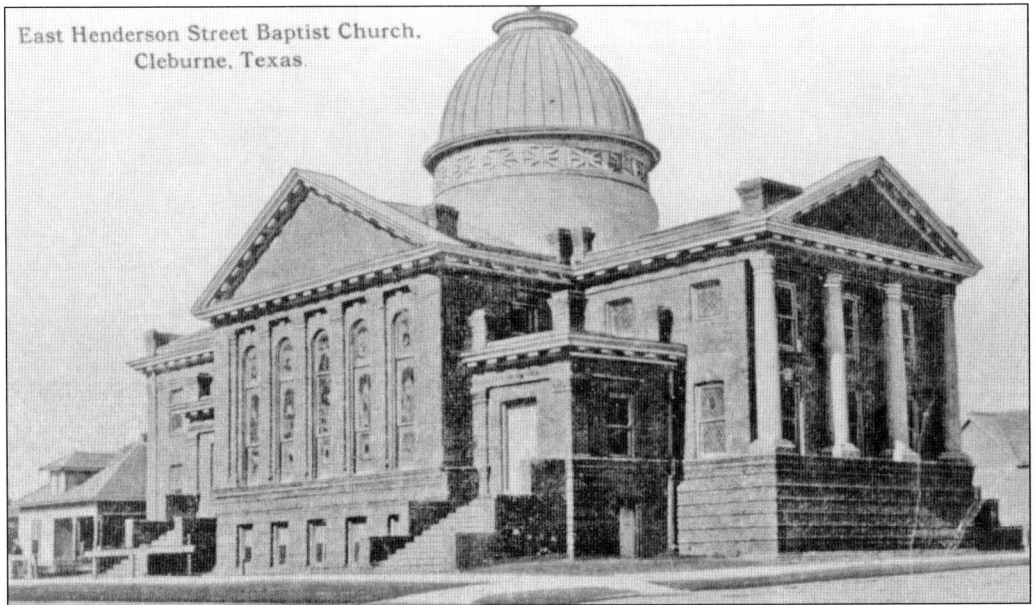

Twenty-one men and women met in 1897 to organize the East Cleburne Baptist Church, which later became Henderson Street Baptist Church. The meeting was held under three wagon sheets near the present site of the church on East Henderson Street. The church group was formed following a revival meeting held with First Baptist Church. Their church was built with bricks made on the property, and the cornerstone was laid in 1907. (Courtesy of Layland Museum.)

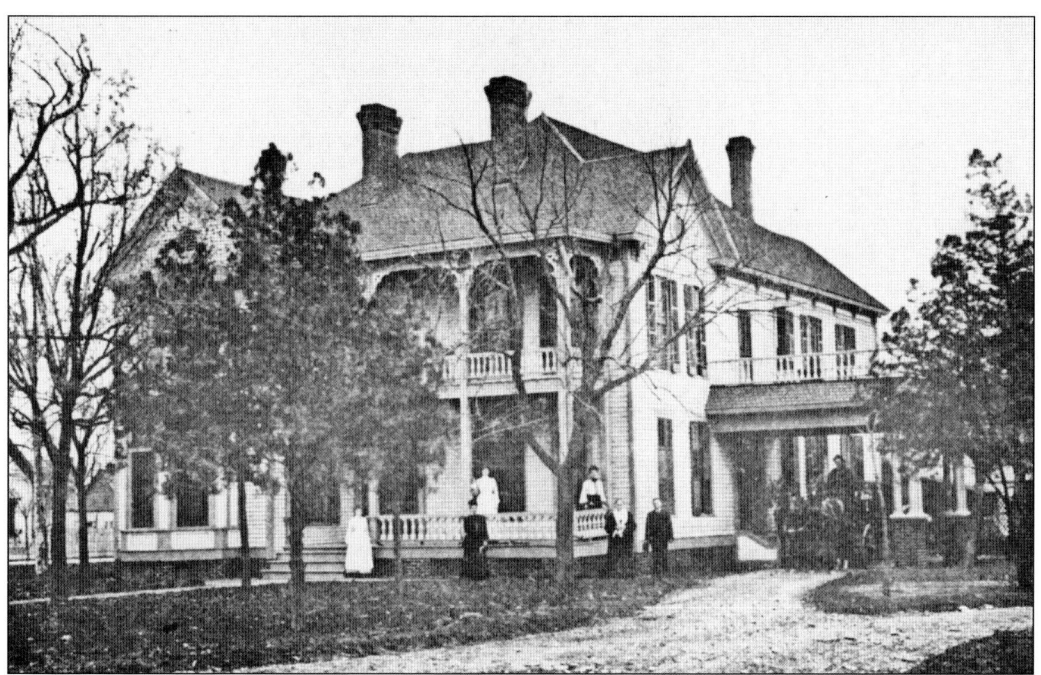

Dr. Robert Lee Yater and surgical staff are shown at the first hospital in Cleburne, opened in 1905 and closed in 1910. He and his six brothers opened Yater Sanatorium, complete with a horse-drawn ambulance, at 414 North Main Street. He earned enough money to attend Baylor Medical School by running a grocery store. (Courtesy of Layland Museum.)

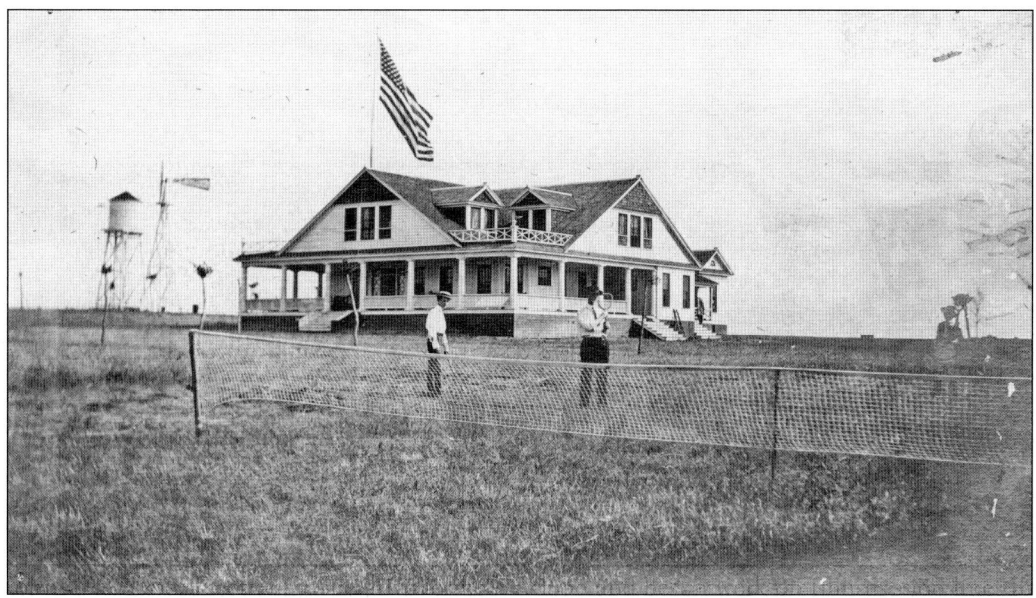

Organized in 1905, Cleburne Country Club offered golfing, tennis, fishing, and swimming in the lake at the 100-acre location 4 miles southwest of Cleburne. The name was changed to Nolan River Country Club by 1950, when the club had 50 stockholder-members, 46 privilege members, and 41 social members. (Courtesy of Layland Museum.)

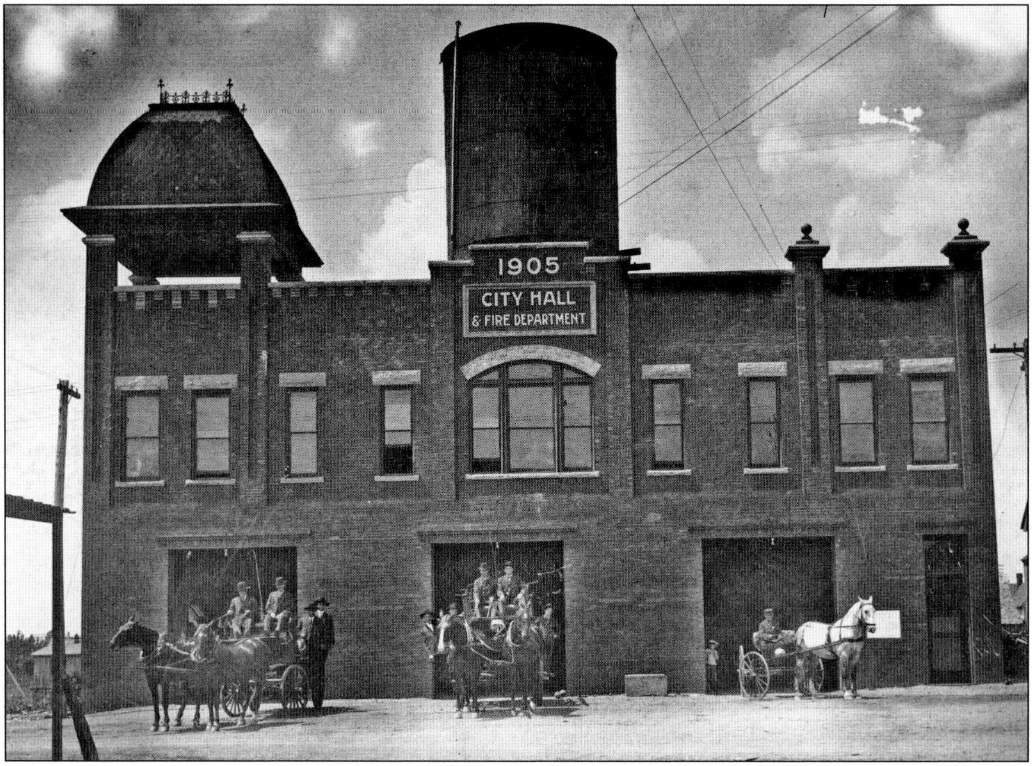

A new fire hall was constructed in 1905 and the first motor-driven firefighting equipment was placed in use in 1913. Fire chief Baylor Bledsoe was on vacation when the courthouse burned in 1912. By 1919, Old Tom and the other horses had been retired in favor of motorized vehicles. Two more new red fire trucks arrived by rail about 1953. (Courtesy of Layland Museum.)

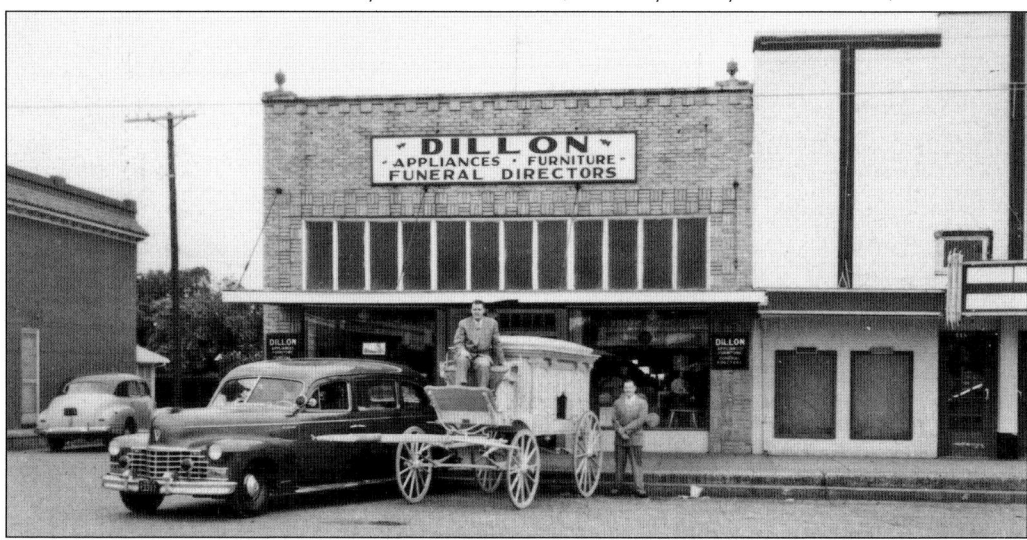

Located at the corner of North Caddo Street and Wardville Street, Dillon Funeral Home was founded in 1905. P. C. Dillon had three hearses and a carriage for funerals. A horse-drawn ambulance was used until they purchased a motorized vehicle with two-way radios. At the scene of an accident, the doctor or a family member could be called. (Courtesy of Layland Museum.)

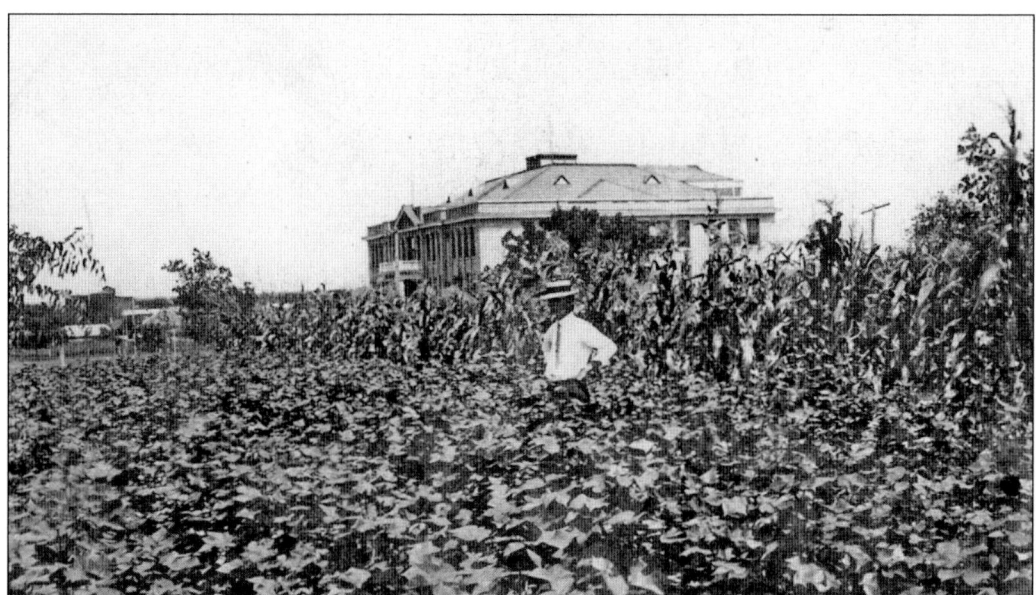

The Fulton Building was almost surrounded by cotton and corn when constructed on land donated by Isabel Kelley, B. J. Chambers's daughter. It opened in 1908 at 311 Featherstone Street; there was a basement with two lunchrooms, one for boys and one for girls, with a kitchen so students could prepare light lunches. The two-story, light gray brick structure was used as a high school, then a junior high, and later for other educational purposes. It was 95 feet by 141 feet and had water, electricity, fire escapes, and steam heat from the boiler in the basement. Besides classrooms, there was also a bicycle room, offices, and an auditorium. It cost $75,000 to build, including the furnishings. A new Fulton School was built in a U shape in 1952 around the old building, and the old one was torn down, as pictured below. (Above, courtesy of J. Gary Shaw collection; below, courtesy of Layland Museum.)

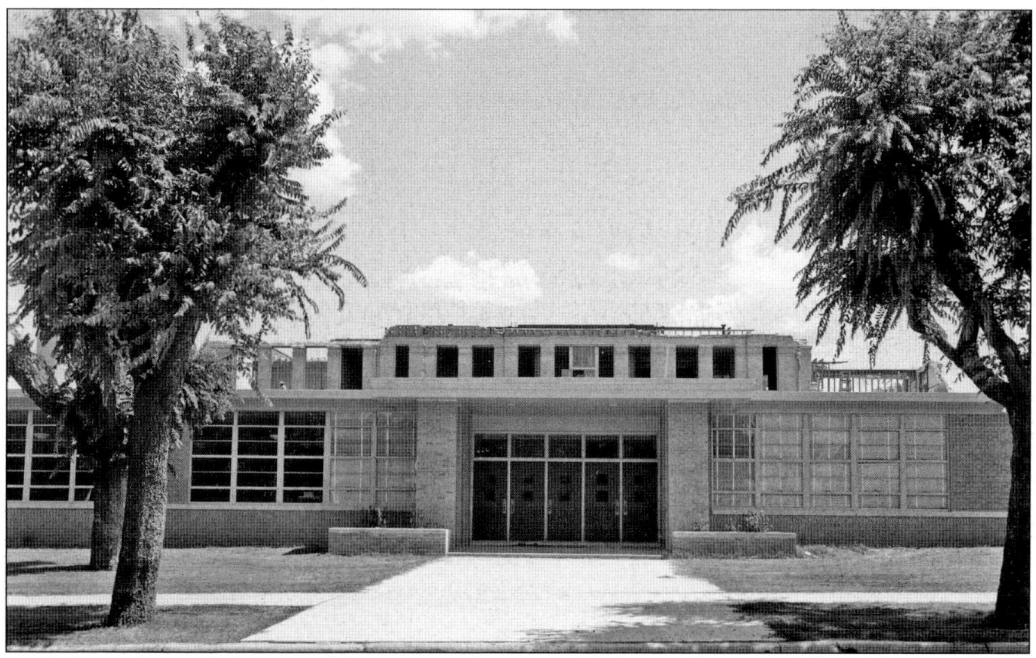

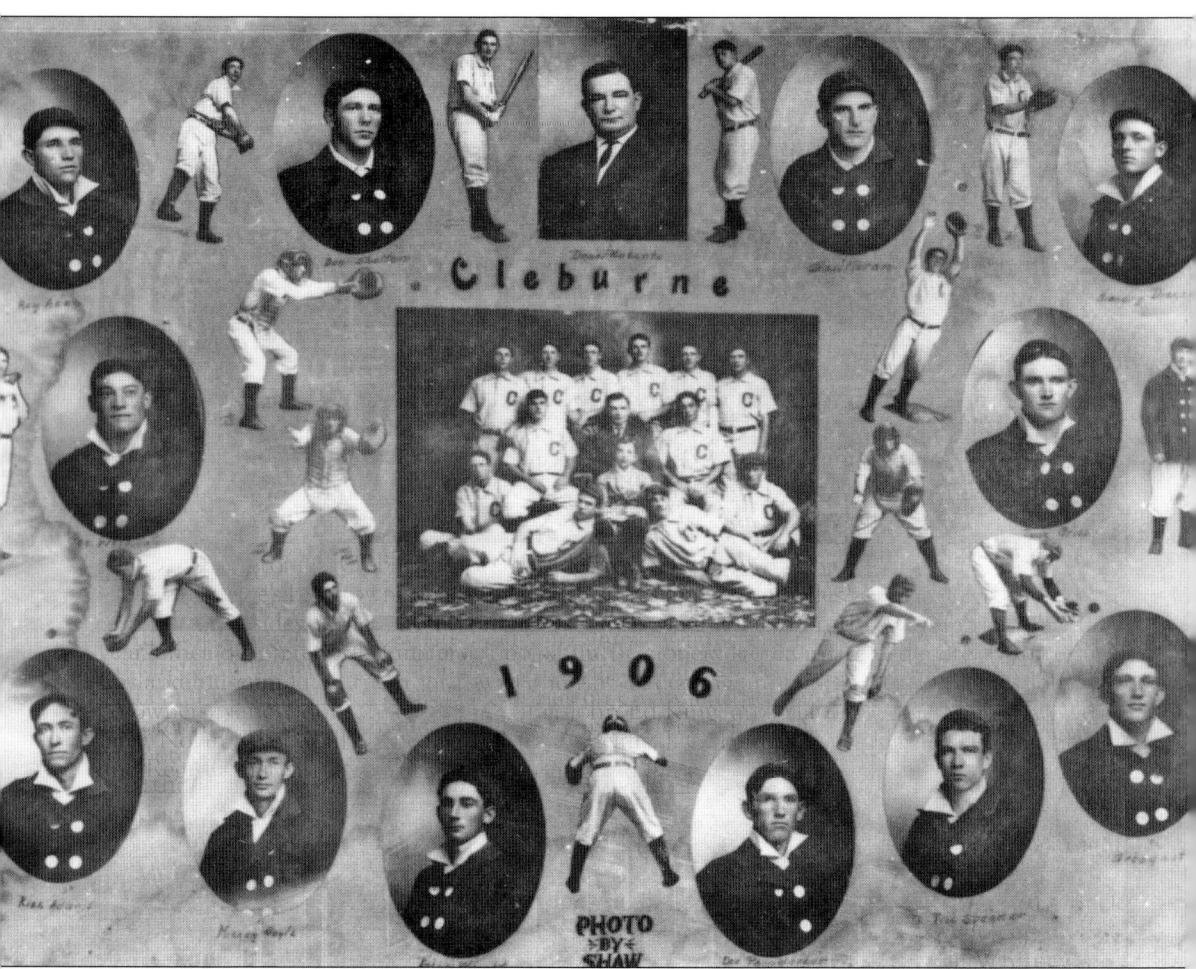

The Cleburne Railroaders, owned by Doak Roberts, was a Texas League baseball team that played in Gorman Park in the early 1900's. The Railroaders were considered one of the best teams in the early 20th century. Tris Speaker batted and threw left-handed and was one of six players to go on to play for the major leagues. He was known as one of the best offensive and defensive center fielders in history. Inducted into the Baseball Hall of Fame in 1937, Speaker had played for the Boston Red Sox and the Cleveland Indians and was on the World Series teams in 1912, 1915, and 1920. He left the major leagues in 1928. Pictured clockwise from top center are Doak Roberts, Charley Moran, Hickory Dickson, Dode Criss, Parker Arbogast, Tris Speaker, Dee Poindexter, Bobby Wright, Mickey Coyle, Rick Adams, George Whiteman, and manager Ben Shelton. The park was located on the corner of Hillsboro Street and Westhill Drive, now a part of Hulen Park. (Courtesy of Layland Museum.)

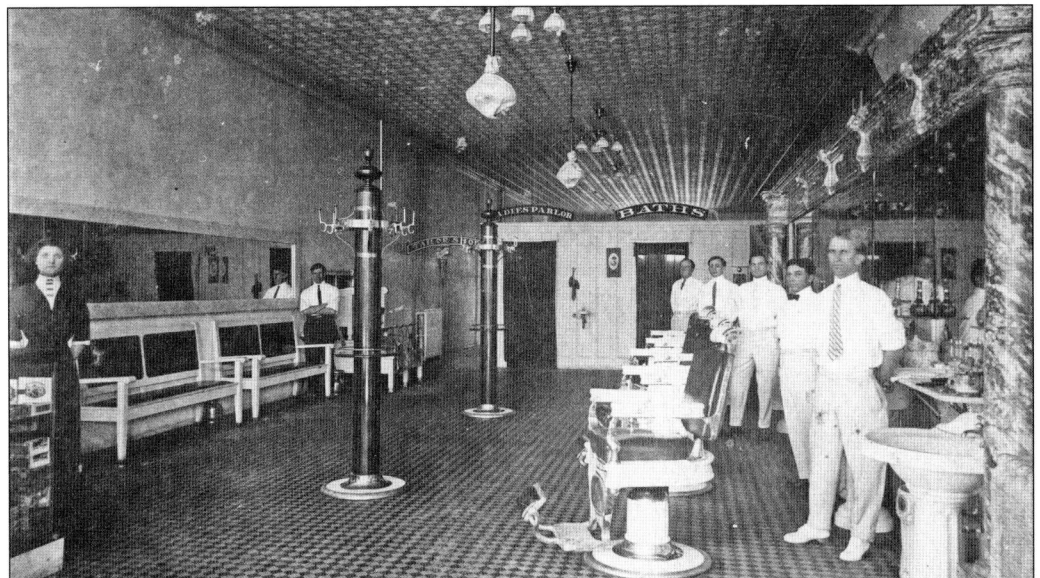

Peacock Barber Shop flourished at 109 East Henderson Street for 26 years. Sam Peacock's customers in the 10-chair shop could get a shave, haircut, and shoes shined. A cast iron heater provided hot water for bathing, necessary after a trip on the coal-powered locomotives. Lela and Everett Gober purchased the west half of the building in 1937 and operated the barber and beauty shop until 1950. (Courtesy of Layland Museum.)

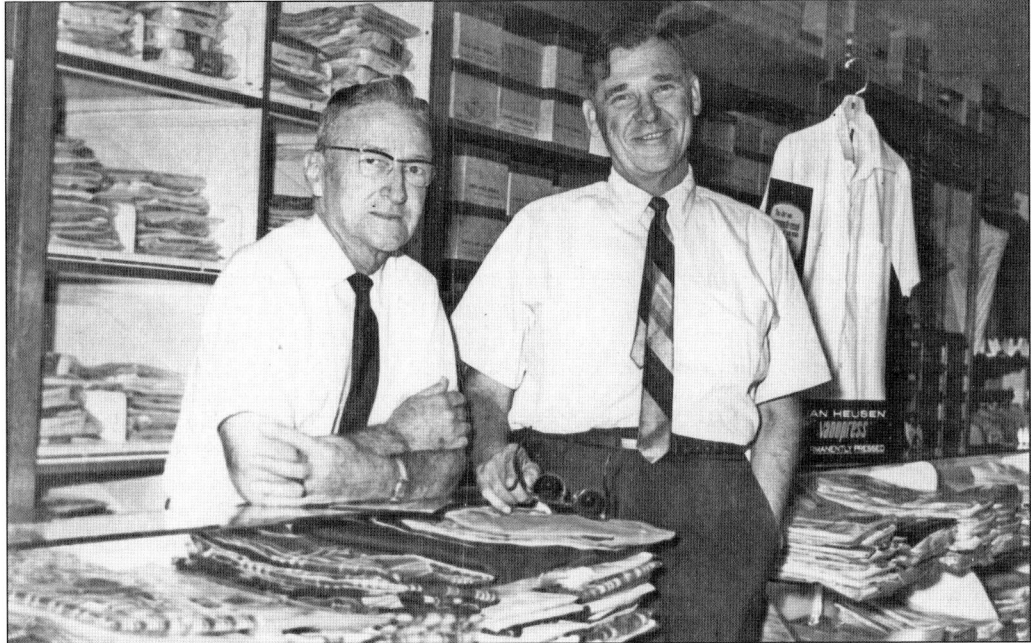

W. T. Bradbury opened Bradbury's Men's Store in 1910 on the south side of the square. Their motto was "The place to buy clothes." Many family members sold suits, shirts, and ties through the years, including the two men pictured above from left to right Robert "Bob" Bradbury and George "Buster" Bradbury. The store location moved twice but was at 106 South Main Street for about 50 years. It closed in 1983. (Courtesy of John Bradbury.)

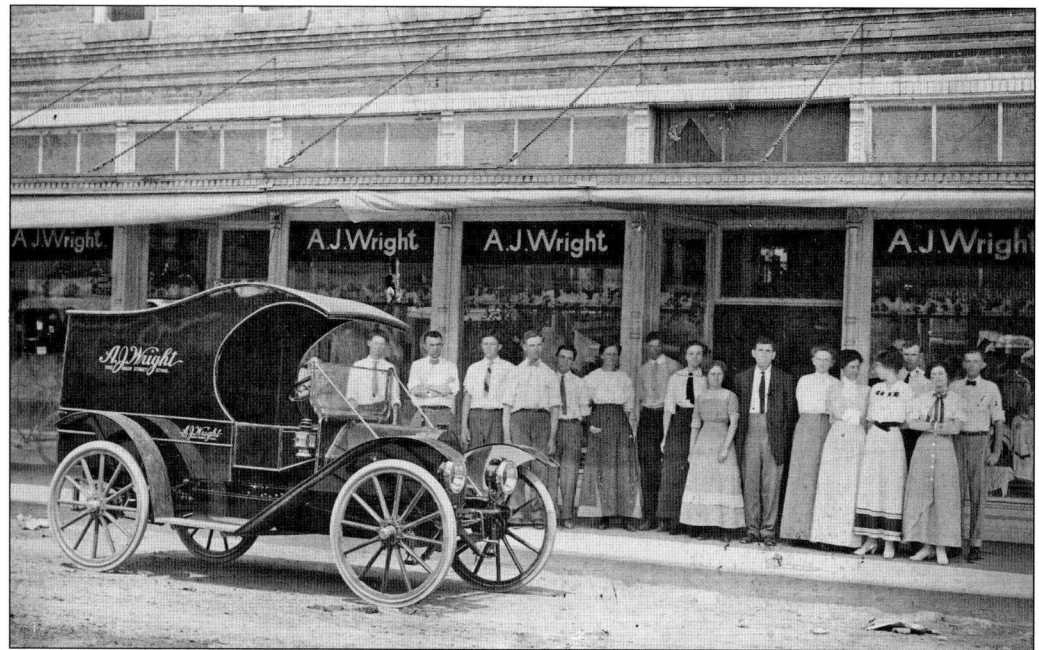

Rev. Harry Luck, founder and president of Cleburne Motor Car Manufacturing, built one of the first automobiles manufactured in Texas. The 1910 Chaparral had solid rubber tires and a 20-horsepower, air-cooled engine. The third vehicle produced, nicknamed the "Luck Truck," was purchased by A. J. Wright for deliveries. In the 1960s, Smikes Watson reproduced the Chaparral for use at Six Flags Over Texas in Arlington. (Courtesy of Layland Museum.)

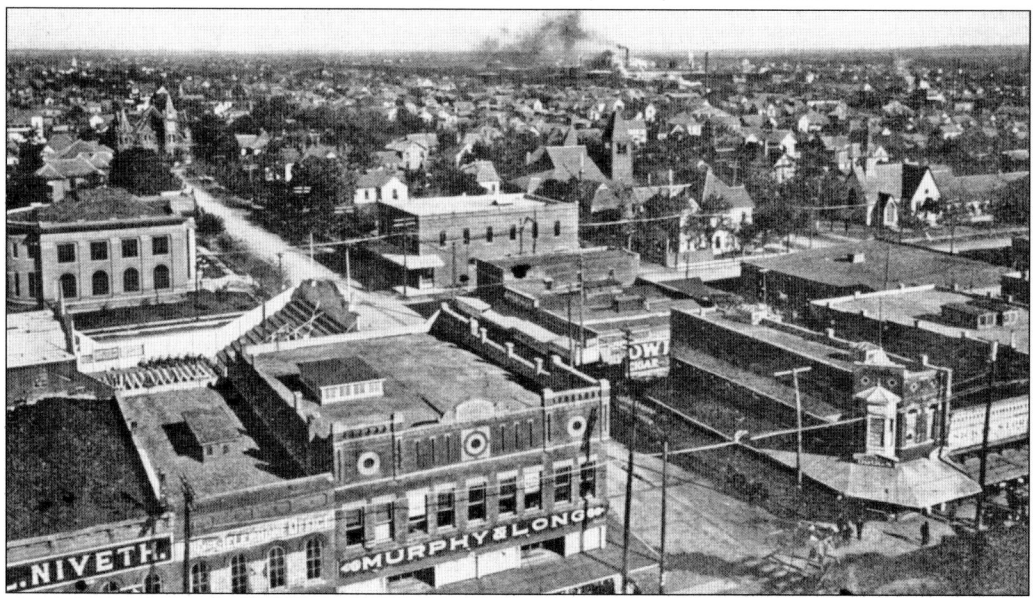

Behind the Murphy and Long building, Brown's Airdome, operated by Annie Clements, was an outdoor theater located south of the Carnegie Library. Red Clements, Bryan Miller, Tootsy Milam, and Van Rucker were prop men who pulled curtains and ran lights. During summer months, live plays and concerts were held. To show motion pictures—usually a silent film—employees stretched a bed sheet on the stage for a screen. (Courtesy of J. Gary Shaw collection.)

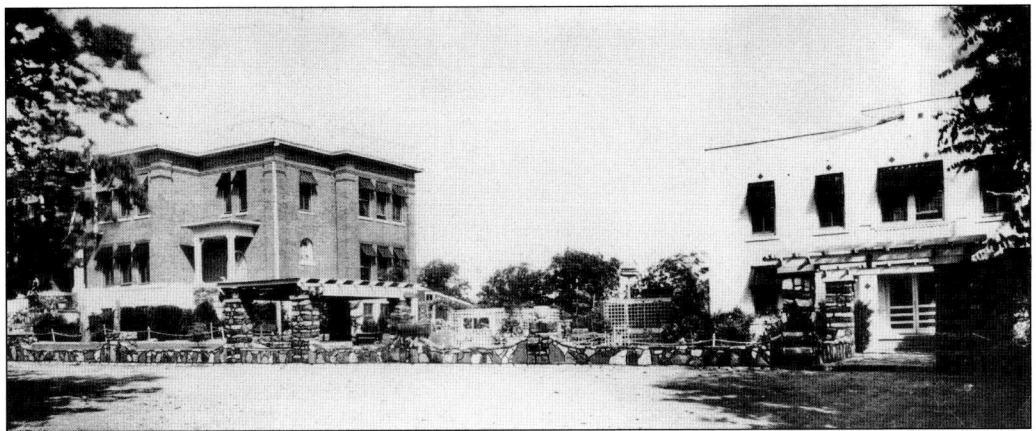

Clebarro College opened in 1909 in a three-story brick building, adding a woman's dorm three years later. Classes were offered in teacher training, music, expression, oratory, and culture. The school closed in 1917 due to the war. In 1919, Dr. C. Cooke and Dr. B. H. Turner reopened it as Meadowlawn Sanitarium. The hospital operated until Cooke donated part of the land for a new school, which was named in honor of him. (Courtesy of Layland Museum.)

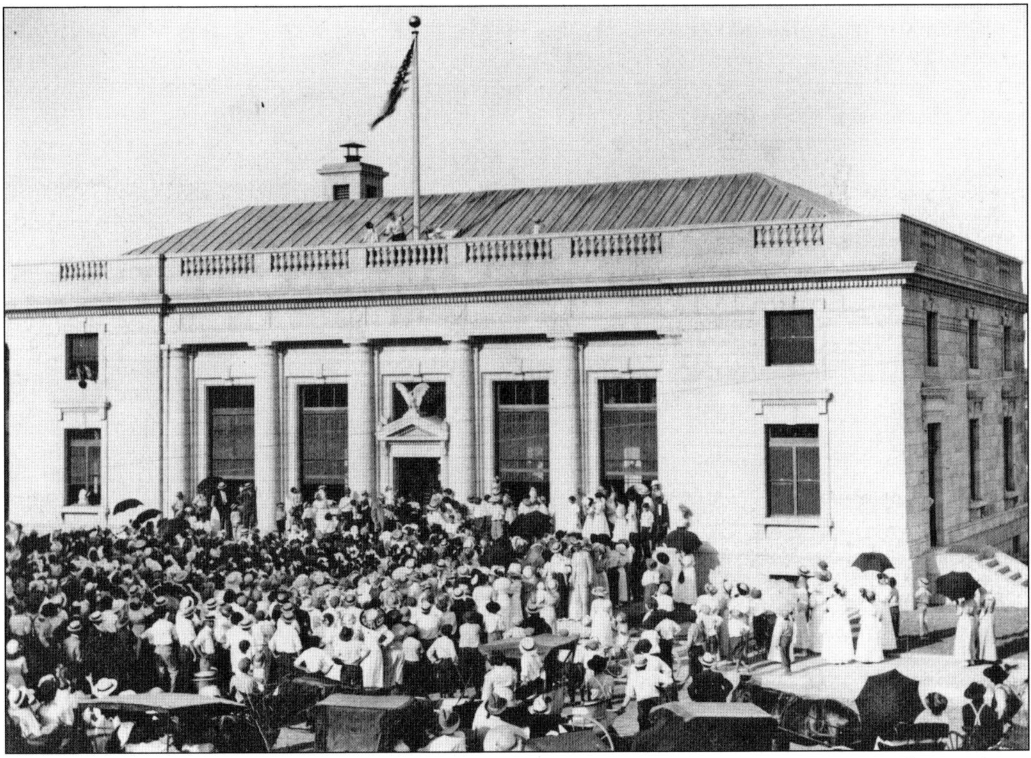

The first post office opened in a one-room house at 112 North Main Street in 1867 with Josephine Wren serving as postmaster. In 1912, an impressive neoclassical revival structure was completed on Robinson Street, and a public dedication service was held. This building served area citizens until 1991, when a new facility opened. (Courtesy of Layland Museum.)

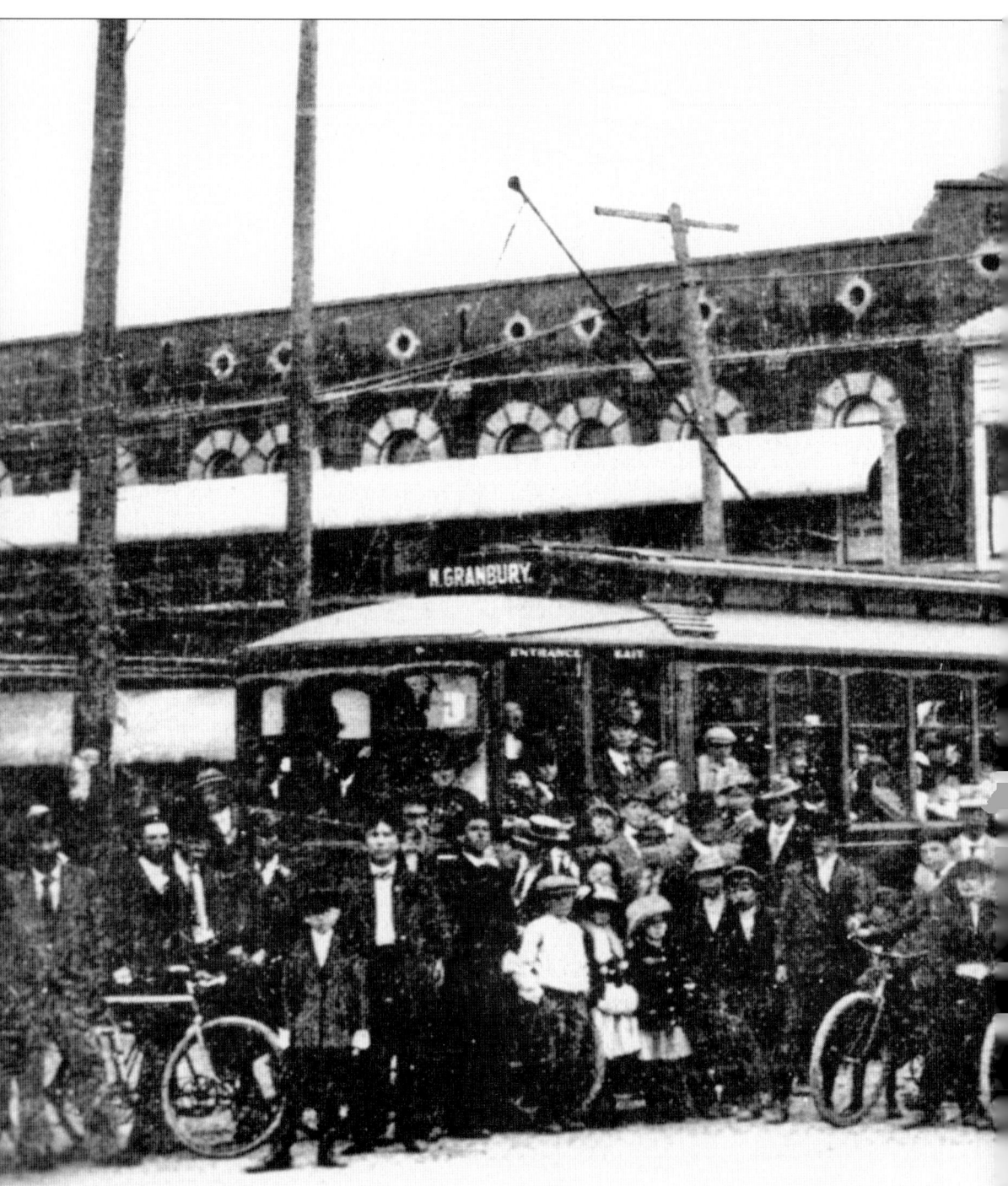

Cleburne Street Railway Company filled its cars to capacity on opening day in February 1911. The trolleys ran from 5:00 a.m. to 11:00 p.m., taking passengers through town and to Lovelady Park. The line ran as far east as Chase Street and as far west as Sunset Avenue and on to the park. It ran north all the way up Granbury Avenue and on North Robinson Street. Twenty-six prominent businessmen were guarantors for the system. The fair was a nickel. The line had four

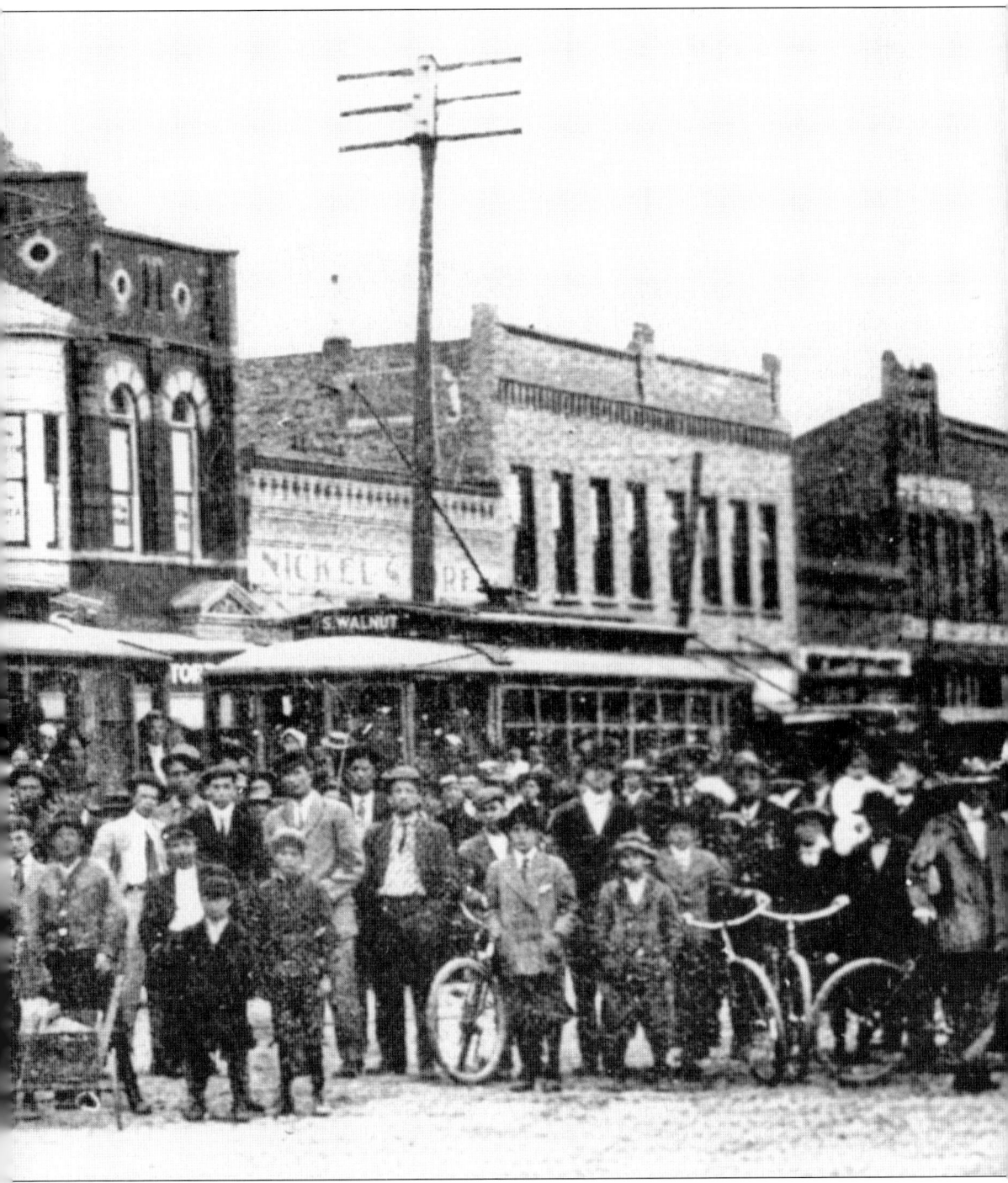

summer cars and eight regular cars. In the first two weeks of service, the daily average was over 2,000 riders. The company closed in 1915 after an accident. Lovelady Park, south of McAnear Creek, was shaded by pecan trees and had a pond for boating, a skating rink, and picnic tables. (Courtesy of Layland Museum.)

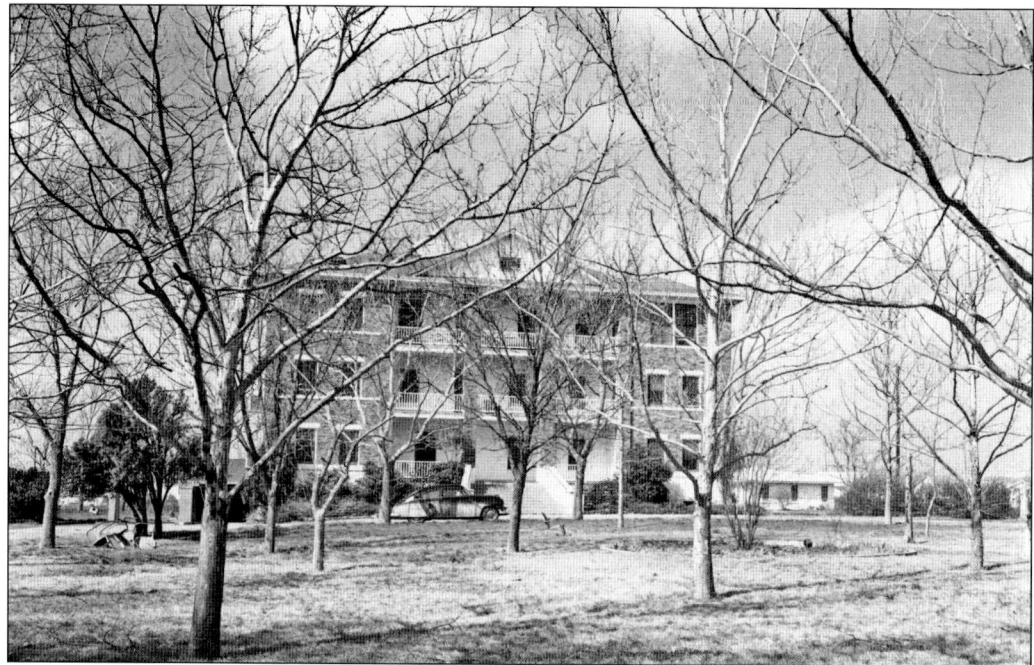

In 1912, Dr. C. C. Cooke and T. S. Jackson helped build the three-story redbrick Cleburne Sanitarium near the end of Smith and Featherstone Streets. Dr. R. L. and Jennie Harris purchased the facility in 1919 and began adding modern equipment and city utilities. Harris and his brother operated it as a hospital until 1936. Later it became a nursing home before closing. (Courtesy of Sandra Davis Jones.)

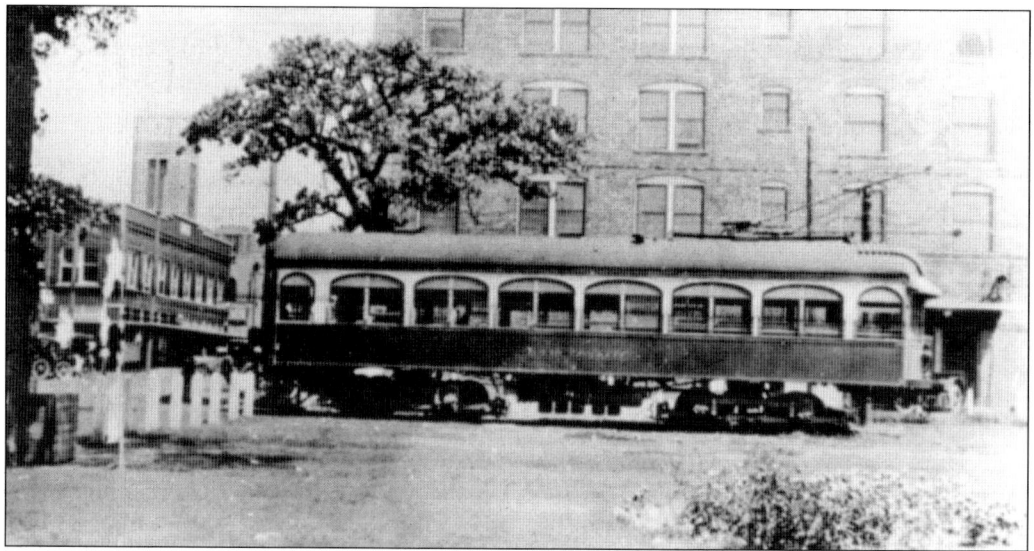

North Texas Traction Company began service in 1912 between Cleburne and Fort Worth. Each electric car held about 40 commuters. A one-way ticket was 88¢, and the cars were able to operate up to 80 miles per hour in open space. Local merchants ordered supplies, including food and furniture, and had them delivered to Cleburne on the interurban. Passenger service ended in 1931. This photograph shows a car in the yard south of the Liberty Hotel. (Courtesy of Don Ross Collection.)

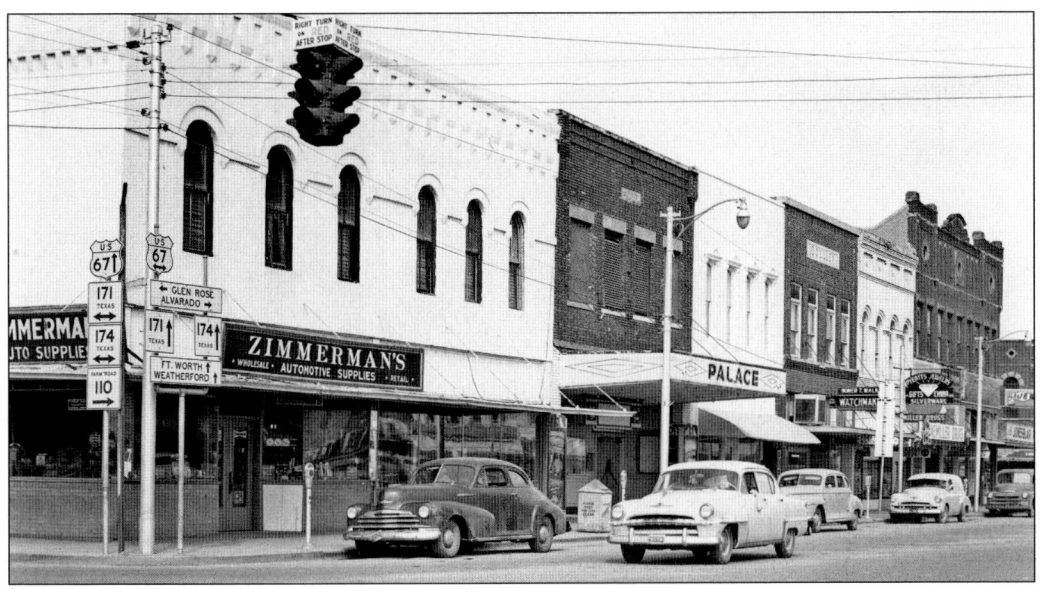

E. J. Zimmerman started City Electric and Auto Supply in 1913, furnishing parts for the growing automobile market. Known today as Zimmerman Sons and Company and managed by Paul Talley, it is located on North Main Street. This firm wired the first house in town and made and sold the first crystal radio sets. Pictured is Zimmerman's on the north side of the square in the 1950s. Below is J. Frank Thompson demonstrating the crystal radio. An electric power plant was constructed in 1888 near the site of the waterworks. The city was lit with 500 sixteen-candle lamps until the business burned in 1892. The Cleburne Electric Light plant was established in 1895 and merged with Texas Power and Light in 1912. (Above, courtesy of Layland Museum; below, courtesy of Paul Talley.)

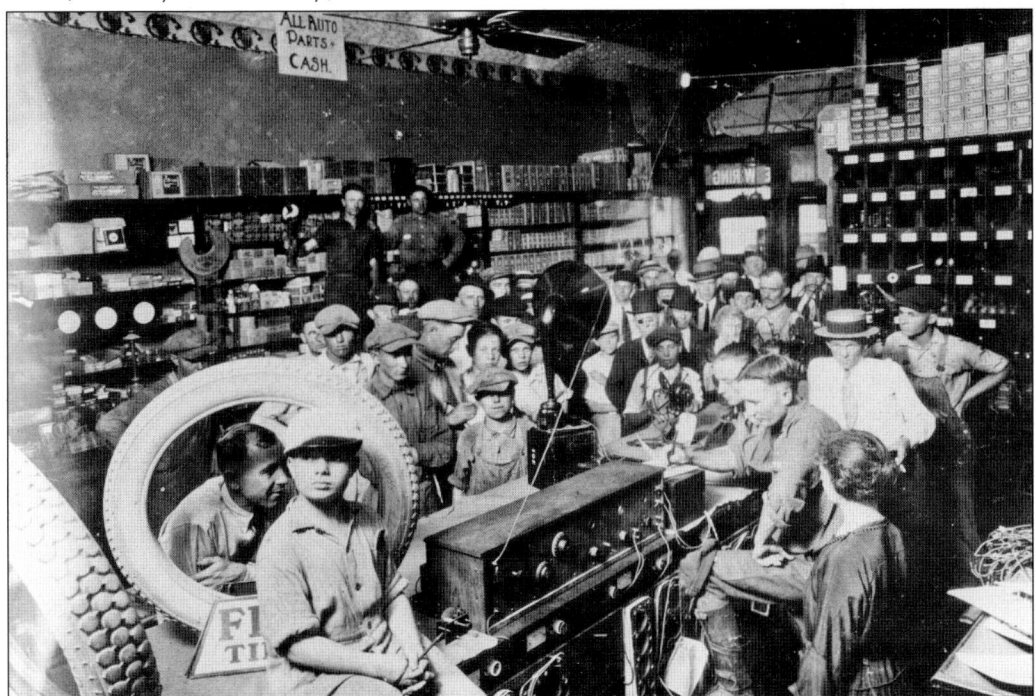

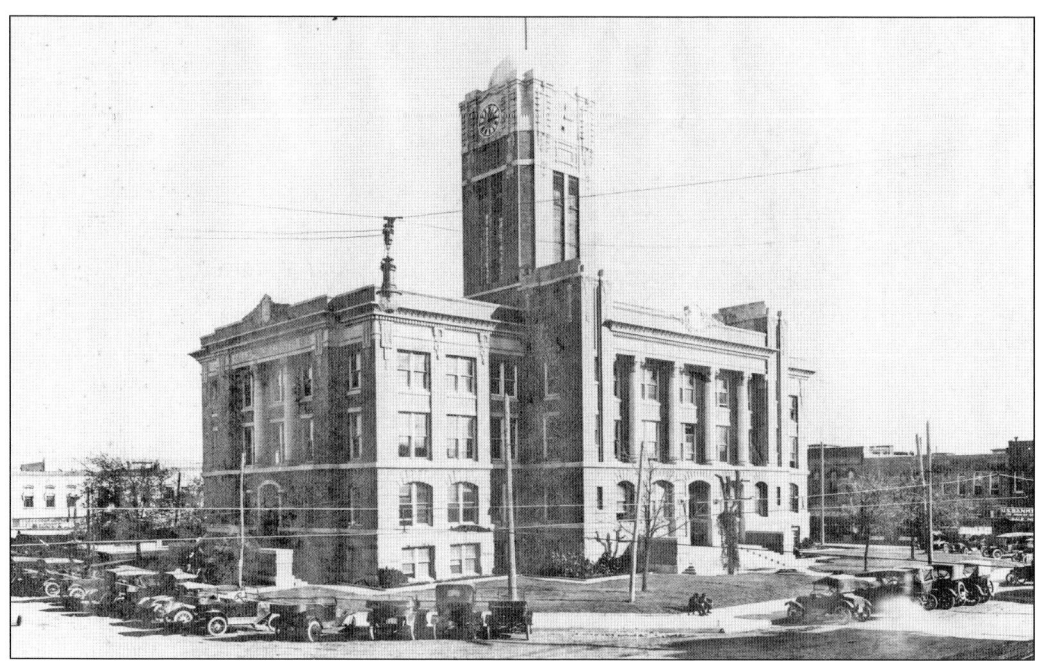

Texas red granite from Burnet County and dark, highly polished Georgia creole marble were used to build the current six-story Johnson County Courthouse. Completed in 1913, this neoclassical revival structure boasts a stained-glass dome and open rotunda. E. J. Zimmerman volunteered his time as superintendent of construction. After a preservation and renovation process was completed in 2001, county offices moved back into the historic structure. The Johnson County commissioner from 1920 to 1924, Roy L. Doak (far left), and county court reporter Homer Wicker (far right) are pictured in a courthouse office. (Above, courtesy of Layland Museum; below, courtesy of Marshall Wicker.)

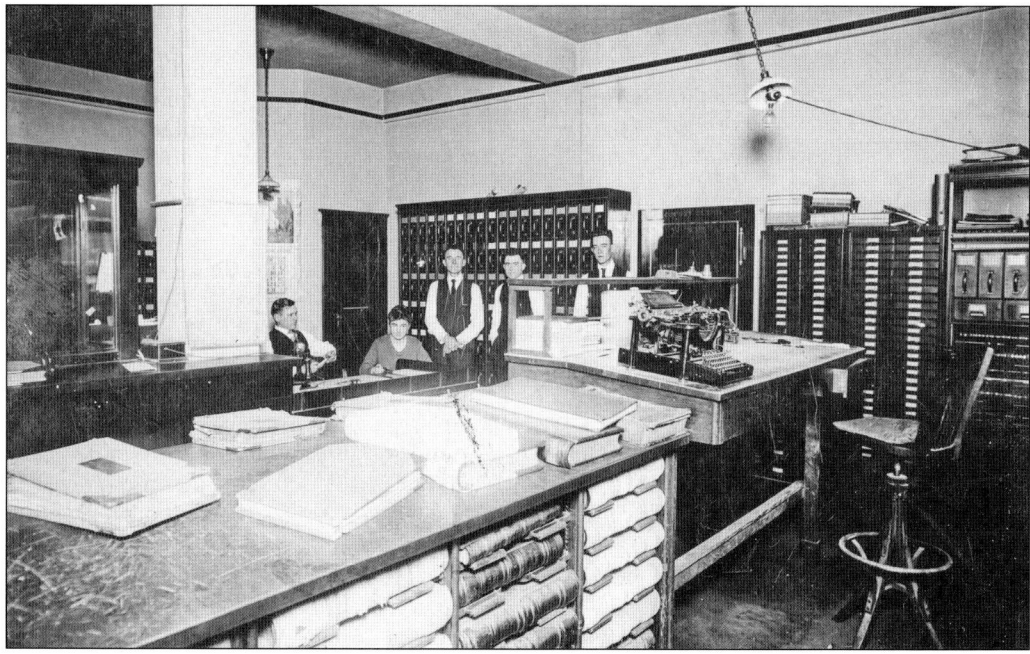

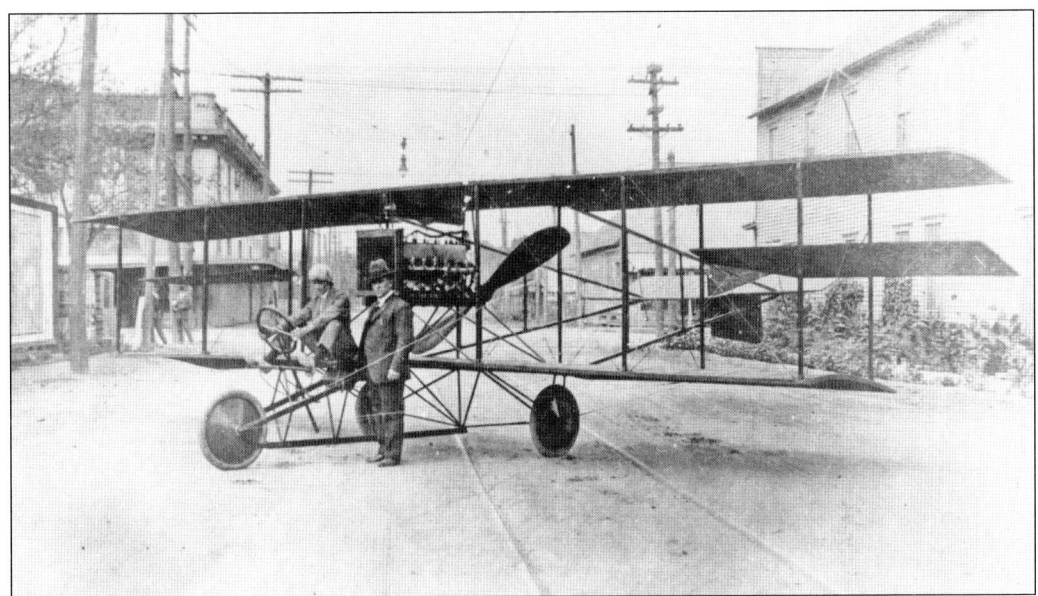

"Old Soggy No. 1," the first airplane built in Texas, is shown in Cleburne in 1912. At the controls is Floyd H. "Slats" Rodgers, who built it with help from his friend and Santa Fe engineer John C. Fine (standing). The airplane construction began in Cleburne and was completed in Keene. Rodgers recouped some expenses by setting up a tent and showing off the plane, charging 50¢ admission to see it. In three days, he made $700. (Courtesy of Layland Museum.)

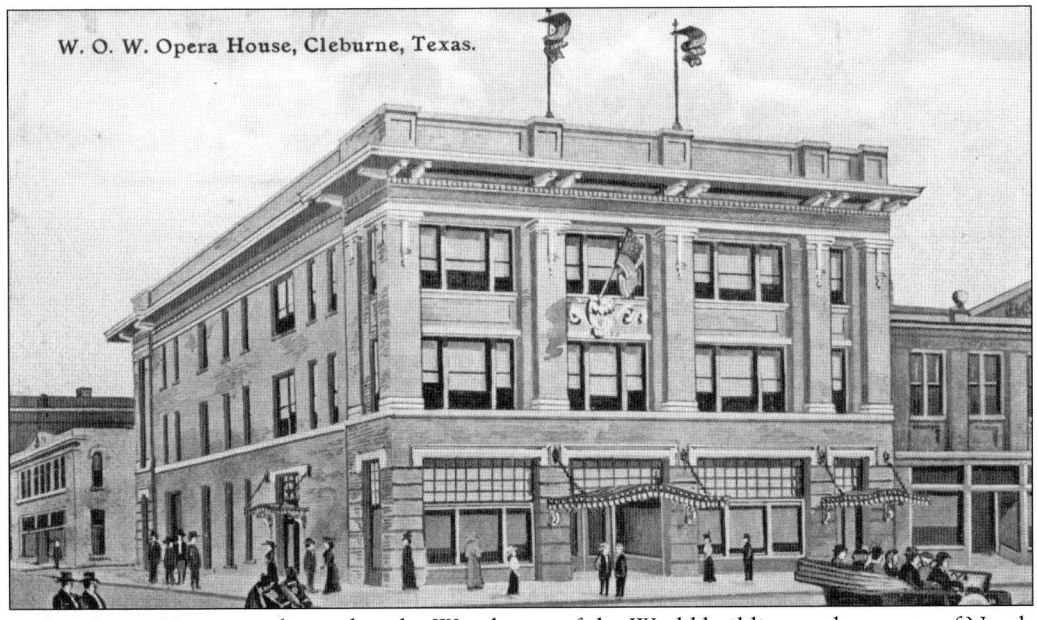

WOW Opera House was housed in the Woodsmen of the World building at the corner of North Main Street and Wardville Street. Later the offices of Texas Power and Light were on the ground floor, which is currently occupied by the Red Cross office. Upstairs has housed the WOW Life Insurance offices since 1914, when it was built. (Courtesy of Layland Museum.)

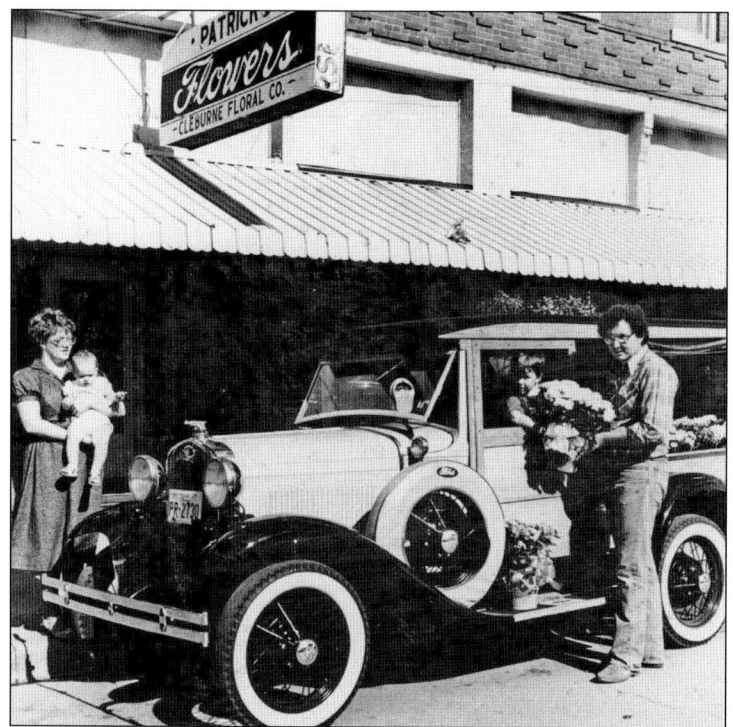

Patrick's Cleburne Floral, owned by the founder's grandson John Joiner Patrick and wife, Brenda, began in 1916. Jack Joiner Patrick first opened a greenhouse that included a large conservatory on the eastern edge of town, then moved the business to Caddo Street. This is one of Cleburne's oldest businesses still operated by members of the original family, including Tara Patrick, the forth generation to continue the tradition. Pictured from left to right are Brenda, holding daughter Tara; son Bryan in the car; and John. (Courtesy of John and Brenda Patrick.)

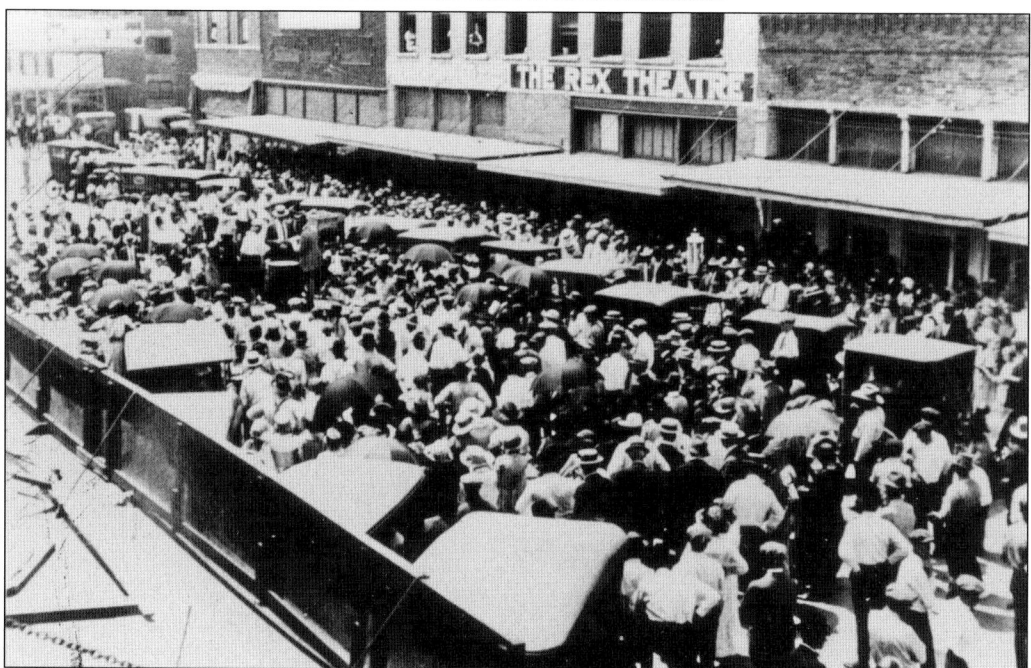

The first moving picture show in Cleburne was the *Great Train Robbery*, shown under a large black tent provided by a traveling carnival about the same time the Best Theatre opened in 1904. Bill Bransom operated the Best, which showed mostly Westerns. W. C. McDonald opened the Rex Theatre in 1914 on the north side of the courthouse square and could seat 500. Admission was 5¢. (Courtesy of Layland Museum.)

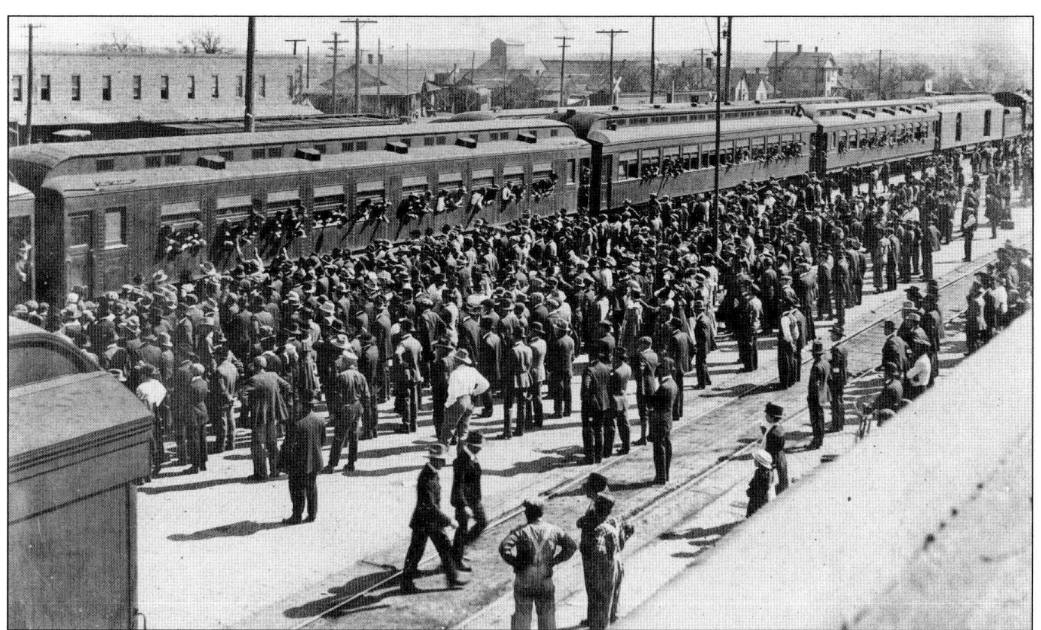

Hundreds gathered at the Santa Fe tracks to honor World War I soldiers as a packed troop train traveled through Cleburne. In the background is a large building east of the tracks that housed a barbershop, a tailor, and other companies, the Missouri, Kansas, and Texas Railway depot, and a milling company. Remains of the milling company were still standing in 2009. Citizens also supported the war effort by rallying for war bonds, walking west on East Henderson Street. Visible in the far background is the dome of East Henderson Street Baptist Church. During this time period, the influenza pandemic hit, keeping doctors and undertakers busy. (Both, courtesy of Layland Museum.)

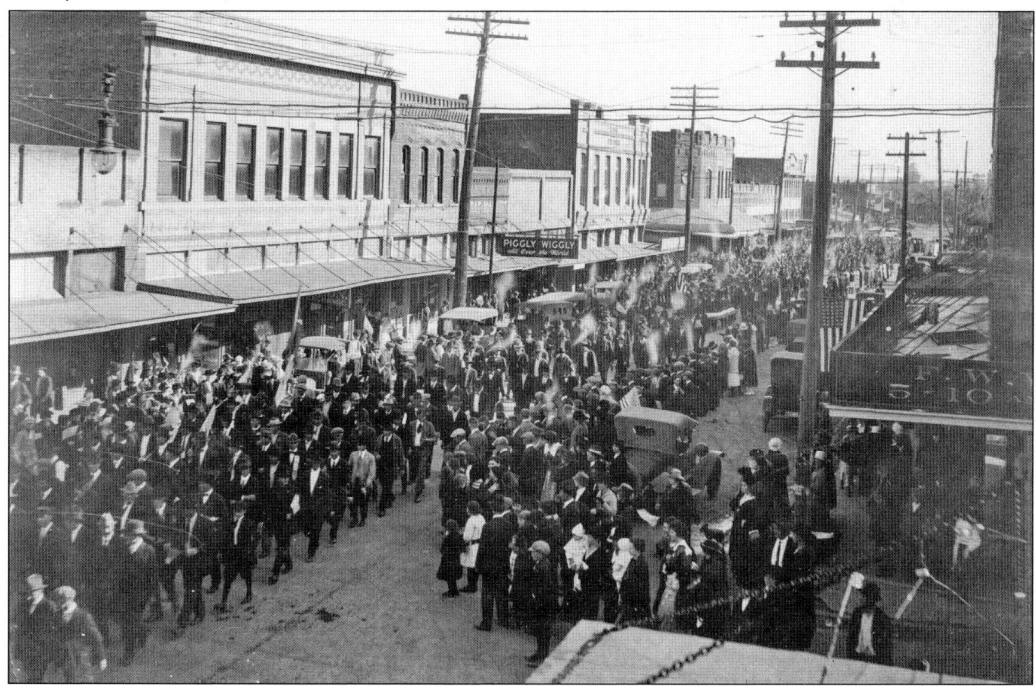

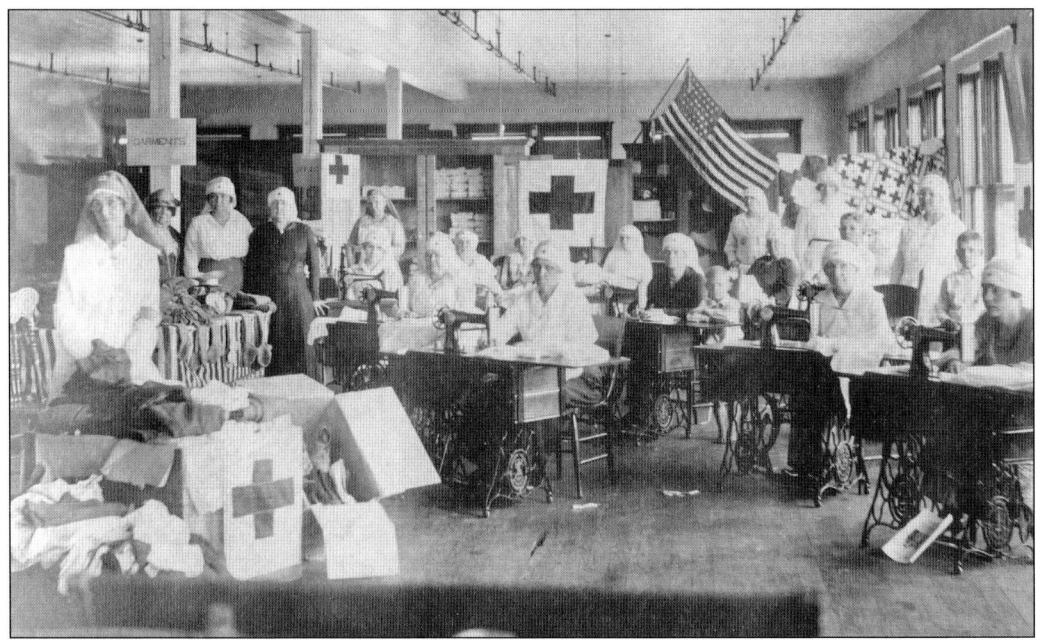

Uniformed Red Cross ladies used Singer sewing machines in the upstairs room of the fire station and made garments or bandages for the World War I effort. The flag in the background shows 46 stars. The woman standing at far right is Laura Jane Couch Sowell with her son David S. "Dave" Sowell Jr. to her right and another son, Thomas Milton "Doc" Sowell, on her left. Others in the photograph are unidentified. (Courtesy of the Sowell family.)

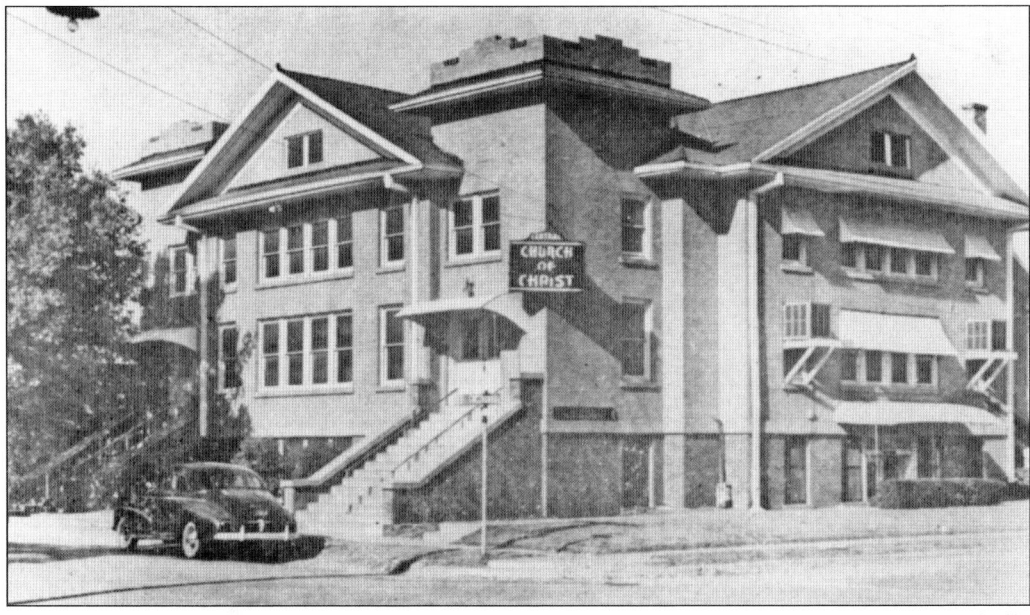

The Central Church of Christ completed its building on the corner of Robinson and Wardville Streets in 1917 and served its congregation for 38 years. A new building was constructed in 1954 on the corner of Robinson and Brown Streets. This congregation and Westside Church of Christ combined and now worship together at the church on Westhill Drive. (Courtesy of Layland Museum.)

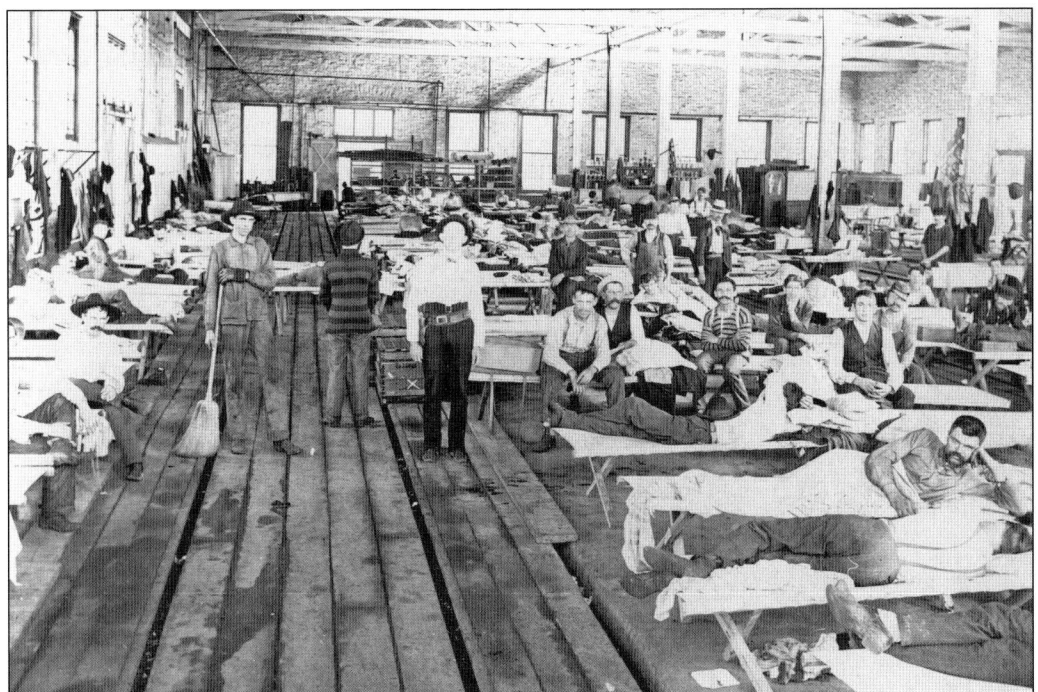

Santa Fe employees went on strike for higher pay in 1922, and many of them lost their jobs. Those who continued to work during the strike lived in a dorm on site. Businesses closed, and the governor sent Texas Rangers to keep things under control. All four city banks failed in the 1920s, which further depressed the economy. (Courtesy of Layland Museum.)

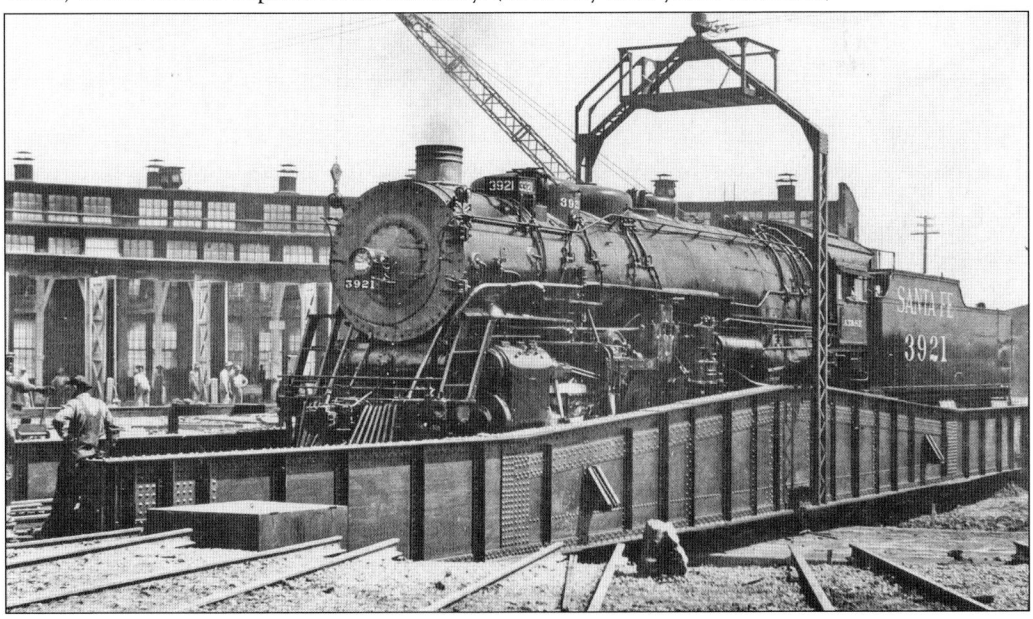

In 1908, the roundhouse was extended and an 85-foot turntable added. Also added during the same year was a new coach shop and paint and woodworking department. Much of the shops had been destroyed by fire in 1904. In 1946, the turntable was replaced by a new version, extending it to 120 feet. (Courtesy of Michael Percifield.)

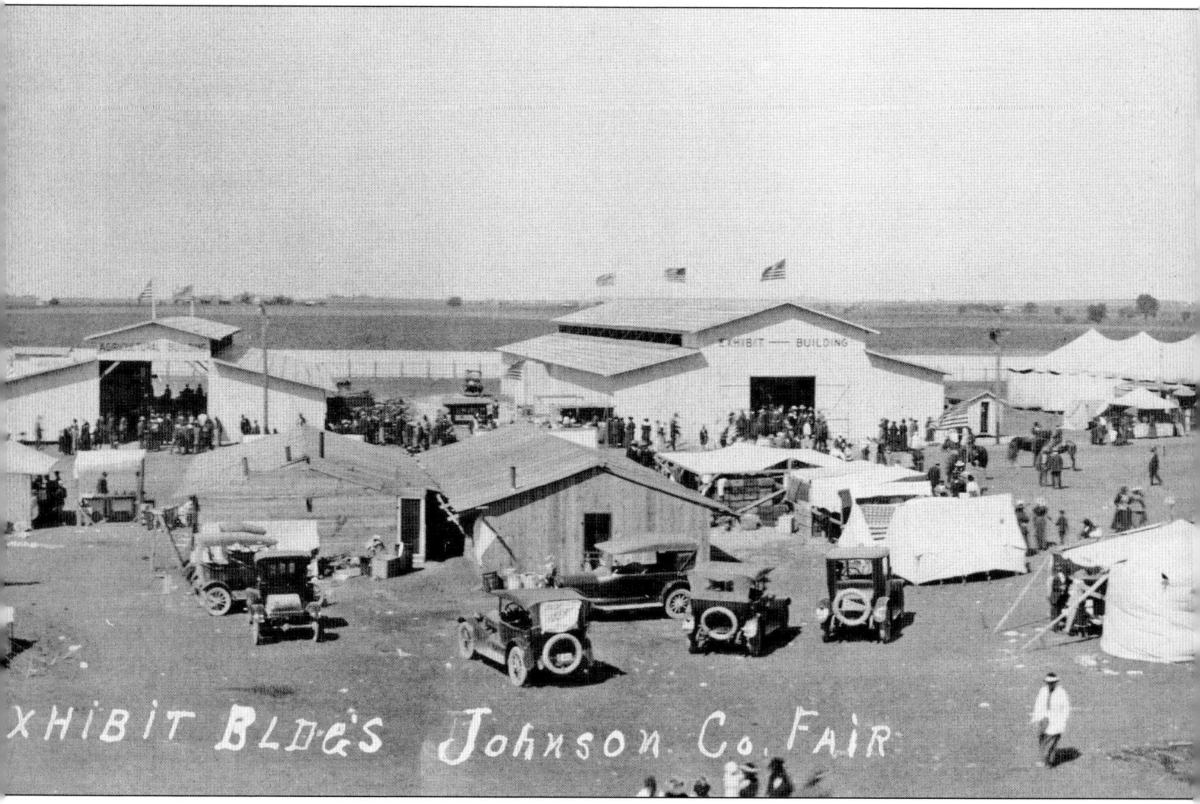

EXHIBIT BLDG'S Johnson Co. FAIR

Johnson County Agricultural Fair was located near Kilpatrick and Granbury Streets with about 15,000 people a day attending the five-day opening in October 1917. The grandstand was packed for automobile and horse races. Tents and agricultural buildings housed livestock shows, canning, art and needlework displays, a culinary competition, and a baby contest. The opening was preceded by a parade, and a large carnival was set up on the grounds. Joe

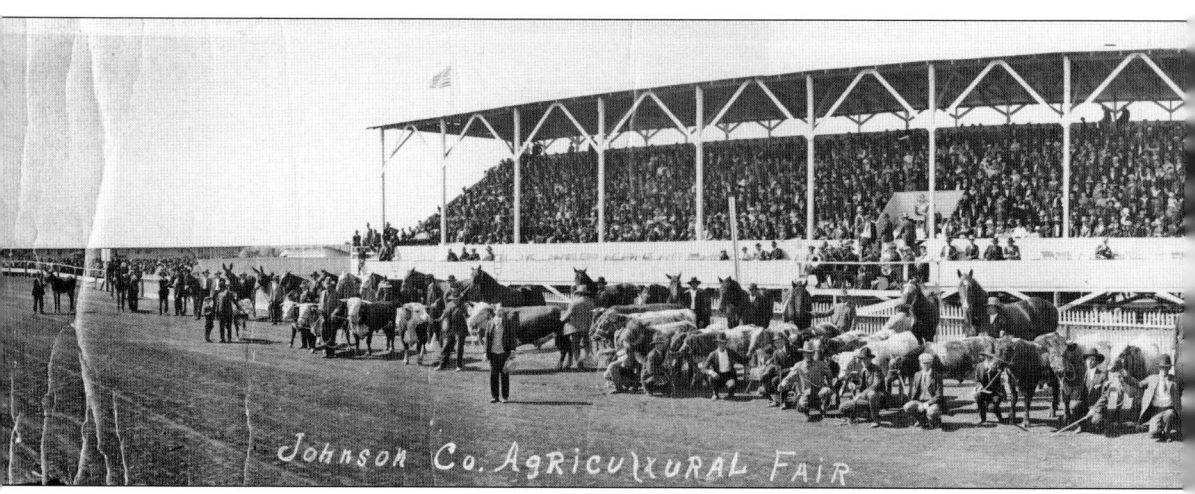

Johnson Co. Agricultural Fair

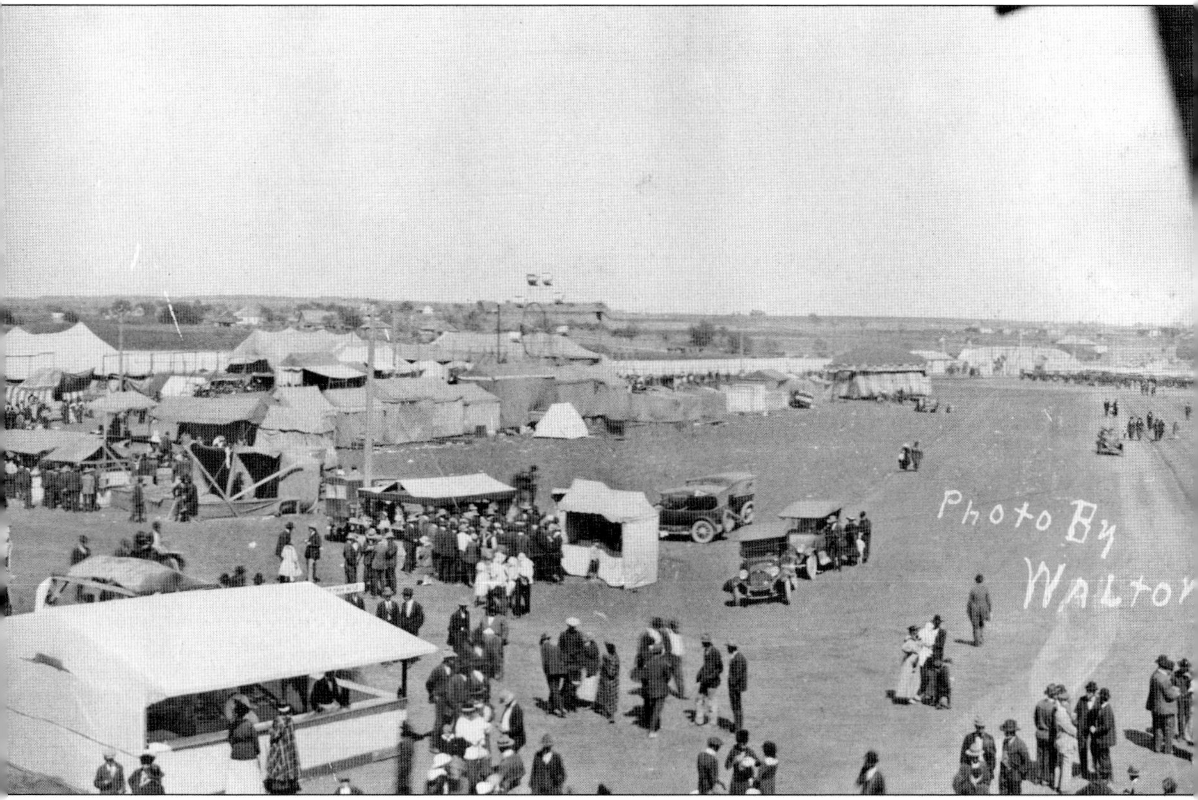

F. Cornish of Temple organized the fair construction and the opening. Shares were sold to area individuals and businesses to fund the project's beginnings. The county also operated a dipping vat for cattle at this location near Kilpatrick Street. The grandstand and many of the buildings were destroyed by a tornado in 1922. (Both, courtesy of Layland Museum.)

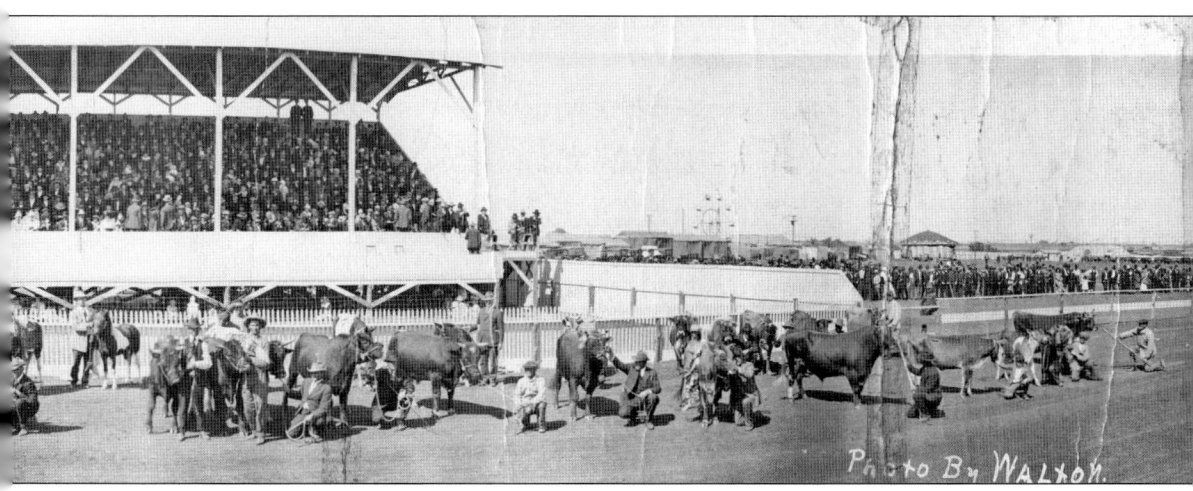

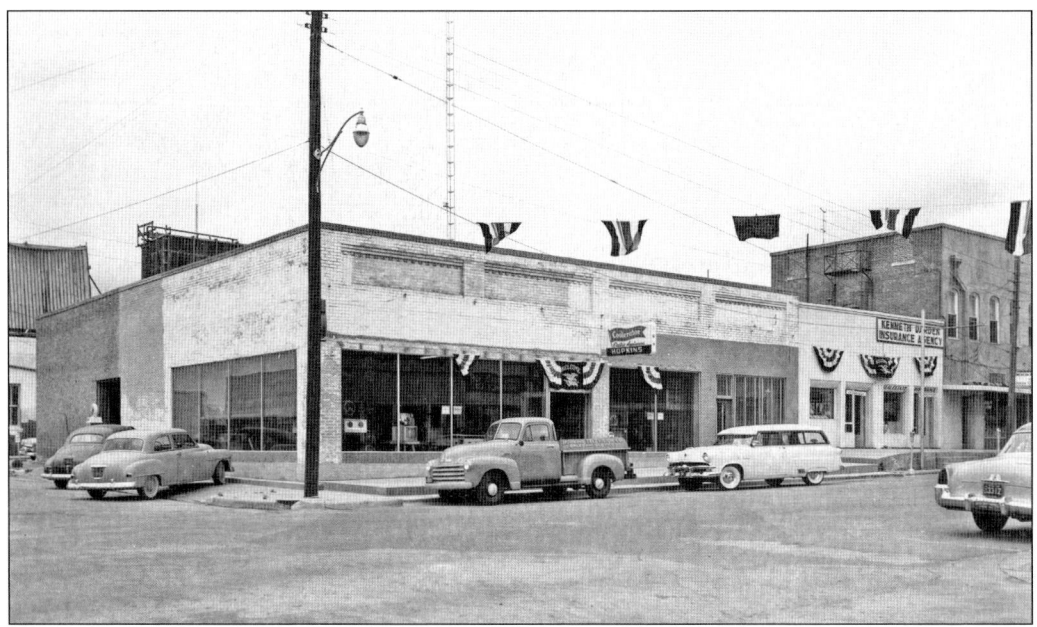

Milas Martin Hopkins opened a garage and gas station in 1924 a block west of the courthouse on Henderson Street. Son Milas Merrell "Hop" Hopkins joined the family business in 1946. They learned to change with the times, selling appliances and then televisions. The first color television set in town was displayed in their window for everyone to watch. They sold the company in 1993. (Courtesy of Layland Museum.)

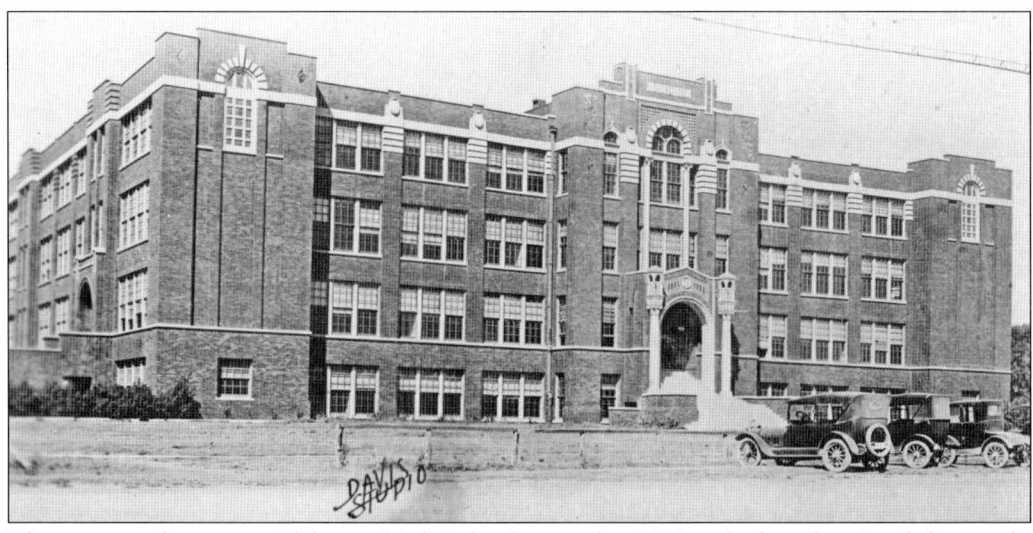

The spacious three-story Cleburne High School opened in 1919 with three boys' and three girls' houses in place of homerooms. Supt. Emmett Brown implemented this system. The girls' houses were Barton, Willard, and Adams. The boys' houses were Riley, Wilson, and Edison. Students in each house sat together in the central auditorium for pep rallies, competing for the spirit stick, and for southern assembly shows. (Courtesy of Sandra Davis Jones.)

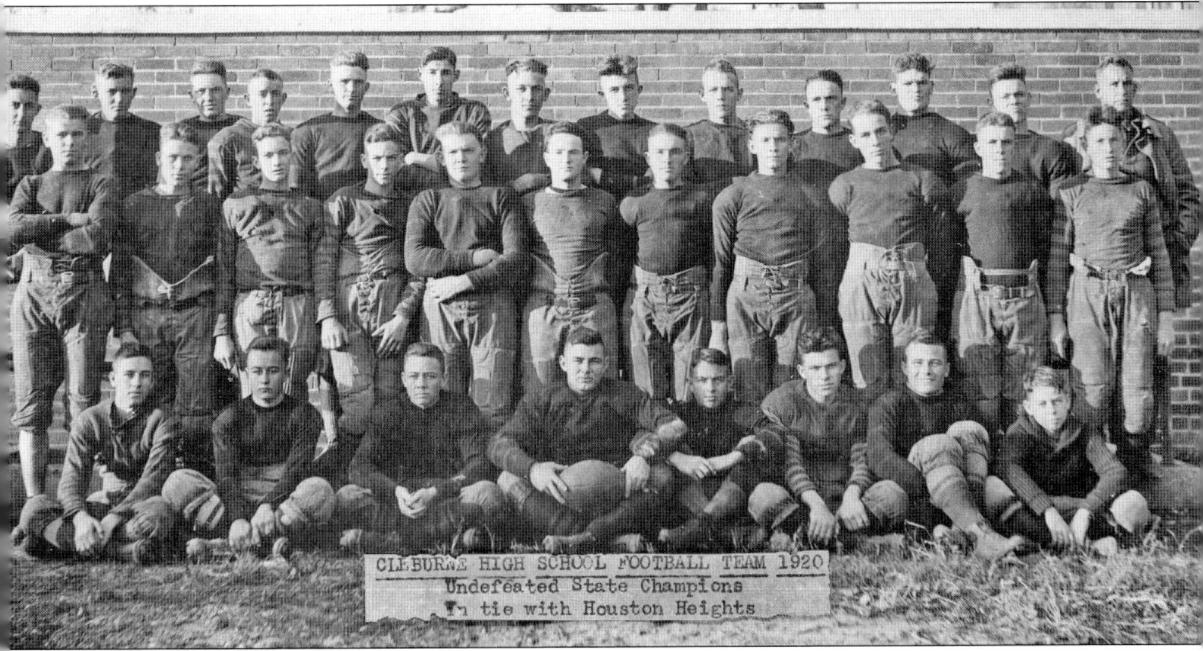

The Cleburne Yellow Jackets battled Houston Heights to a scoreless deadlock in Austin to share the 1920 state football championship. It was the first state meet of its kind. A special train carried 500 Cleburne fans, athletes, and the 15-member band with director Admire Lewis to the game. Team members were, from left to right, (first row) Byron Rhome, Lang Holt, Reuben Ransome, Joe Rhome (captain), Luther "Snag" Hill, Noel Pittman, Bolton Head, and Sid Norwood; (second row) Curtis Poindexter (captain), Ben Gaby, Duncan Robinson, Sam Allen, Louis Poindexter, Red Westbrook, Marvin Farris, Barton Hinton, Allen Ferrell, Frank McClendon, and Clark Lee; (third row) Joe Bailey Meacham, Claude Lockman, Fred Cornelius, Jimmy Wyman, Swan Taylor, Albert Sowell, Marion Tommy, Calvin Dickey, Clarence Smith, H. L. Bicknell, Doss Richardson, Ronie Carter, and Fred G. Erney (coach). Rhome Field, located behind the 1920 high school, was named for Joe Rhome. (Courtesy of Layland Museum.)

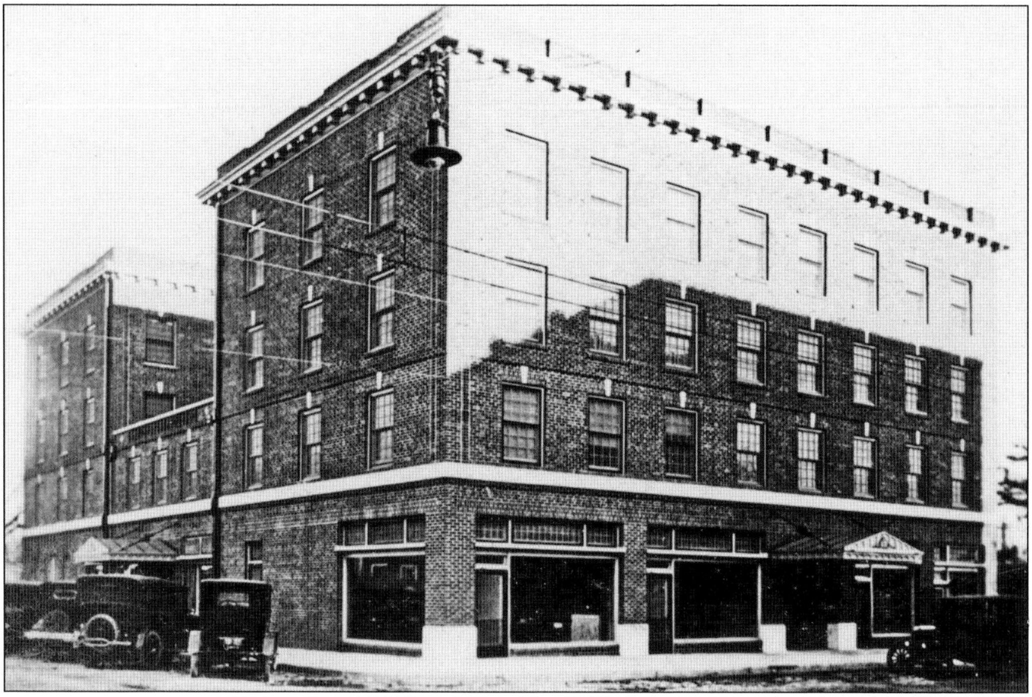

The first electric elevator in Cleburne took guests to the 69 rooms, a ladies parlor, and a banquet hall in the four-story Liberty Hotel. A. J. Wright opened the brick hotel in 1924 at a cost of $200,000, which included a coffee shop where the counter seated 20. Black and white terrazzo tile covered the lobby and dining room floors. Santa Fe crew members often used this hotel for boarding until the railroad built a dorm. In 1932, Lawrence Welk's band, the Hotsy-Totsy Boys, played for a packed crowd. Pictured below are, from left to right, employees Osborn Wilson, Guy Jay, Steve Amos, Mitchell Husk, and Clarence Gambel, who for over 50 years operated the switchboard and lobby counter at night. The interurban ticket office was across the street, and its yard was next door. (Both, courtesy of Layland Museum.)

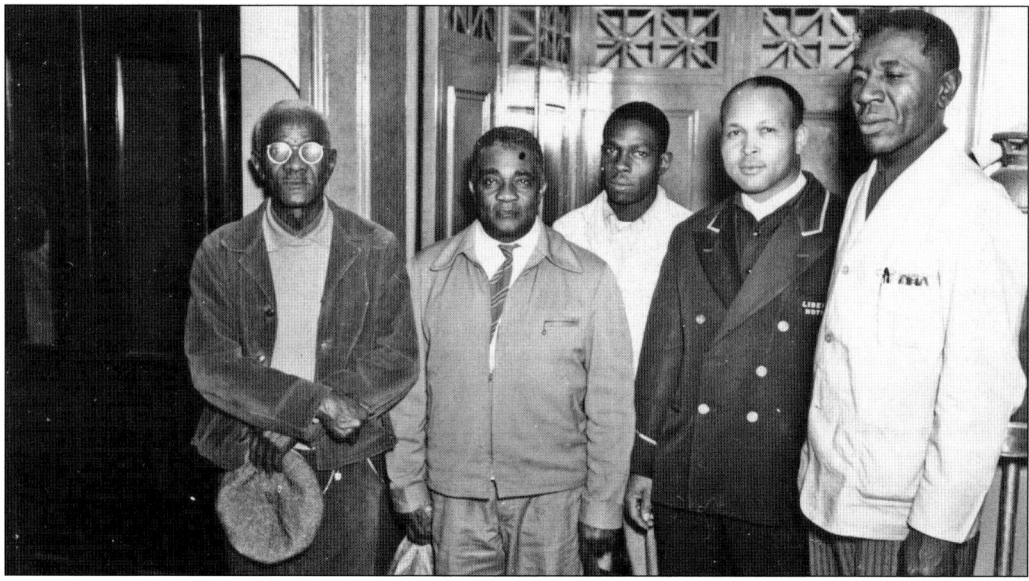

# Three
# 1926–1950

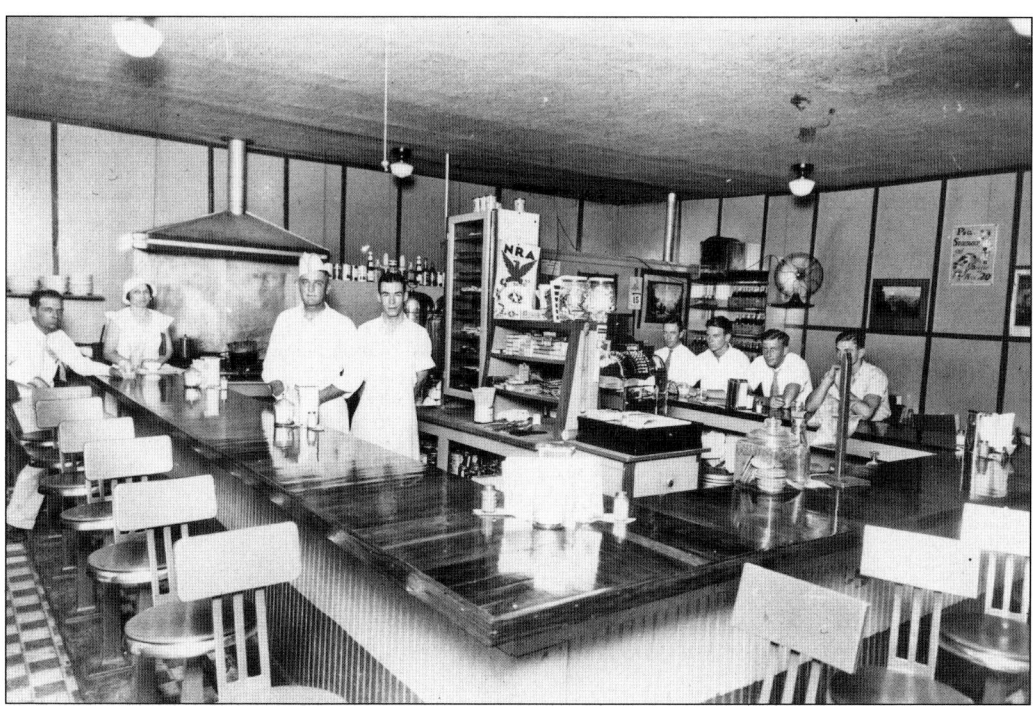

Ralph Chafin began a tradition of family-owned cafés in the 1920s when he opened one on the square. Standing behind the counter in this 1933 photograph are Ralph Chafin and cook Buddy Lightfoot. Seated at the end of the counter is Gurtha Chafin. Chaf-In, now owned by Dan Roberts, still specializes in home-style cooking and baked items and is located on West Henderson Street. (Courtesy of the author.)

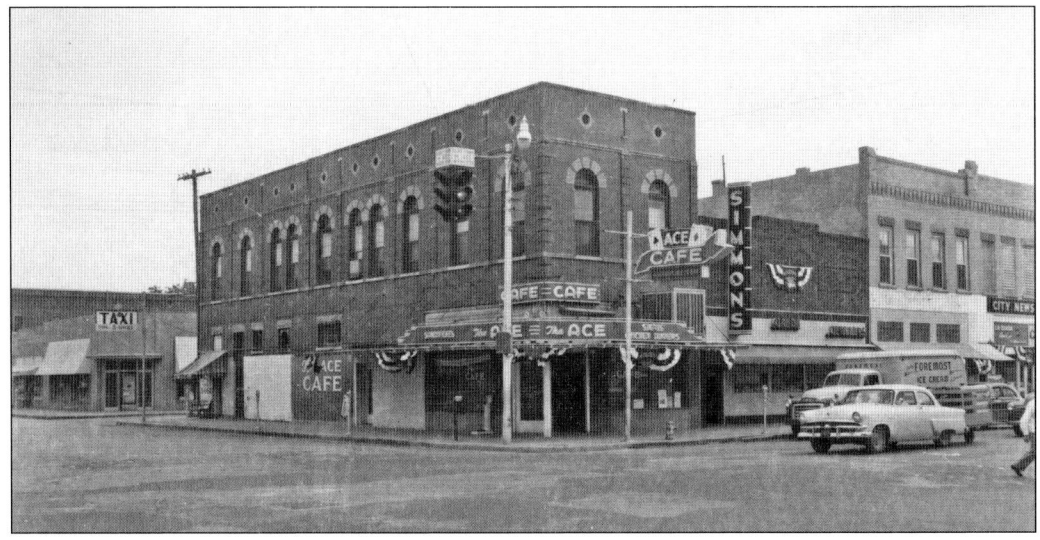

On the northeast corner of Henderson and Caddo Streets stood the Ace Café, opened by Rupert "Whitey" White in 1926. He not only had good food, he also had one of the first televisions in Cleburne in 1948. Customers packed the café on Monday nights to watch wrestling. (Courtesy of Layland Museum.)

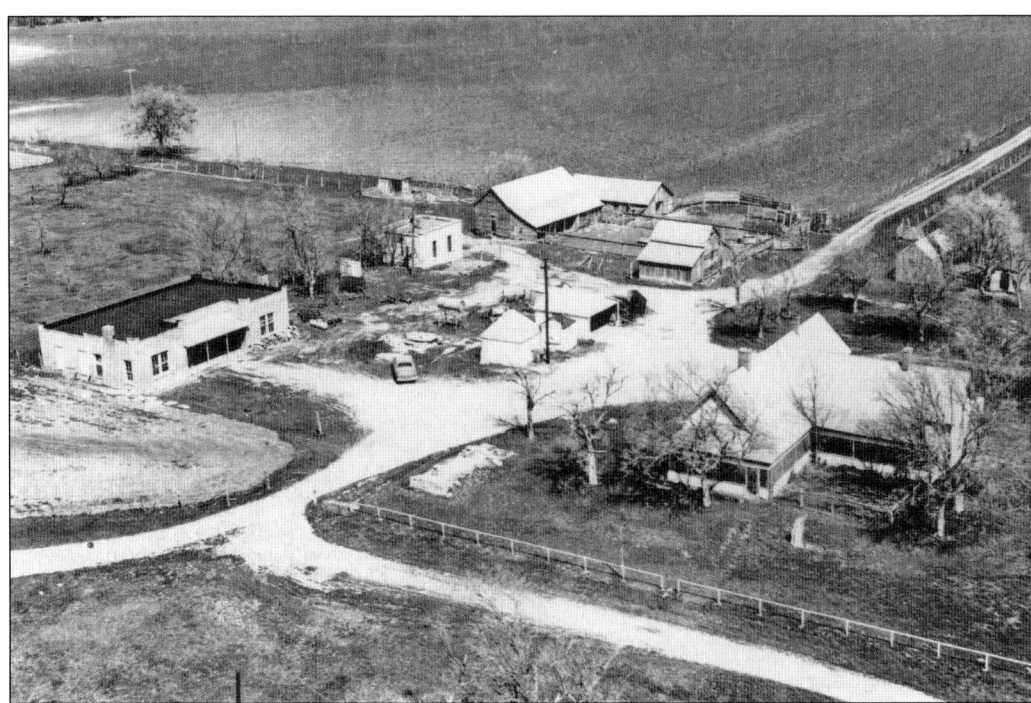

From 1888 until 1944, a county farm served as a home for poor people, the mentally ill, wayward girls, and convicts. They ran a dairy; raised sugar cane, cotton, oats, and hogs; and had a large vegetable garden. The cemetery was moved in 1963 to Rose Hill Cemetery to make way for the building of Lake Pat Cleburne. (Courtesy of Layland Museum.)

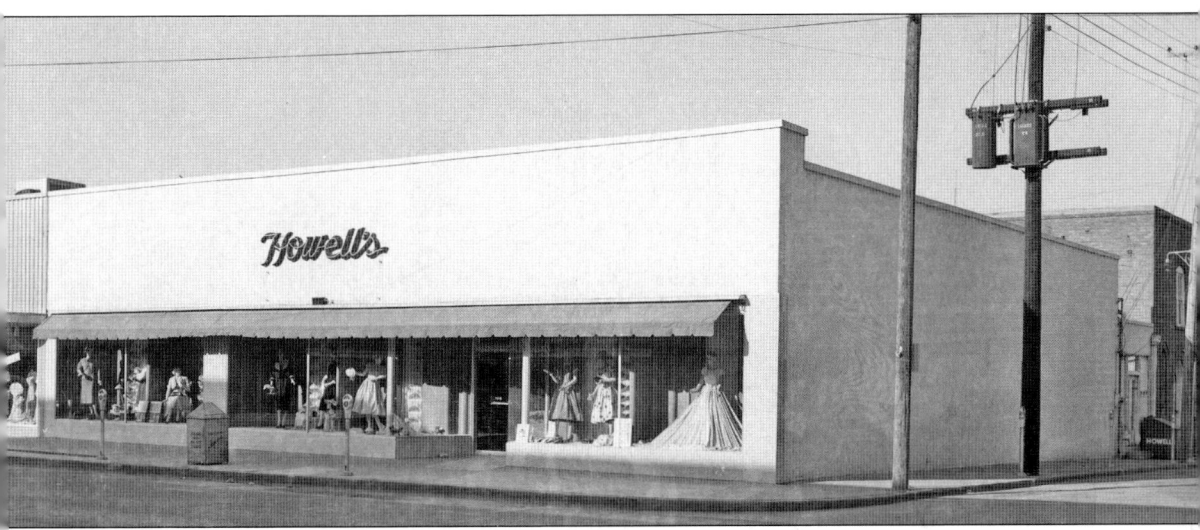

When W. E. and Florence Howell opened Howell Dry Goods in 1927, they carried a full line of dresses, hose, millinery, patterns, piece goods, and notions in a small space. They expanded, as did the departments, carrying fine china, crystal, and ladies ready-to-wear. The last store owner was Margaret Griffith, and the store remained on South Main Street until closing. (Courtesy of Layland Museum.)

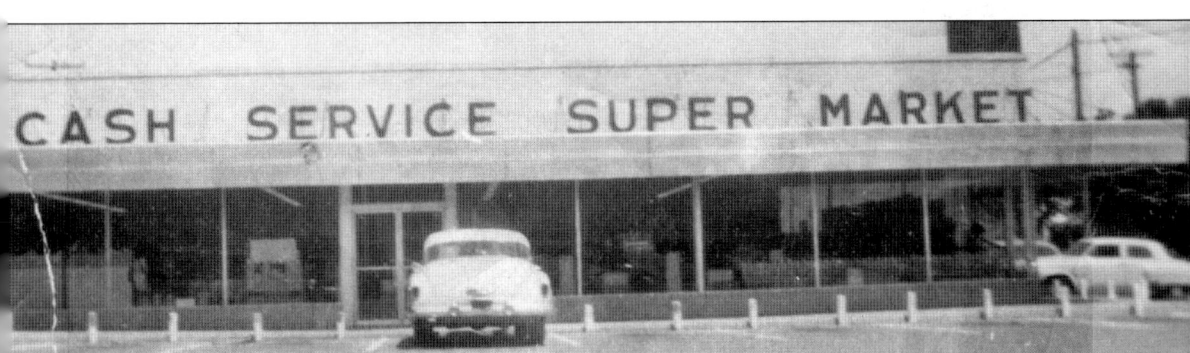

S. B. Riza established a feed equipment manufacturing company in 1925, and Madsen Chair Company opened in 1935. Cleburne was growing and needed a modern grocery store. Cash Service Super Market, located on South Caddo Street where Caddo Street Grill is in 2009, was opened in 1927. Aubrey Preston, the owner, had the first frozen food department in town. (Courtesy of Margaret Lee Preston Frasier.)

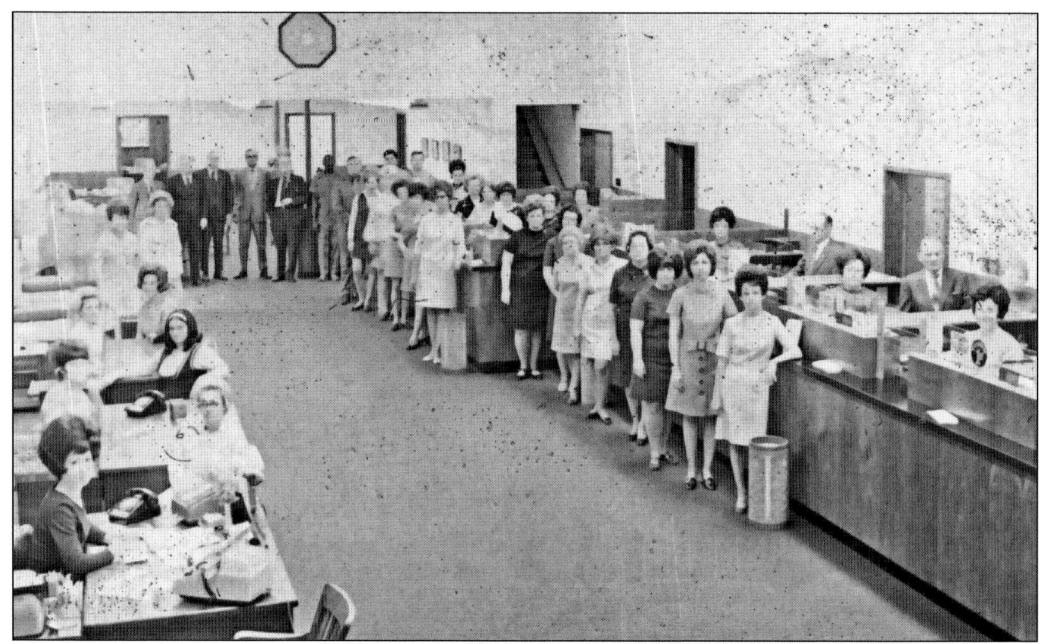

First Financial Bank began as City National Bank in 1927. Pictured is opening day at 115 North Main Street, where the bank moved in 1950. The name changed to First National Bank four years later. By 1978, growth necessitated building a larger facility, so the bank moved up the street. In 1990, it became part of First Financial Bankshares, and it merged with Cleburne State Bank in 1999. (Courtesy of Bob Force.)

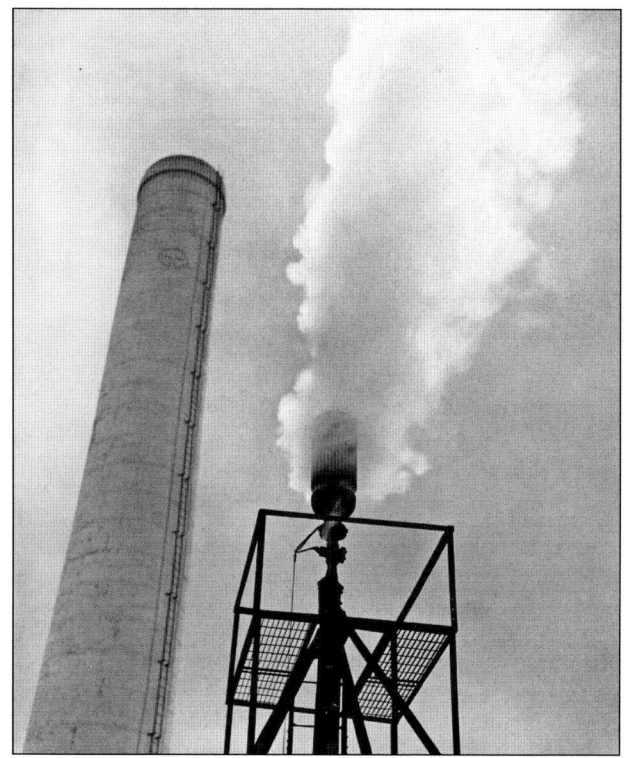

Towering 230 feet above the rail yard and sunk 17 feet into the ground, this concrete smokestack was completed in 1929. It is about 20 feet in diameter at the base and 7 feet at the top. The new powerhouse contained three boilers and operated around the clock, providing steam and oxygen. The steam-driven whistle blew several times daily according to the employees' work schedule. (Courtesy of Layland Museum.)

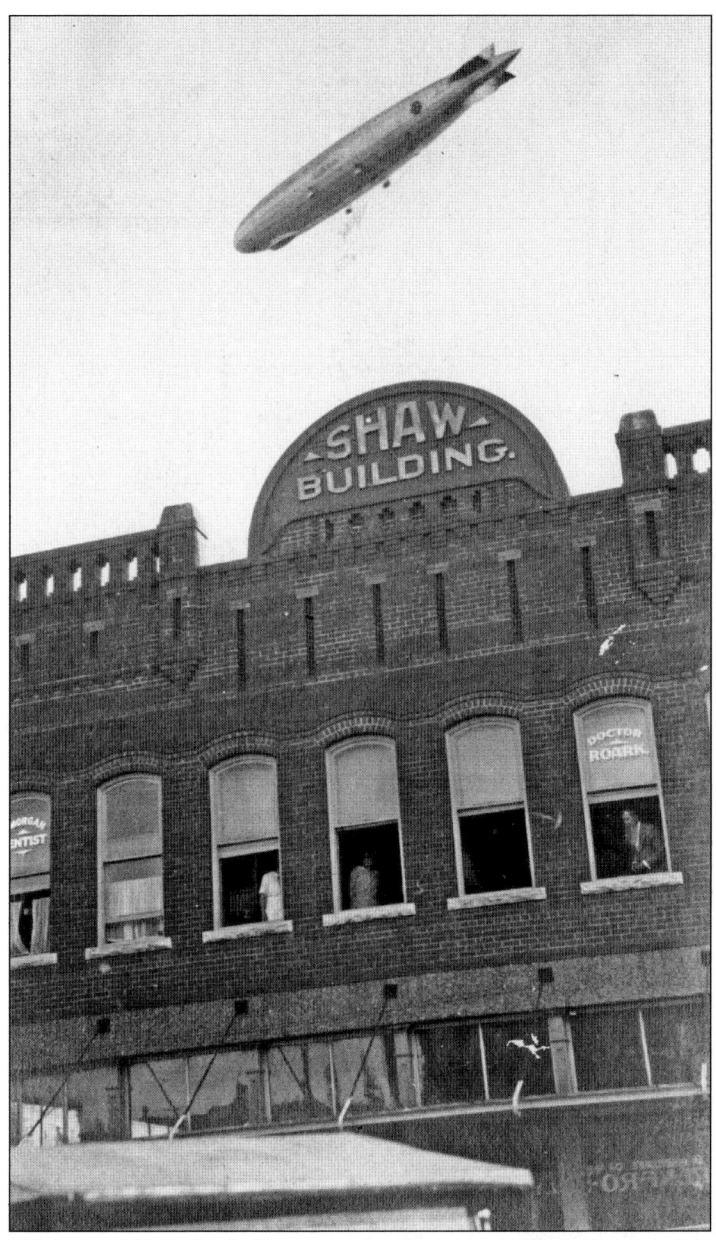

Hannah Rosendahl turned all the lights on in her home on North Anglin Street the evening of June 12, 1932, so her son Charles Rosendahl, commander of the USS *Akron*, could find his childhood home. The fire department rang bells and ran their search light into the air. People lined the streets. Rosendahl circled the town before dropping a weighted letter to his mother from the navy dirigible. At 785 foot long, this helium-filled airship was one of the largest flying objects in the world. There was a crew of 82 on board, and it could store 20,000 gallons of gasoline. The local newspapers, the *New York Times*, and *Time* reported on this exciting event. Rosendahl graduated from Cleburne High School in 1910 and was named to the Wall of Fame in 1983. During his career, he commanded the USS *Los Angeles* and directed the rescue efforts after the *Hindenburg* crash in 1937. He retired as a vice admiral. His extensive lighter-than-air collection, including memorabilia and books, is available at the University of Texas at Dallas. (Courtesy of Layland Museum.)

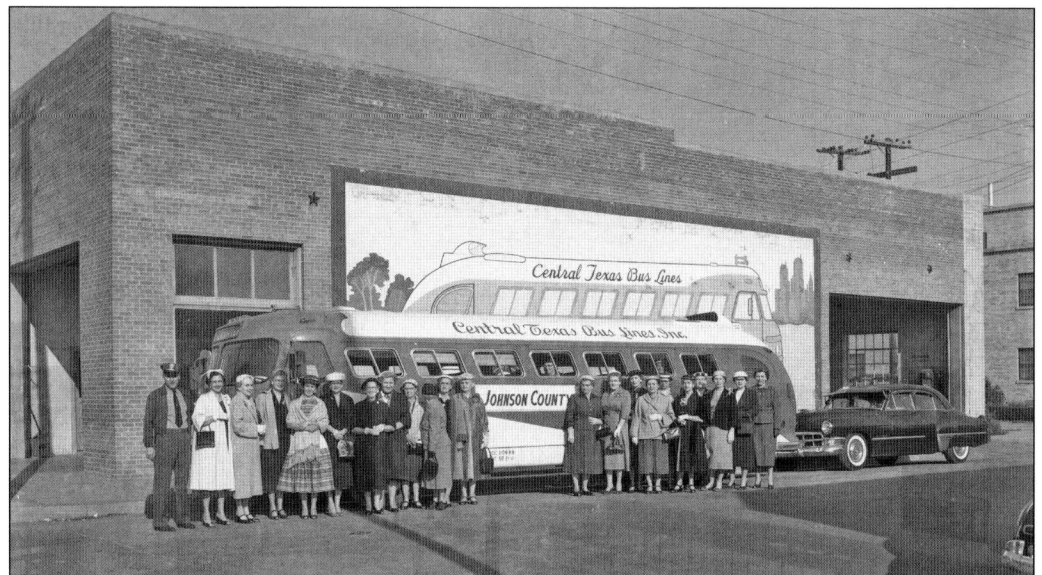

George Wellington Hyde purchased a bus line for $5,200 and began operating Central Texas Bus Lines in 1933 with two buses and two employees. By 1945, he ran buses in four directions out of Cleburne, had 15 employees, and carried about 30,000 passengers monthly. Offices were located on the corner of Robinson and East Henderson Streets. The business became Central Texas Trailways when Paul Smith purchased it in 1960. (Courtesy of Layland Museum.)

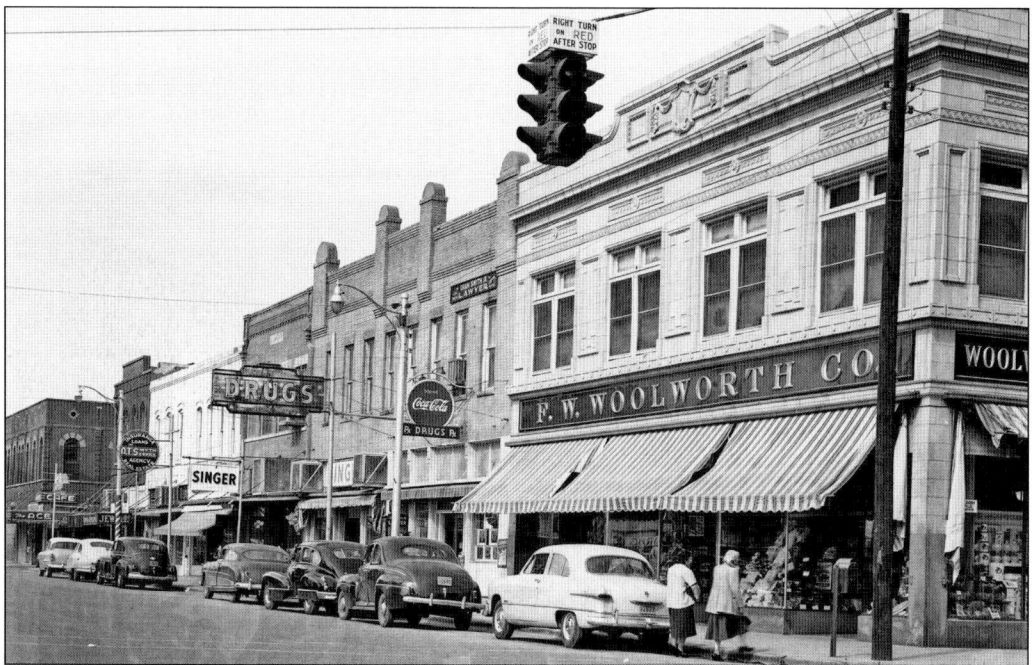

Paul Colquitt and Frank Lacewell established a drugstore in 1935. They also owned a drugstore on the west side of the courthouse, next door to Woolworth's, that began as Foster-Fain. During the 1960s, Lamar Sloan purchased the business on the east side of the square, and he operated it until Royce Cheyne bought it in 1975, changing the name to Royce's Pharmacy. (Courtesy of Layland Museum.)

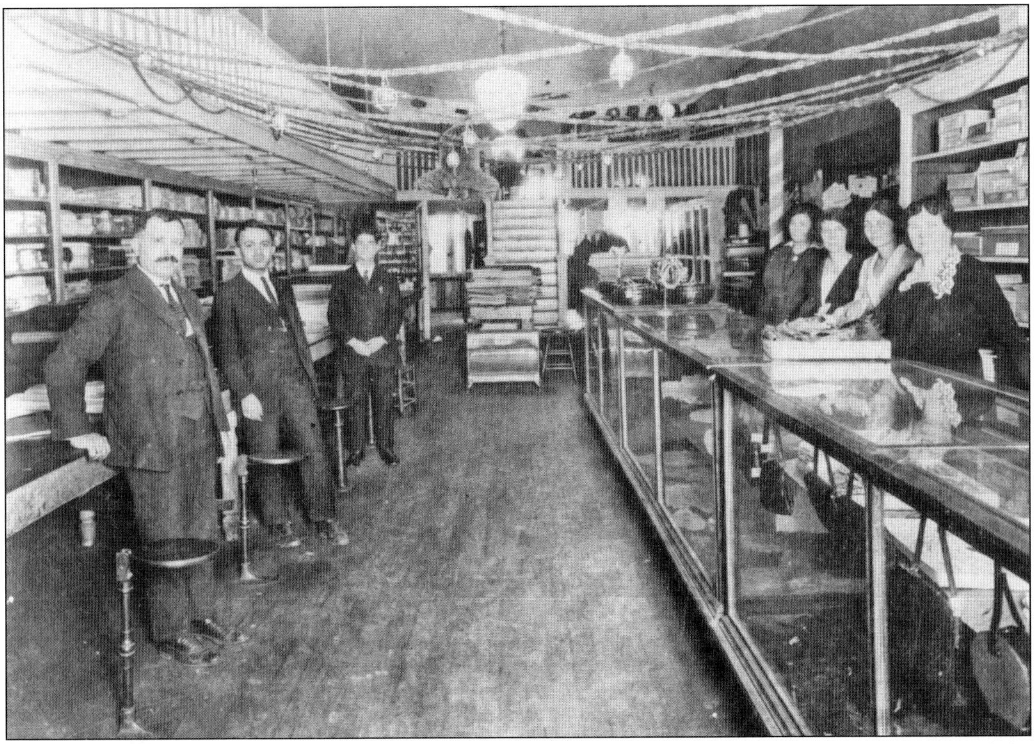

The E. Altaras Dry Goods store on the south side of the courthouse square was decorated for Christmas and filled with bolts of fabric and dry goods in 1936. Opened about 1920 by Nancy and Emil Altaras, this family business thrived until 1979. Many young girls and their moms shopped here for wedding dress fabric, lace, and beading. Emil Altaras is pictured second from the left. The 1920s photograph below shows a view looking east on Chambers Street from the intersection of South Main Street, with Altaras Dry Goods the second store in the block. (Both, courtesy of Tommy Altaras.)

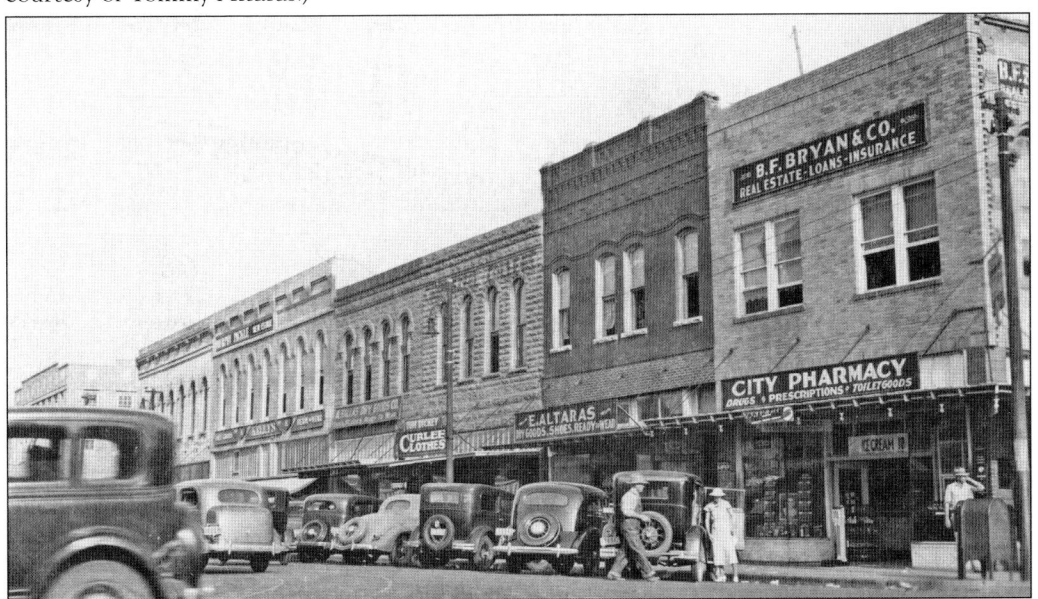

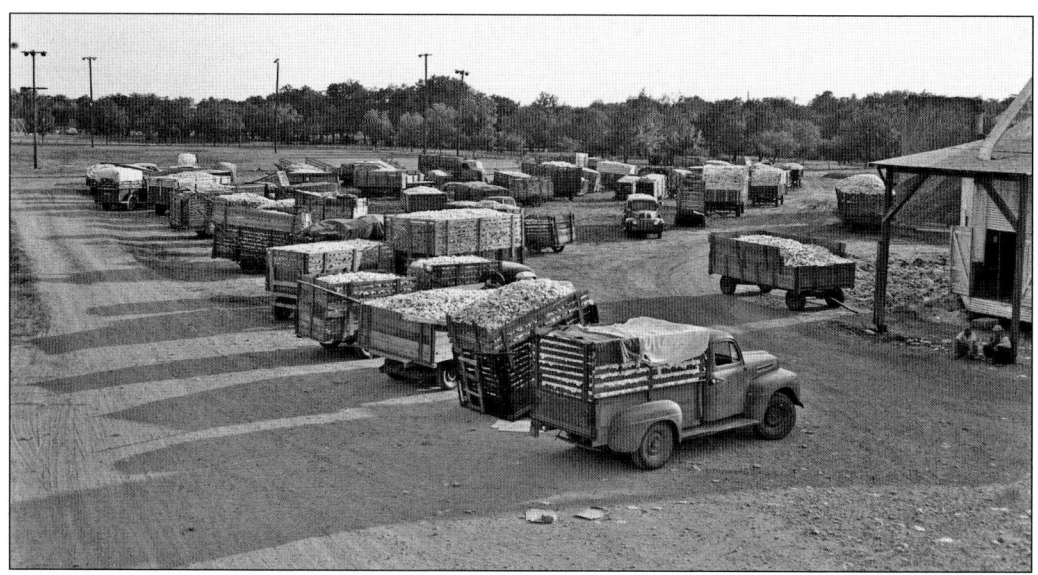

During the mid-1930s, Santa Fe was the largest industry next was the dairy business. The county boasted of over 3,700 farms. Pictured are trucks lined up around Producers Gin, and a baseball field can be seen in the background. Cleburne also had bakeries, mills, print shops, wholesale ice cream companies, tailoring establishments, floral companies, utility concerns, hospitals, hatcheries, auto shops, blacksmiths, dress makers, candy stores, and sign painting shops. (Courtesy of Layland Museum.)

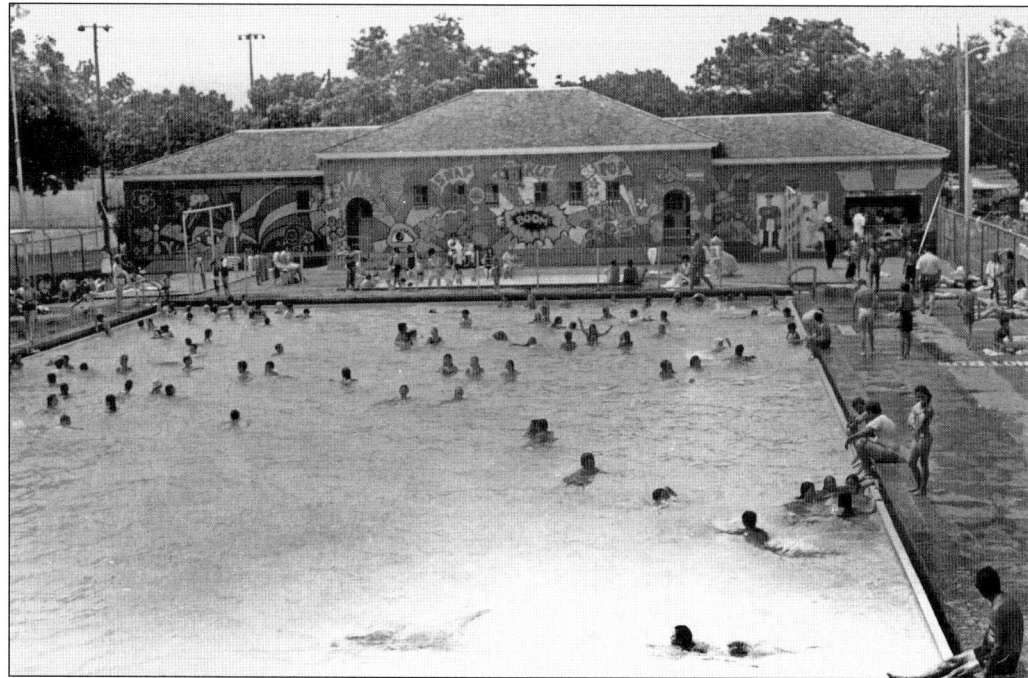

The Cleburne public pool opened in Hulen Park in 1936 on land leased to the city for 99 years by Gen. John Hulen in 1932, acting for the Burlington and Rock Island Railway. The completed project cost just under $40,000, and the cost to swim in the first years was 15¢. In 2002, Splash Station, a 4B sales tax project, replaced the pool. (Courtesy of Bob Force.)

The Yale Theatre could seat 250 when it opened in 1936. Late night movies, live entertainment, and even a "Kiddie Review" showcasing local talent organized by Don Wood were all popular. Later an orchestra directed by Jack Rumbley was added. Giving away Depression glass or money from a local bank brought the crowds until it closed in 1959. Today the Cleburne Masonic Lodge is located there at 111 South Caddo Street. Pictured below is Christmas Eve 1947, prior to a horse and saddle being given away. (Right, courtesy of Oklahoma Historical Society, negative no. 21500.50.2; below, courtesy of Tolbert Mayfield.)

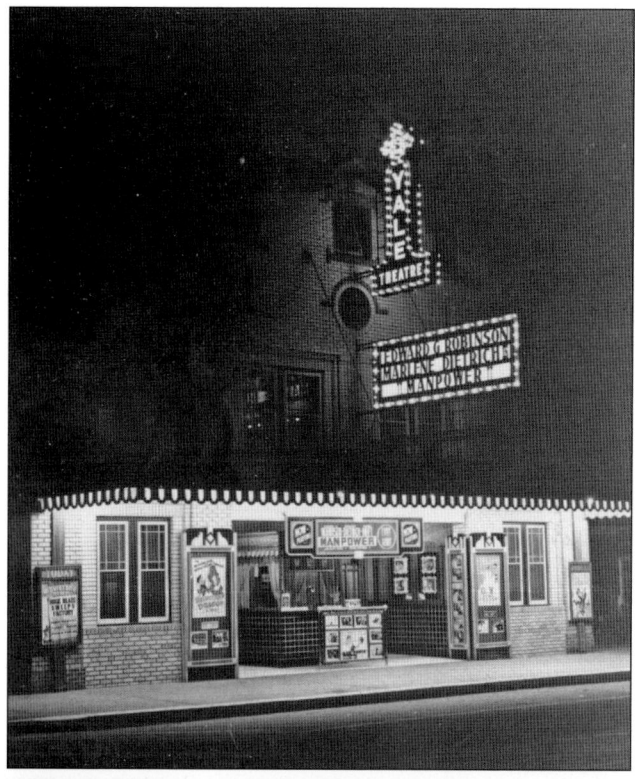

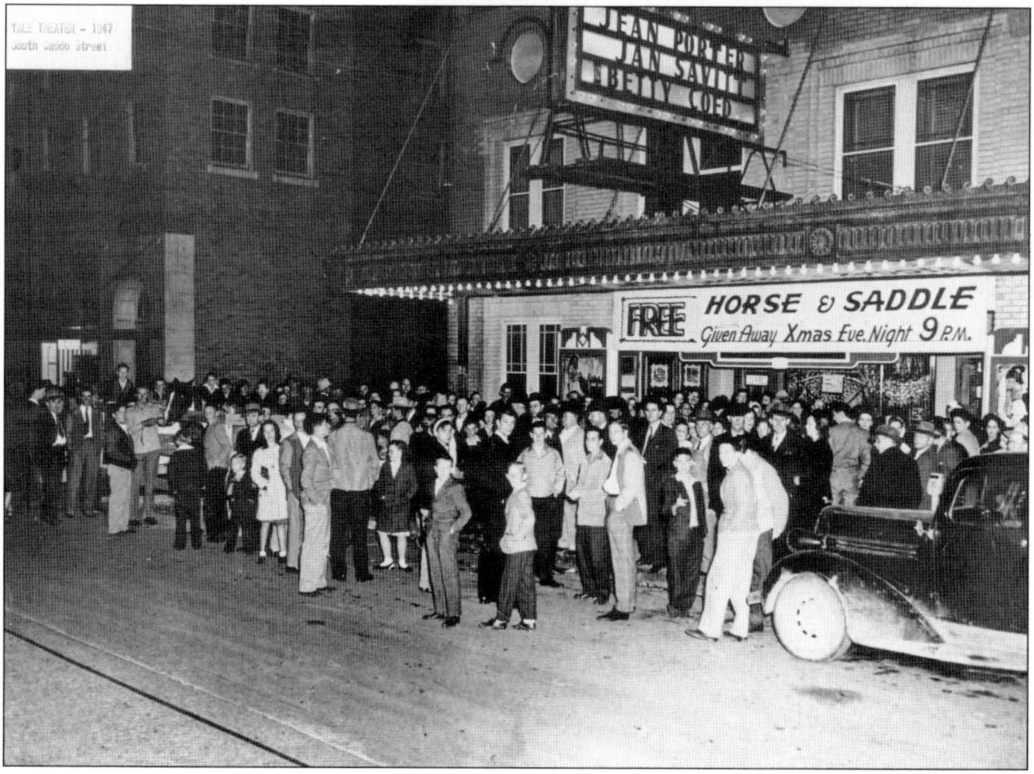

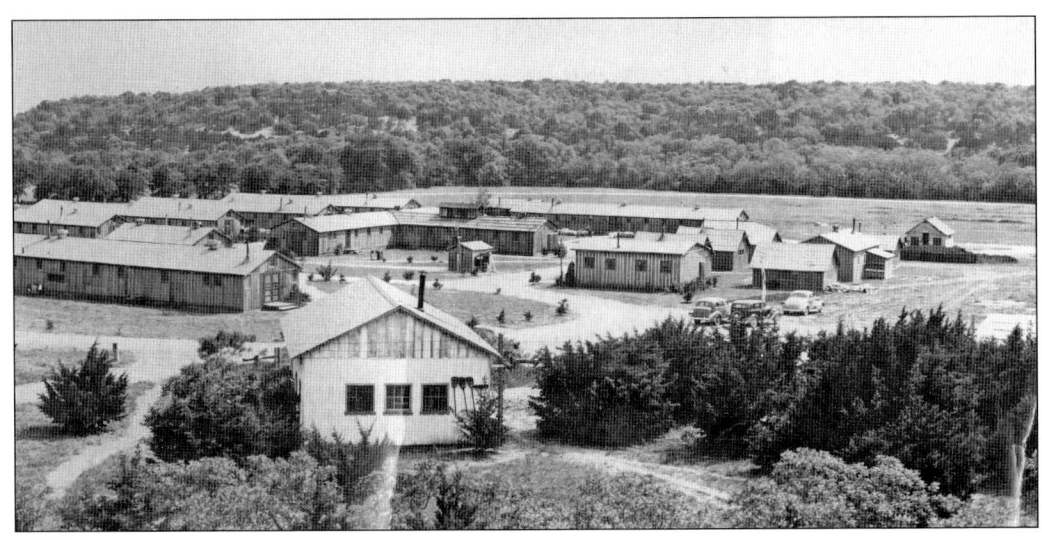

Cleburne State Park, a 528-acre park southwest of Cleburne, encompasses a spring-fed 116-acre lake. The Comanche Indians used this area as a trail from the northwest, and cowboys drove cattle near here on the Chisholm Trail. Land was acquired from the City of Cleburne and private owners by the State of Texas in 1935–1936, and the park was opened in 1938. Pictured is the fishing pier near the concession stand. In 1935, Civilian Conservation Corps Company 3804 of the federal government moved into the site, lived in barracks, and built an earthen dam to impound the lake with a beautiful masonry three-level spillway, then cleared a 3-mile-long roadway around the lake. They were paid $30 a month. The concession building, boathouse, and bathhouse were built in 1936, with additions in 1940. (Above, courtesy of Layland Museum; below, courtesy of J. Gary Shaw Collection.)

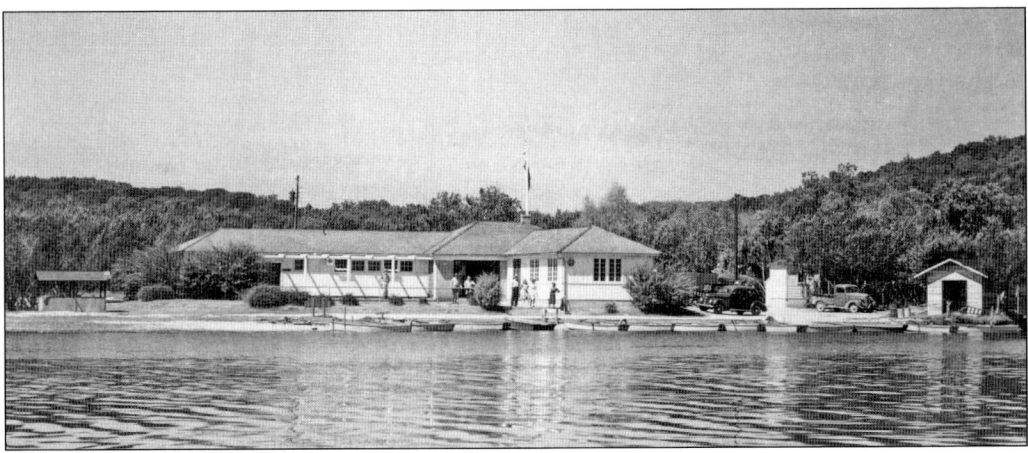

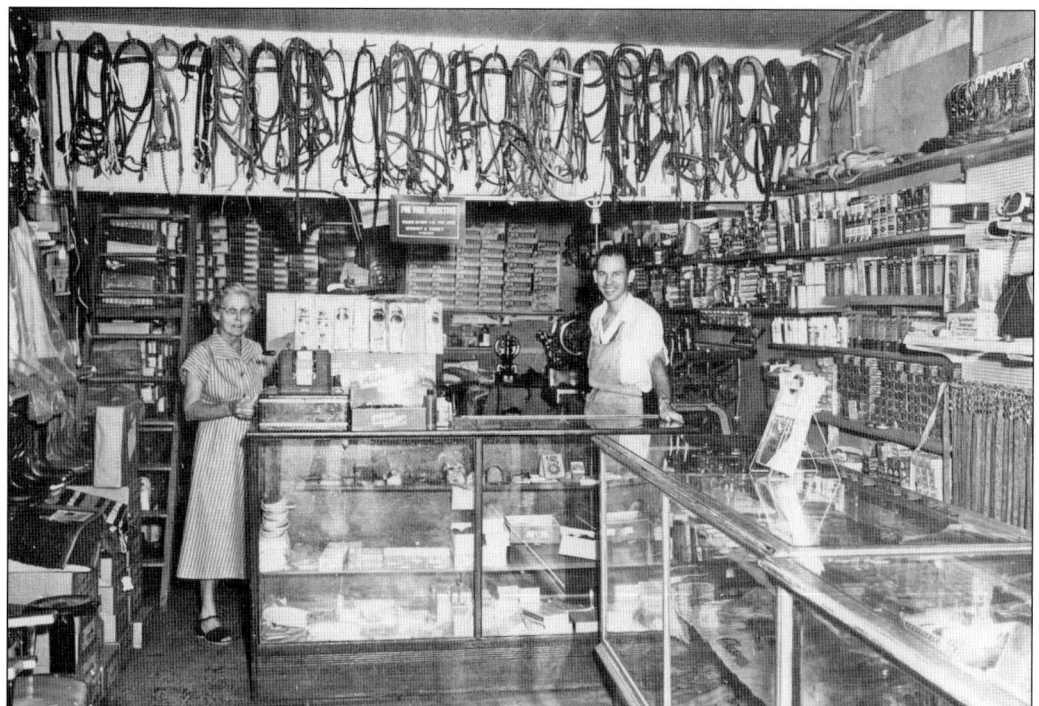

In the beginning, it was known as Pedigo's Shoe Shop, pictured here, but it evolved into Pedigo's Western Wear. Their focus became repairing anything leather, including saddles, plus repairing safes and doing locksmith work. Pictured are Essie Nan Morgan Pedigo and son Robert S. Pedigo at their store on the west side of the square. Later the Pedigo family owned several convenience stores, the Wright Building, and local rental property. (Courtesy of the Pedigo family.)

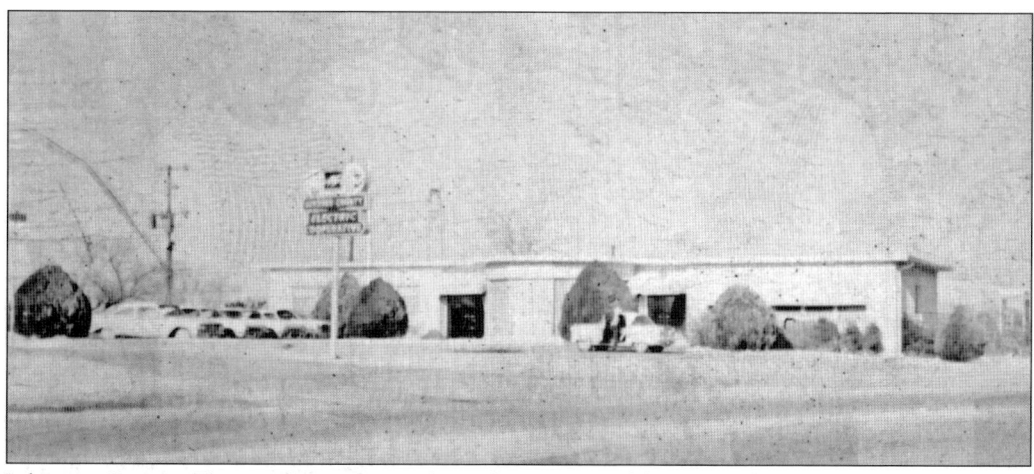

Johnson County Electric Cooperative formed in 1938 and began work on transmission lines to rural residents. In 2000, this co-op combined with Erath County to form United Cooperative Services. Owned by the more than 50,000 customers they serve, the headquarters are located on North Main Street. Members hold an annual update meeting and elect officers. They also are involved in local economic development. (Courtesy of Layland Museum.)

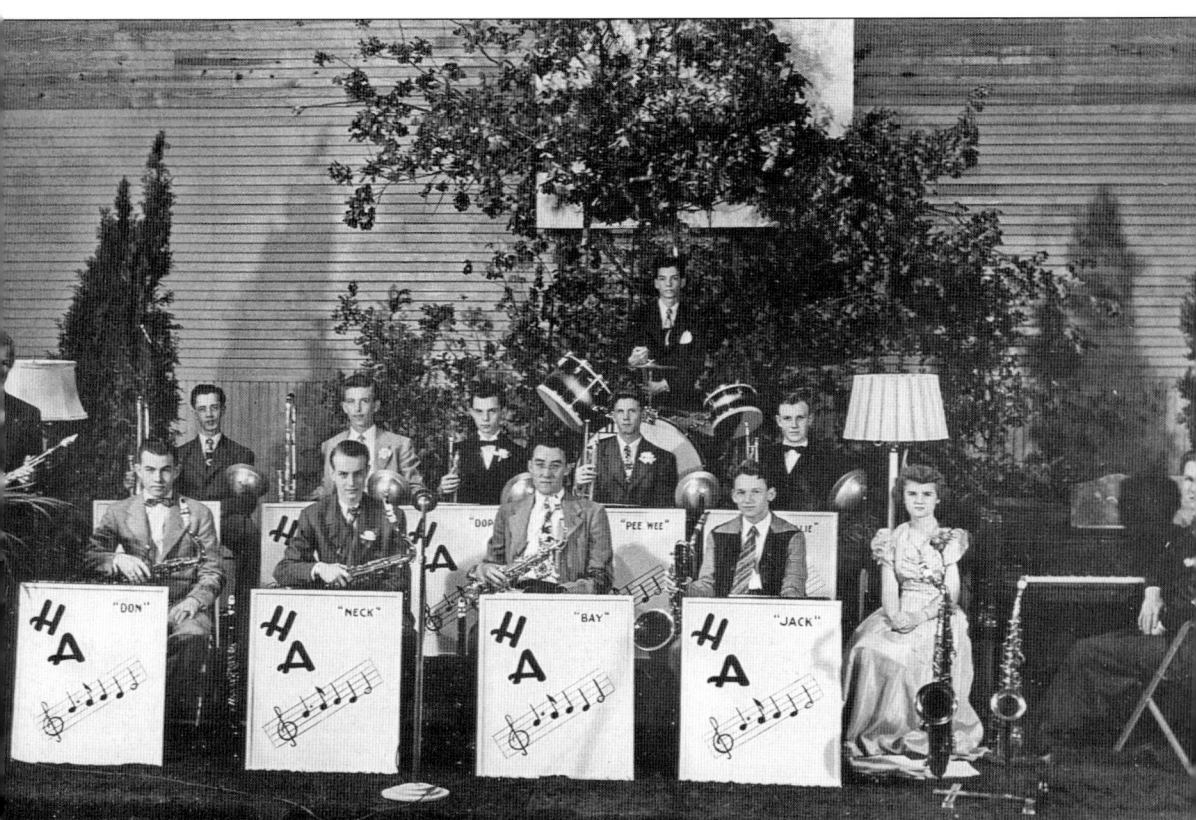

The Harvey Anderson Band provided entertainment for the 1944 Cleburne High School Junior-Senior prom, held in the Brown Gymnasium. Band members are, from left to right, (first row) Harvey Anderson (clarinet); Don Lanman, Tyson Payne Jr., Bay Mitchell Lomax, and Jack Anderson (saxophone); Jean Stewart (vocalist); and Danny Harris (piano); (second row) Robert English and Kenneth Looper (trombone), and Roland "Dopey" Falkenbury, Charles "Pee Wee" Allard, and Allan Willbanks (trumpet); (third row) John E. Weeks Jr. (drums). Others involved with the band but not pictured included Bill Boger (reed), Emmitt Mahanany (trombone), and Nan Bradbury (vocalist). Anderson directed his own band; played the saxophone, clarinet, and flute; and worked with bandleaders, including Harry James, Doc Severinsen, and Sammy Kay. When traveling bands played in Fort Worth, he often joined their performances. Anderson was a graduate of Texas Christian University, where he served as drum major. (Courtesy of Tyson Payne Jr.)

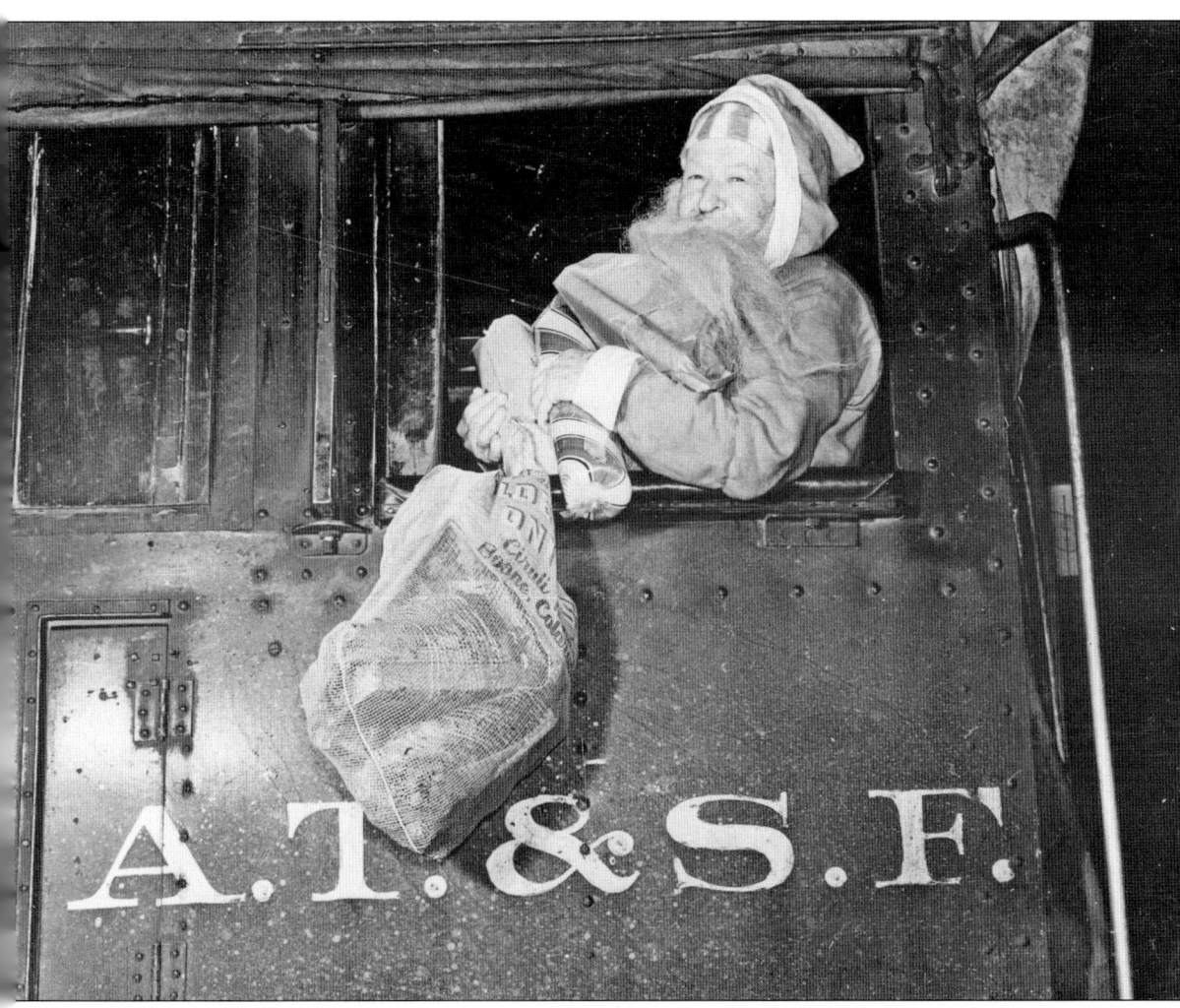

Joe Gerard got the job of running the train from Cleburne to Purcell, Oklahoma, in 1901. He got to know the folks who opened up the Indian Territory and lived in little shanty and tent towns along the way as he traveled the line 22 days a month. During the 1930s, Gerard stretched his $200 monthly paycheck to buy toys and tobacco, tossing them and old newspapers to anyone who left a white flag beside the tracks. In 1936, his wife made him a Santa suit, and local churches and organizations became involved in donating gifts. With a twinkle in his eyes, the "Santa Fe Santa" rode the tracks and gave gifts until he retired in 1943. (Courtesy of Nancy Lee Foley and James Kenneth Lee, great-grandchildren of Joseph M. Gerard.)

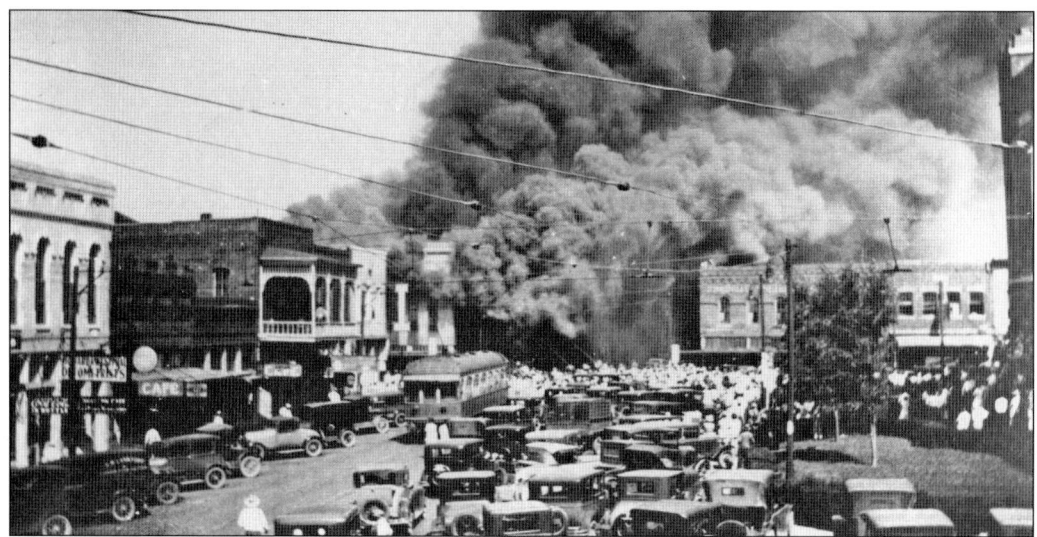

The third floor of the Cleburne Hotel was destroyed by fire in 1928. This dramatic photograph shows Cleburne's busy town square lined with stores and automobiles. The interurban operated until 1932. Besides being a hotel, other businesses were located on the bottom floor over the years, including Stewart's Grocery, a book and stationery store, and a feed store. (Courtesy of Layland Museum.)

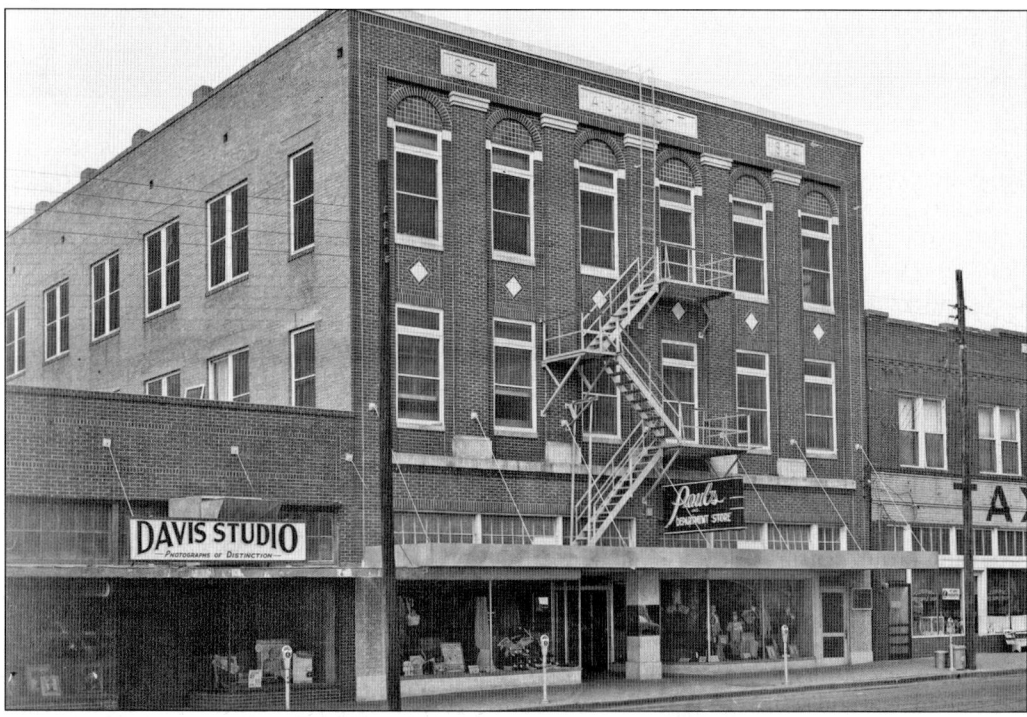

Paul's Department Store had inside doors connecting it to Duke Ayers and to a ladies store, McCullough and Cole. Photographer James A. Davis operated Davis Studio for 47 years at 10 ½ Caddo Street, and later his children, Gayland Davis and Dorothy Davis, operated the business on South Caddo Street (as pictured) until 1975. Roy Lanman owned the Yale Taxi stand pictured at right. They operated 15 taxis 24 hours a day. (Courtesy of Layland Museum.)

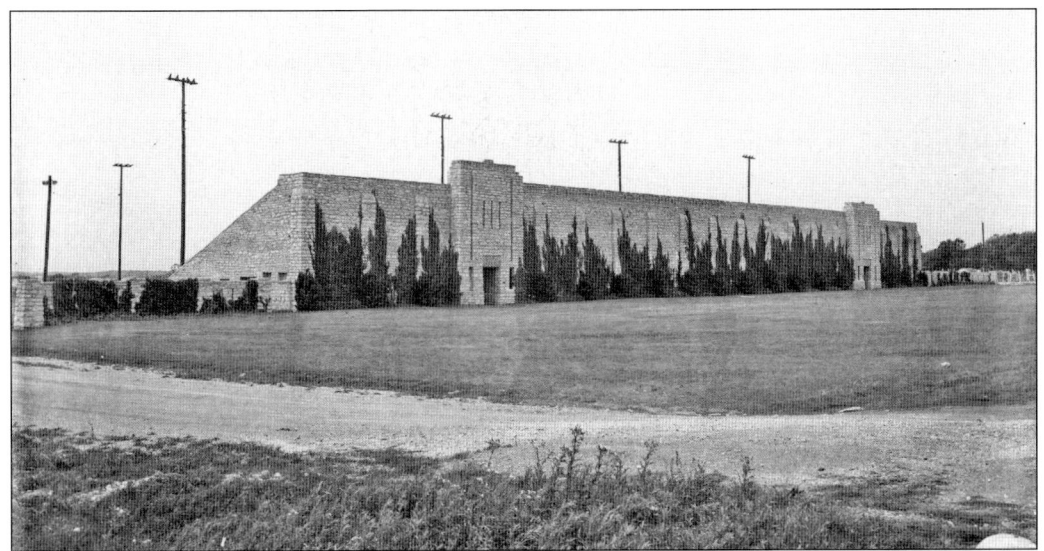

Yellow Jacket Stadium was completed by employees of the Public Works Administration in 1941 using native limestone. The PWA helped provide jobs during the Depression. The stadium cost $80,000 with $15,000 coming from the school district. The press box was reconstructed in 2008. Called "The Rock" by many, the stadium is still in use and now seats 5,400. (Courtesy of Sandra Davis Jones.)

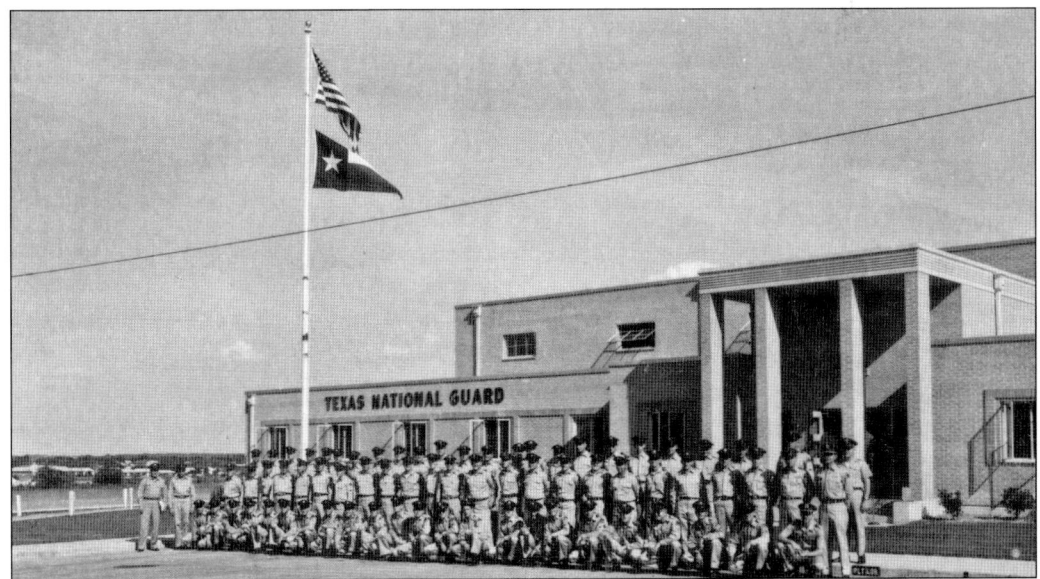

Before the city purchased this building, it was an active armory post for the National Guard. In 1944, the U.S. government leased the property for use as a German prisoner of war camp. Many prisoners worked on area farms and ranches, and some returned years later to thank the community for taking good care of them. (Courtesy of Layland Museum.)

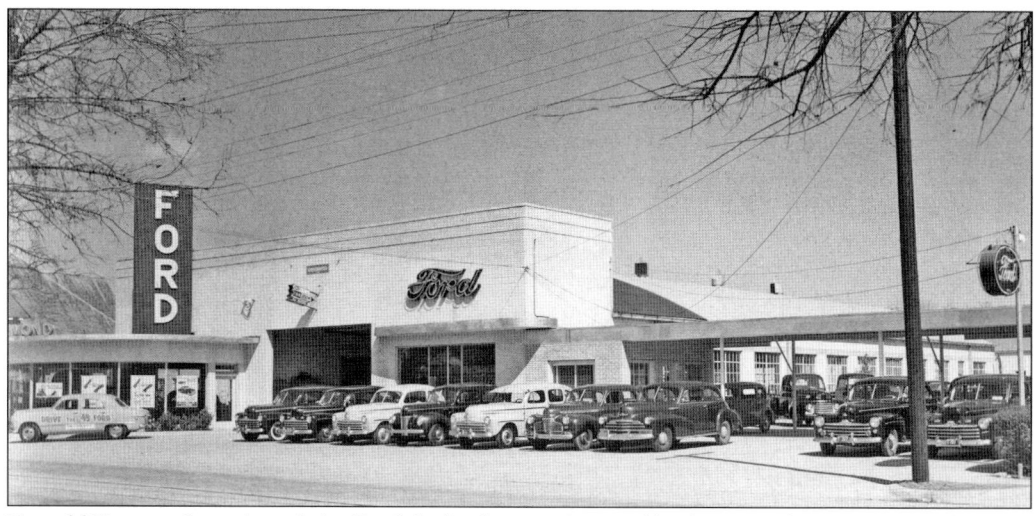

Donald Diamond purchased the Ford dealership in 1944 and built a new showroom at 420 North Main Street two years later; now this is the location of Zimmerman's. John Sledge purchased the dealership in 1972 and moved it to the current facility at 3600 North Main Street in 1988. He was known for his recorded radio commercials: "This is John Sledge. We want your business; we need your business." (Courtesy of the Diamond family.)

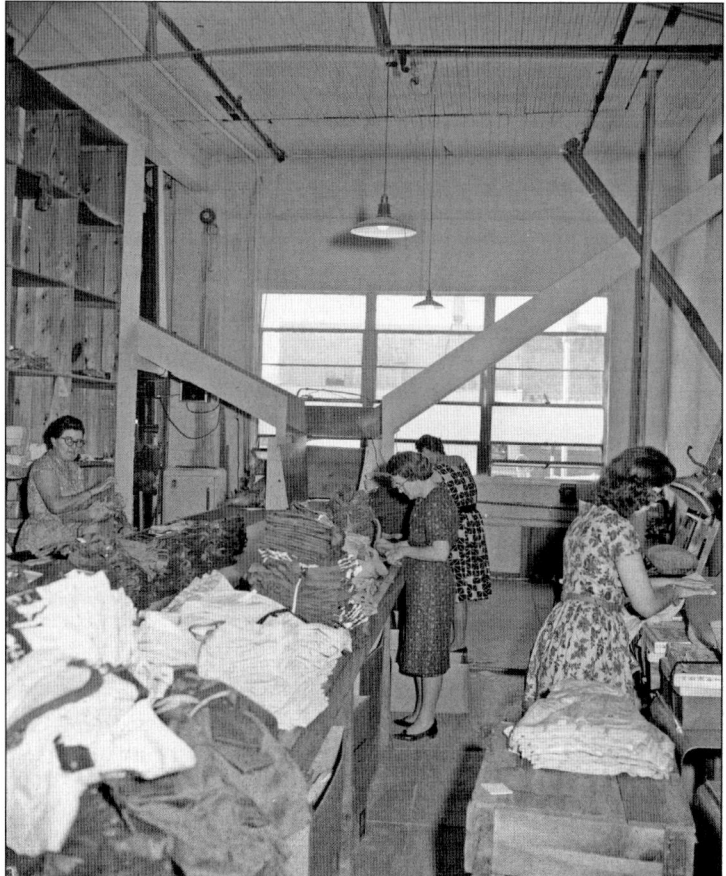

Fleta and George S. Walls founded Walls Manufacturing in 1945 with 35 employees and began making the trademark one-piece coverall that became a work apparel staple. Located first on East Henderson Street, the company moved to North Main Street about 1965. Manufacturing has moved offshore, but the administrative staff and outlet store are in Cleburne. Pictured are workers in the sewing room at the original location. (Courtesy of Layland Museum.)

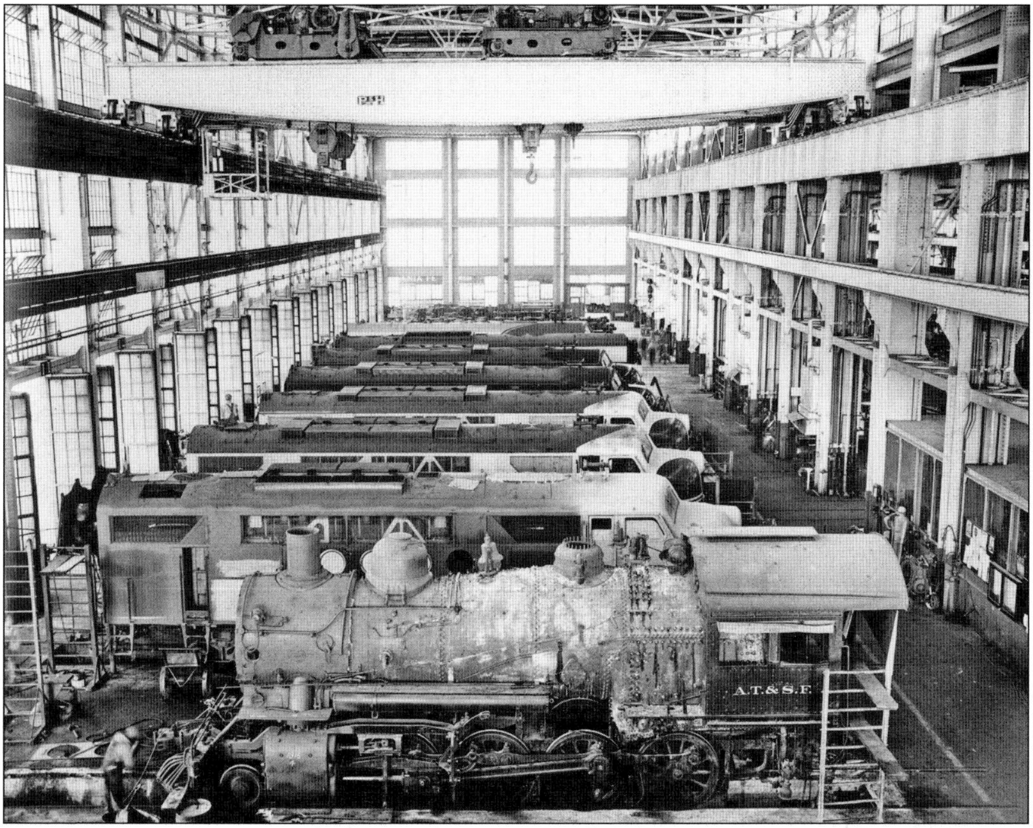

In 1945, the first regular diesel freight service entered Cleburne on the Santa Fe rails, followed by a diesel passenger train the next year. As diesel units replaced the worn-out steam equipment, over 200 workers serviced them by doing inspections and replacing parts for 197 engines in 1950. Some diesel locomotives already had a million miles of use by then. (Courtesy of Layland Museum.)

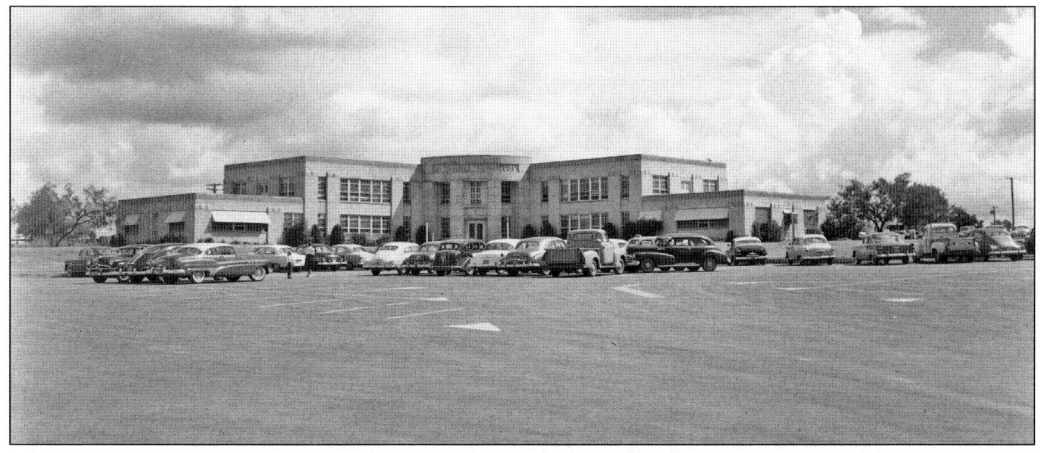

Johnson County Memorial Hospital opened in 1948 with a bed capacity of 47. Cleburne Business and Professional Women raised $10,000 for hospital equipment during their campaign. In 1953, 24 beds were added. By 1961, with the third addition and some minor revisions, the bed capacity reached 150. In 1975, there were 224 beds, with a 7-bed coronary care unit, 8 beds in surgical recovery, and a surgery department on the top floor. (Courtesy of Layland Museum.)

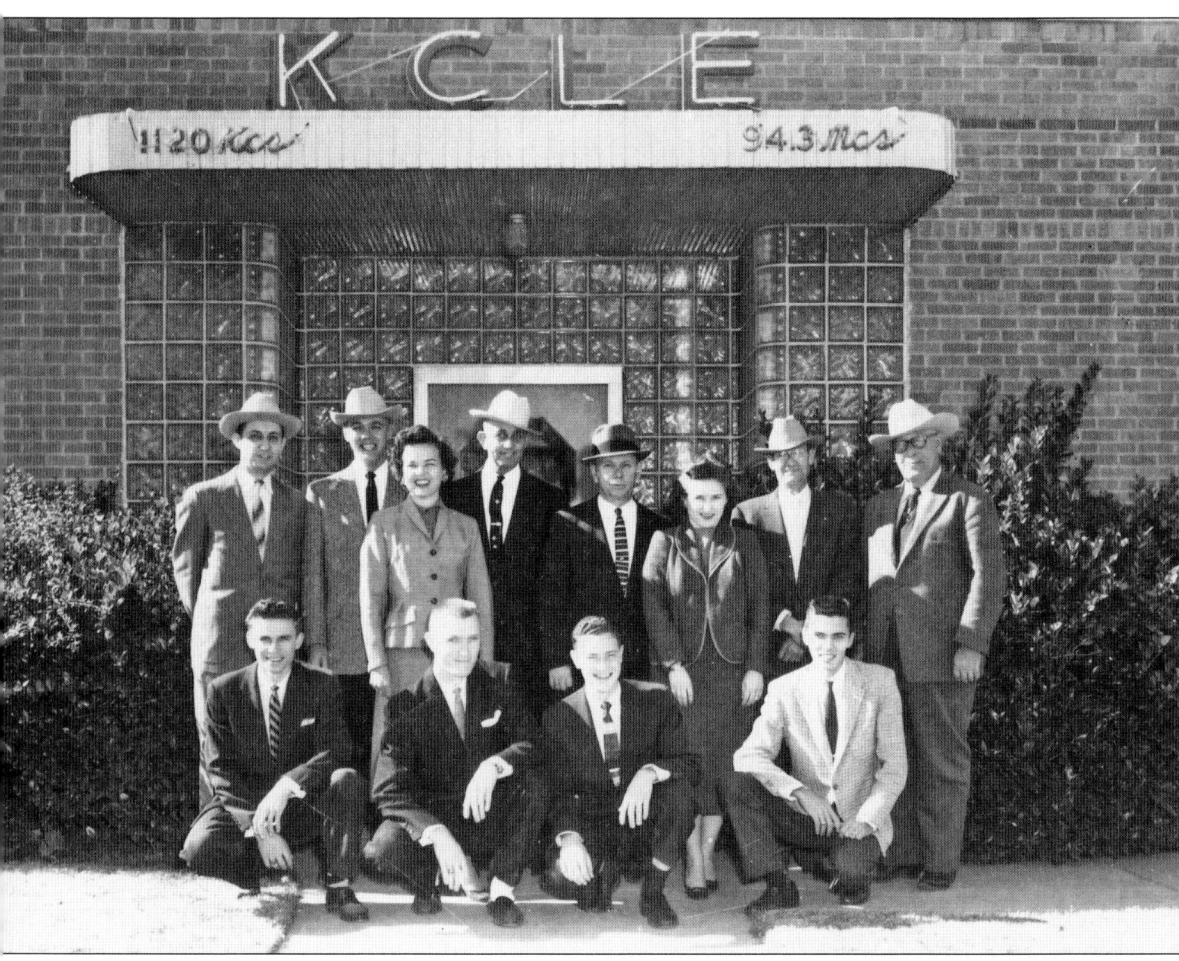

KCLE radio station went on the air on Easter Sunday 1947. This 1958 staff included from left to right (kneeling) Russ Bloxom, Don Harris, Bob Ellis, and Mike Ambrose; (standing) George Marti, John Polson, Jo Marti, Frand Hardgrove, John Butner, D'Voe Lee Smith, John Marti, and Lee "Pop" Myers, who was later known for his voice on commercials, saying "How long as it been since you had a bowl of Wolf Brand Chili?" George Marti opened Marti Electronics in 1960. Later, with his late wife, Jo, he invested in Cleburne State Bank, which merged with First Financial Bank. George served as mayor of Cleburne for a dozen years, was named Engineer of the Year in 1993 by the National Broadcasters Association, and was the first person named to the Texas Association of Broadcasters Hall of Fame, in 2002. Marti Elementary School opened in 2003 and is named to honor George and Jo Marti. Jo began an education foundation and now George and daughter Michelle continue to oversee the Marti Foundation, which assists about 200 students annually with college funding. George Marti had an interest in or financed 12 radio stations, and by 1994, when Marti Electronics was sold, he had equipment in over 80 percent of radio stations worldwide. That included the Marti unit, allowing wireless transmission. Jo operated their Charolais business for over 25 years. (Courtesy of Layland Museum.)

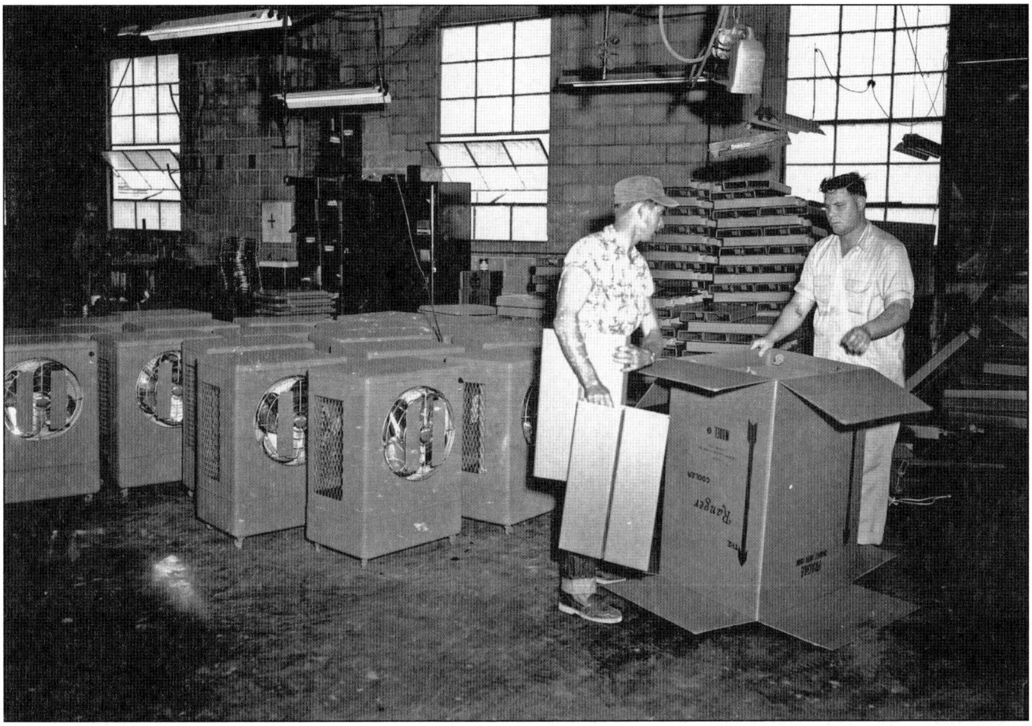

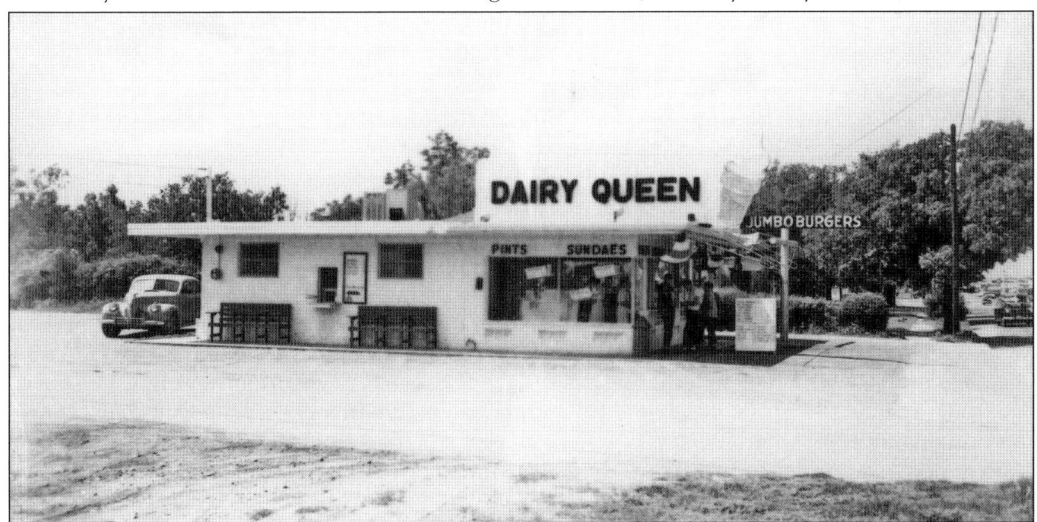

Roberts Manufacturing Company began in 1948 with R. E. "Gene" Roberts as owner, eight employees, and one sales person on South Wilhite Street. The name was changed to Rangaire Corporation in 1962. They have manufactured ice chests, range hoods, industrial and commercial lighting fixtures, heating equipment, radio-intercom systems, and Ranger evaporative coolers. Now they are known as Broan-Nutone Storage Solutions. (Courtesy of Layland Museum.)

Tolbert F. Mayfield opened the first Cleburne Dairy Queen in 1949 at 901 West Henderson Street, serving only ice cream and closing in the winter months. The second location, on North Main Street, was completed in 1955 with a dining room added two years later. A new building replaced the original business by 1959. The Mayfield family has given to many causes, including Hill College and a Cleburne school sports complex. (Courtesy of Layland Museum.)

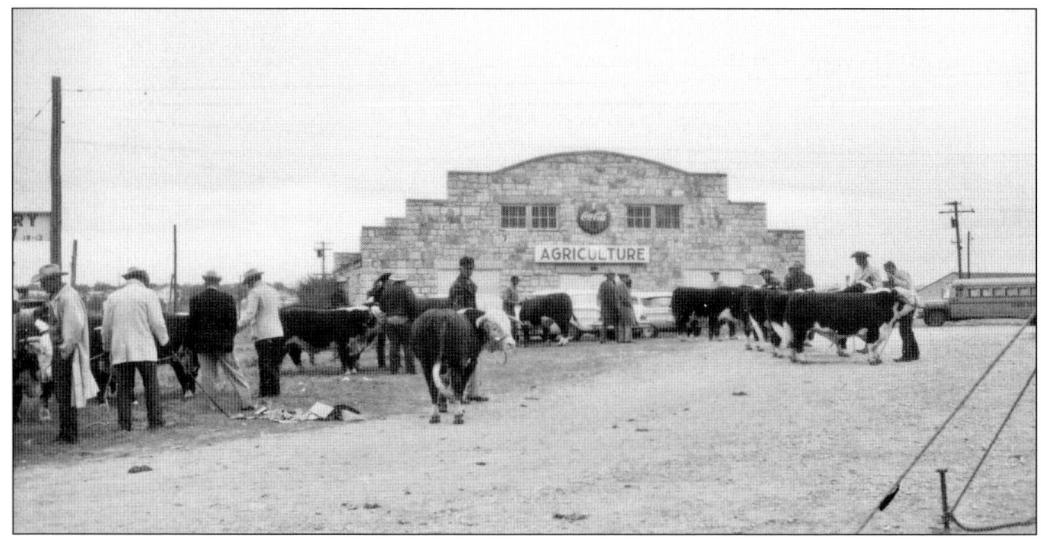

The Johnson County Fair, called the North Central Texas Fair and Rodeo beginning in 1949, was held annually in September on the land now occupied by the Cleburne Chamber and Civic Center. In 1952, the show included a four-day rodeo and exhibits of 800 fowls, Black Angus, Herefords, and 300 head of Jerseys, Holsteins, and Guernseys. The rock buildings had served as a World War II prisoners of war camp. (Courtesy of Layland Museum.)

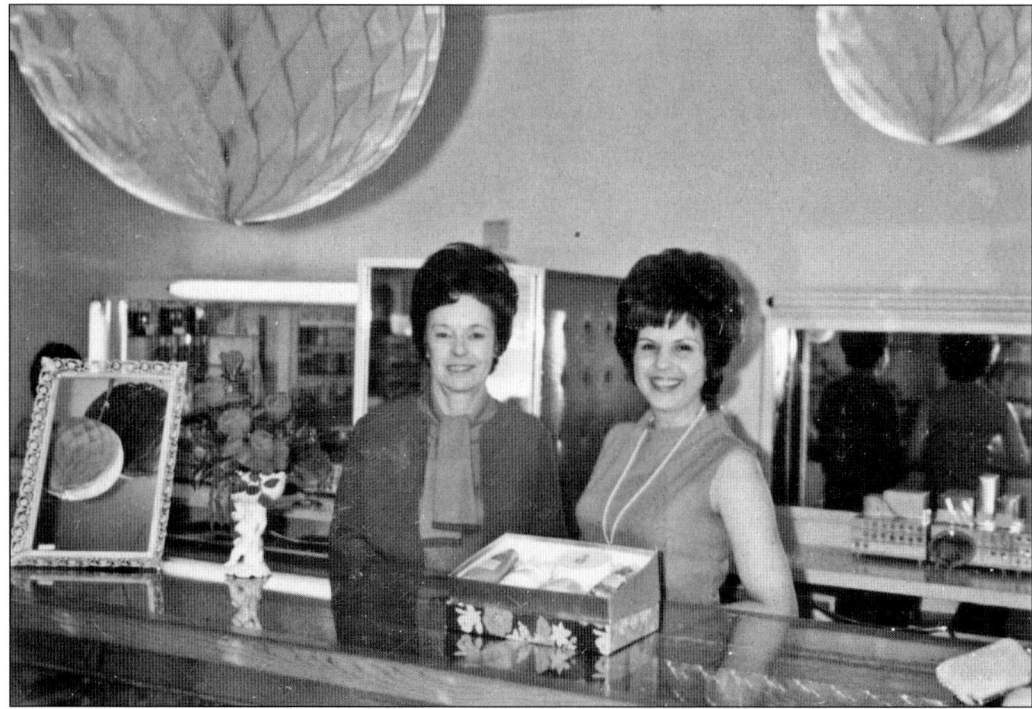

Sammie Smith opened Merle Norman Cosmetics in her Earl Street home in 1947. When Pat Starnes (right) purchased the business about 1970, she moved it to the Cleburne Shopping Center first, then to Ridgeway Drive, where it is today. Other owners have been Susan Carter Haynes and Joan Nowlin, but since 1999, Beverly and Cliff Holden have been the owners. Pictured at left is Betty Bodston, a friend of Pat's who attended the open house. (Courtesy of Pat Starnes.)

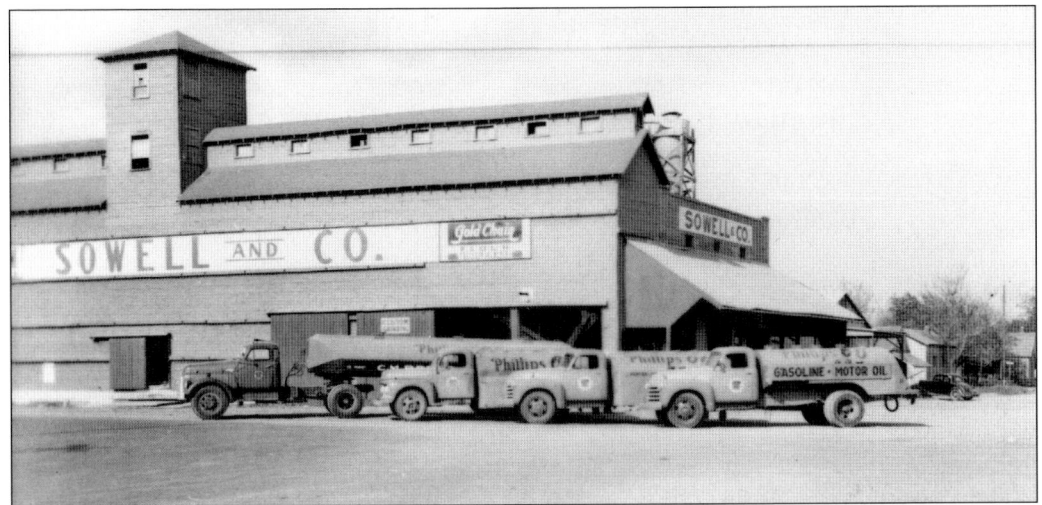

Thomas Milton "Doc" Sowell was in business in Cleburne first with the Cleburne Oil Company and later with the Sowell Tire Company, which began as a Goodyear tire franchise. David S. "Dave" Sowell Jr. was in business with the Cleburne Oil Company and, after World War II, with Sowell and Company at 601 East Chambers Street. They sold feed, grain, and wholesale groceries. (Courtesy of Layland Museum.)

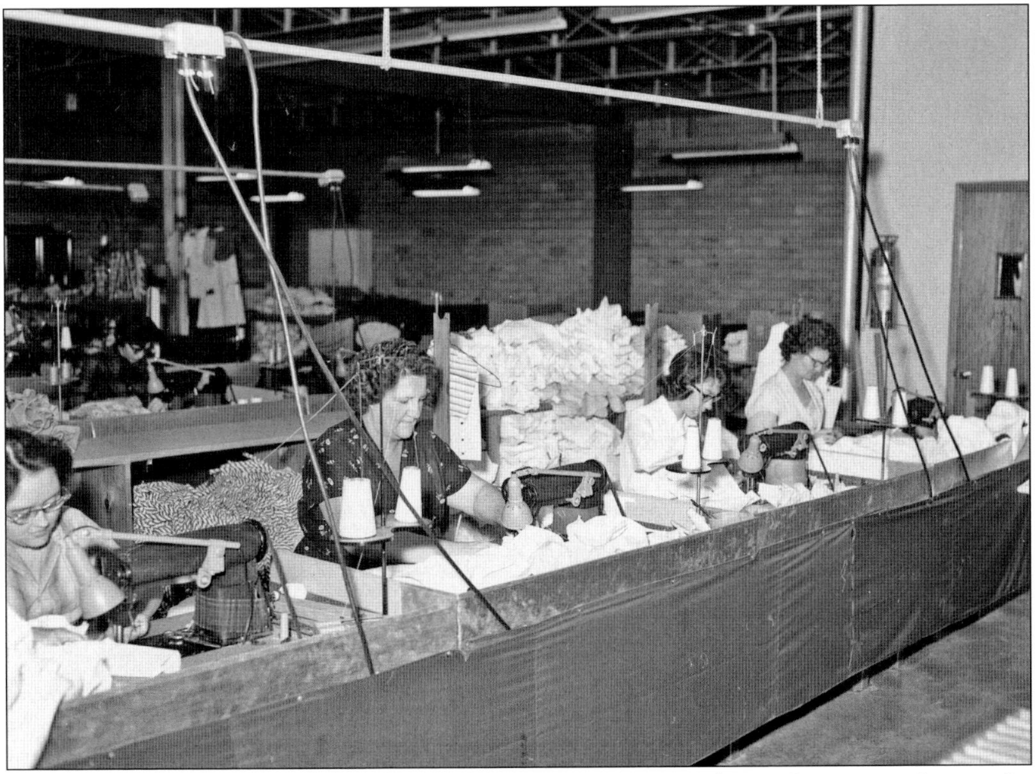

Lorch-Westway Manufacturing opened in 1944 at 1204 West Henderson Street, next door to the 67 Motel. It employed as many as 150 women as factory seamstresses or sales clerks in the outlet store. Popular women's apparel lines included Lorch, Prissy Missy, and Jeanne Durrell. Dorothy Burt served as manager for several years. (Courtesy of Layland Museum.)

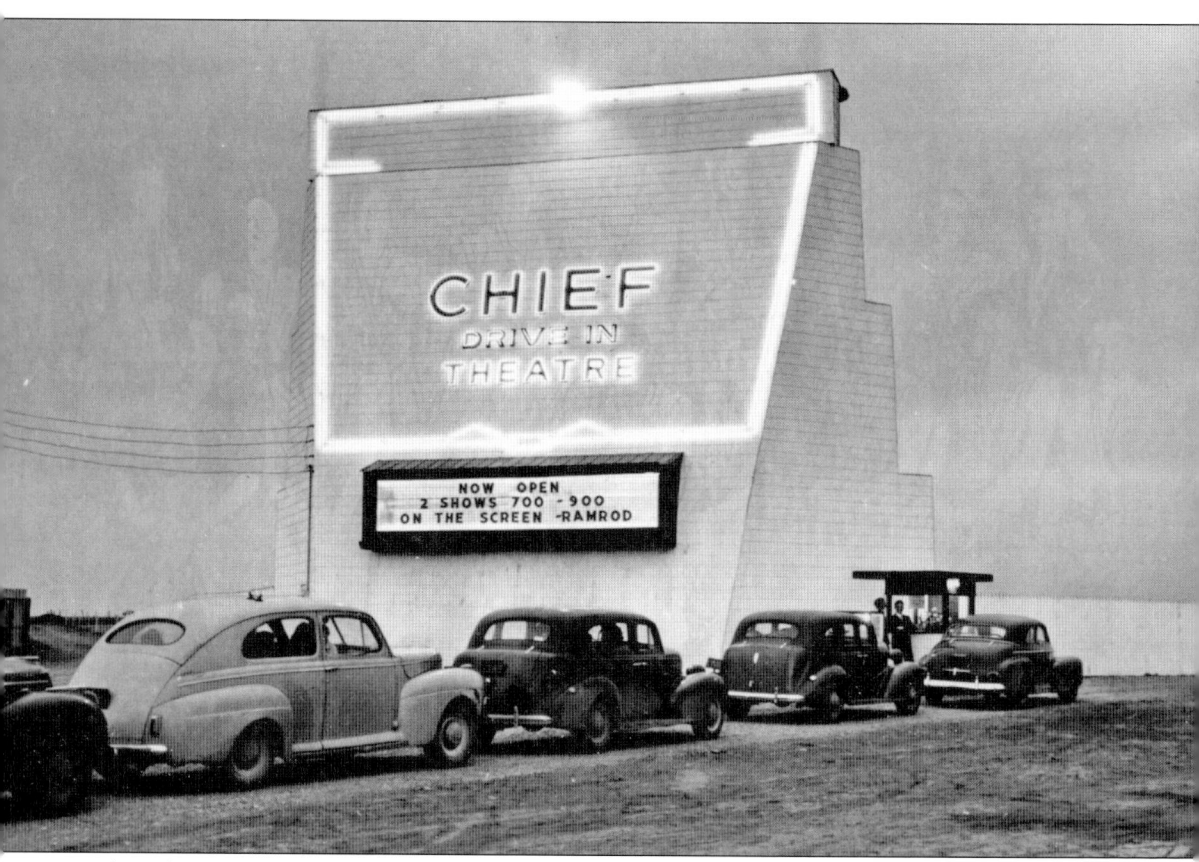

The Chief Drive-In opened in March 1949 with the full-color Western *Ramrod*, starring Rod Cameron. Three hundred cars could park on the grounds, but with carpooling, many more could watch each film. Picnic tables were near the front so families could eat and watch the movie. There was also a concession stand. (Courtesy of Oklahoma Historical Society, negative no. 21500.47.1.)

# Four
# 1951–1975

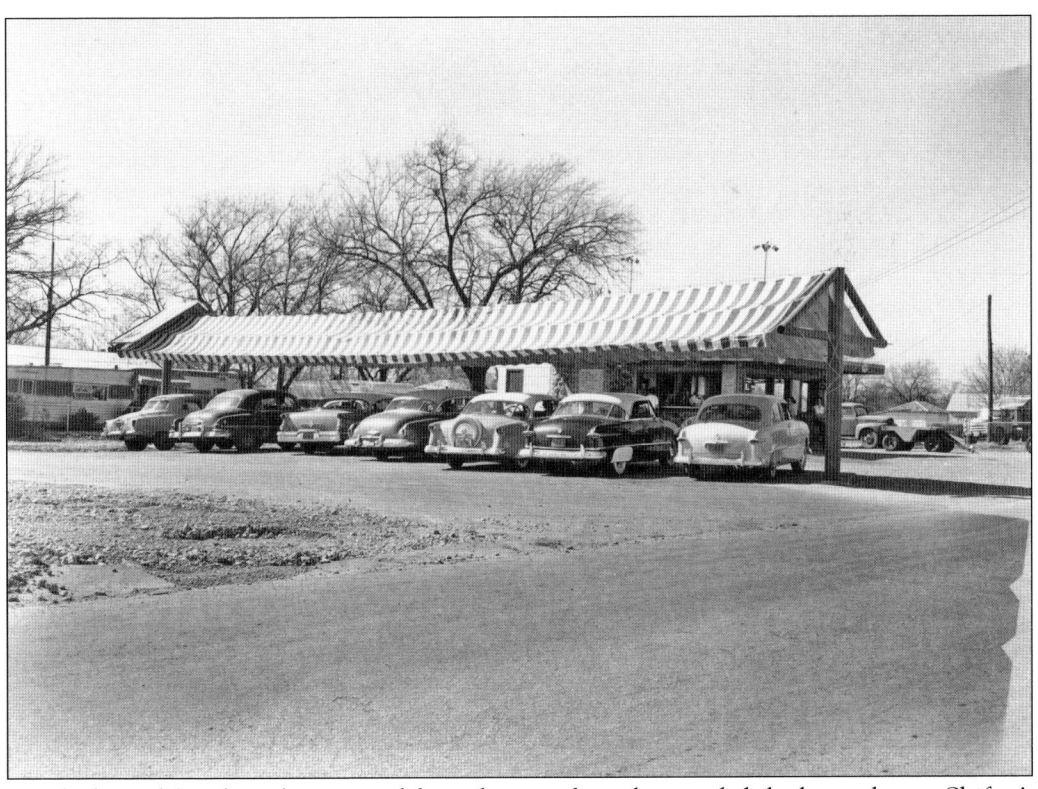

Neatly dressed female carhops served frosted mugs of root beer and chili cheese dogs at Shiftar's on West Henderson Street. Donald and Margie Shiftar made their own chili and root beer and sold an average of 1,000 hot dogs a day. Ed Zimmerman bought the equipment in 1966 and opened a similar place named Zimm's. Safeway purchased the land. (Courtesy of Donald and Margie Shiftar.)

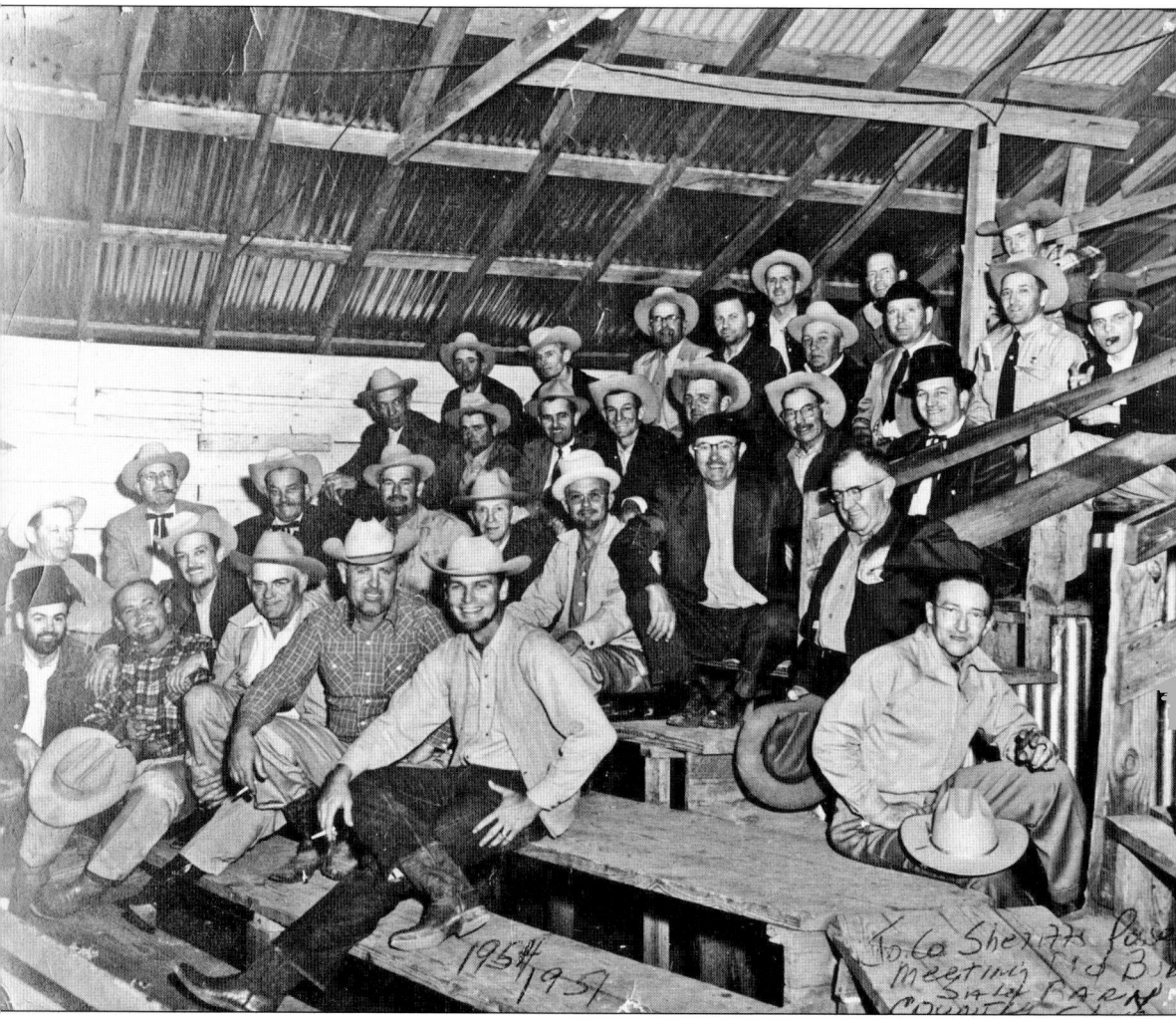

In October 1951, a group of men gathered at the Cleburne Livestock Auction Barn to organize the Johnson County Sheriff's Posse. Charter members pictured are, from left to right, (first row) Leslie Elmore, Homer Ferguson, E. L. Hoffman, Kelly Lillard, and unidentified; (second row) Sheriff Earl King, Louis Tutt, unidentified, Bill Chambless, unidentified, J. W. Howard, Ray Porter, Bud Burleson, Bob Watson (standing), and Bob Bradbury; (third row) Durwood Lankford, Homer Brown, Charlie McCoy, Milton Williams, R. M. Lillard, Creed Rogers, and Lonnie McCoy; (fourth row) Jack McClure, Jack Whitlock, two unidentified, Sam Evans, Clayton Holland, Luke Johnson, and Buddy Simmons; (fifth row) unidentified, W. D. Lee, and unidentified. During the first years, the group leased the grounds and arena from the North Central Texas Fair and Rodeo Association for its events and constructed a clubhouse on site. The first three-day rodeo was held in 1953. The Junior Posse was formed in 1956. Patsy Lillard was elected the first Sheriff's Posse sweetheart. (Courtesy of Sandra Davis Jones.)

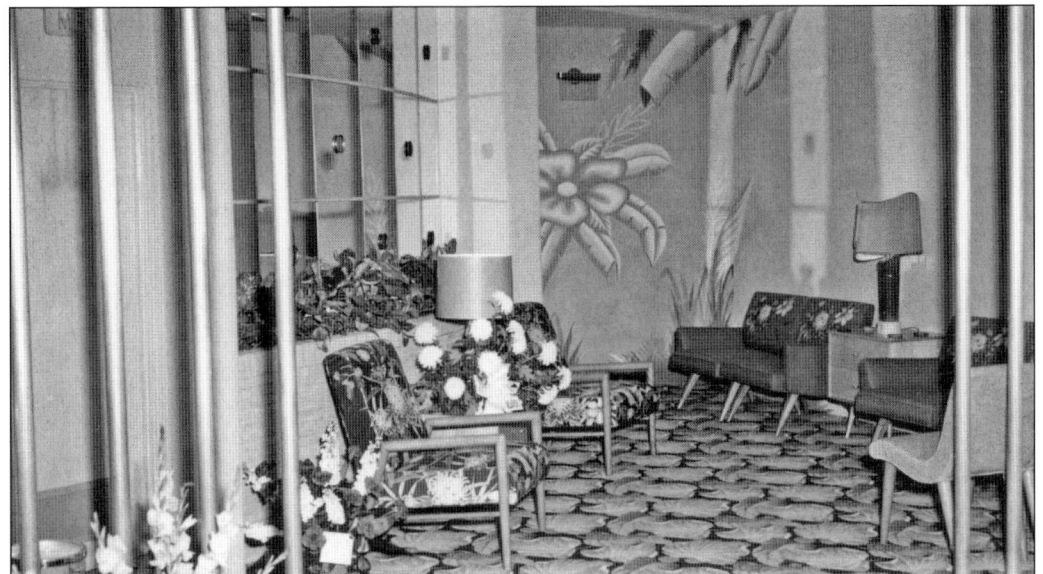

The Esquire Theatre opened at 209 North Main Street in 1951 with the Western *The Santa Fe Trail*, starring Randolph Scott. There was a stage suitable for traveling shows and a screen for movies with sound, 750 seats, and a baby cry room. The photograph above shows large florescent magnolias painted on the walls and floral carpet covering the lobby floor. Early employees who ran the film included Claude Fox, ? McGee, and Red Todd, and for many years, the manager of this and the Chief Drive-In was Nelson Myers. On Saturday mornings, kids lined up for special shows. Years later, the theater was divided and a second screen added. The building was torn down after it burned, and the space is now a parking lot. (Above, courtesy of Oklahoma Historical Society, negative no. 21500.48.3; below, courtesy of Layland Museum.)

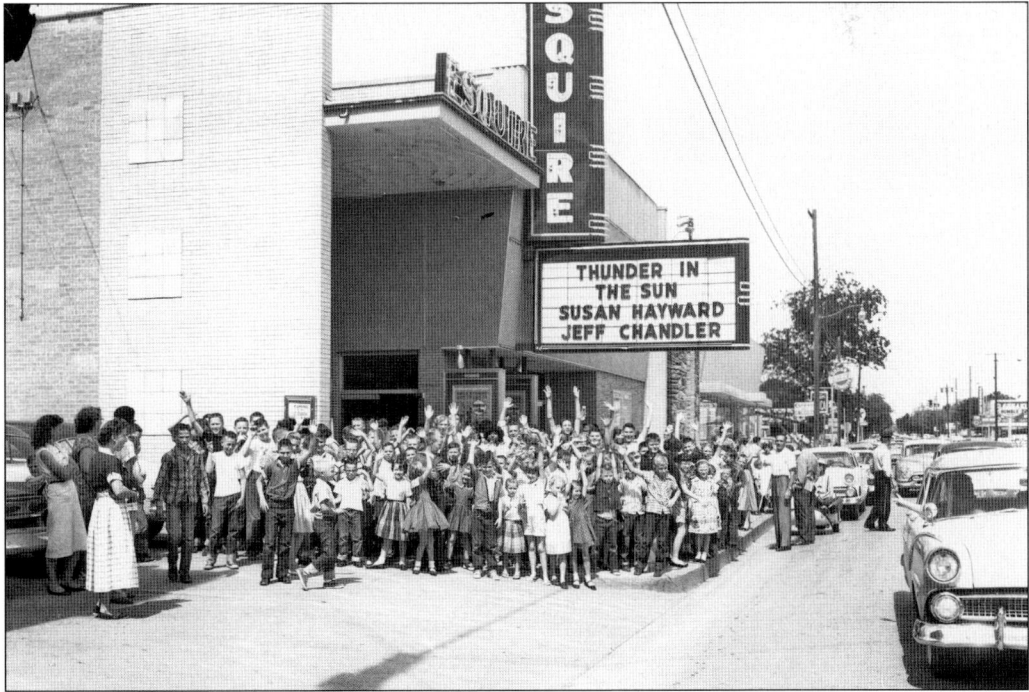

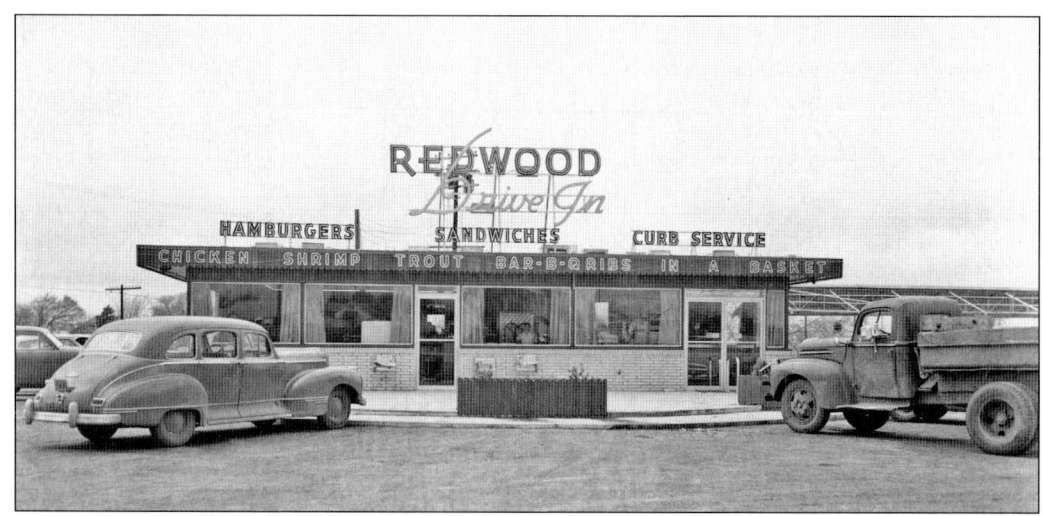

Local musician Harvey Anderson and his band played to an overflowing crowd at the opening of the Redwood Restaurant in 1953. Owners Donald Diamond and wife Faye welcomed the audience with the help of, from left to right, Miss Texas 1953 Paula Lane, Diane Boulware, WBAP personality Bobby Peters, Maryaline Preston, John Butner, Peggy Scallorn, and Gaylynn Baker. Paula, the daughter of dairy owners L. B. and Rosie Lane, was earlier crowned Miss Lake Whitney and Miss Fort Worth Cats. *Cleburne Times-Review* editor Jack Proctor encouraged local young ladies to enter beauty contests and help promote Cleburne. Donald Diamond continued building businesses on North Main Street and in 1955 opened the Traveler's Motel. (Both, courtesy of Layland Museum.)

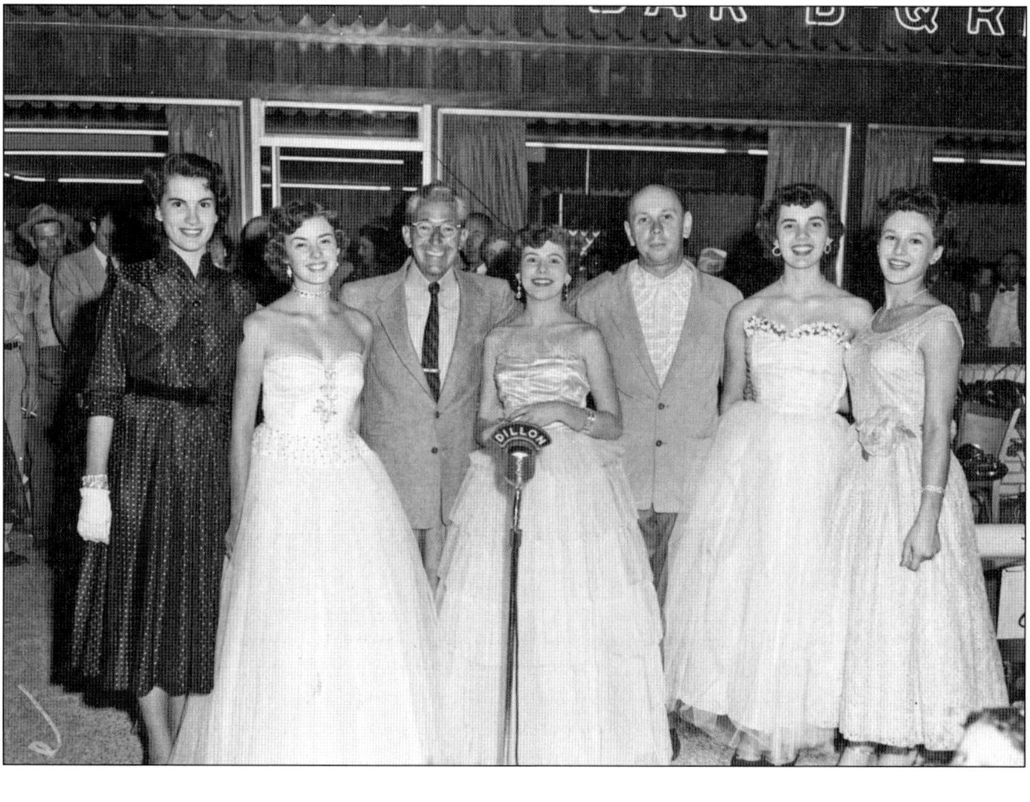

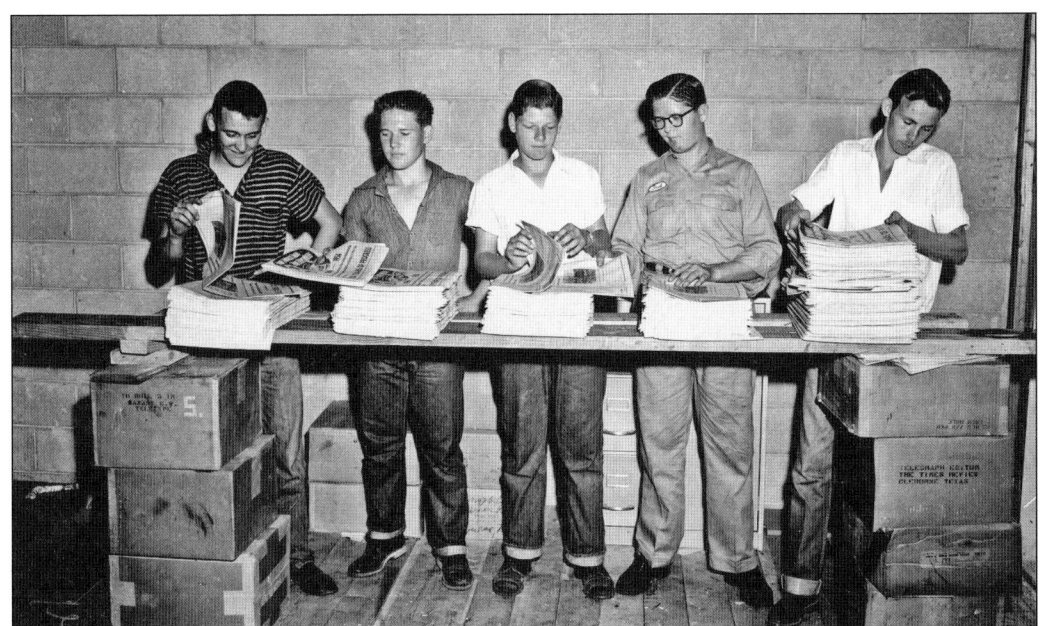

Inserting 12 sections into the 100-page centennial editions are *Cleburne Times-Review* employees, from left to right, Edwin Gilliam, Dean Cheek, Wayne Birchfield, Fred Birchfield, and Ronald Crowley. In 1928, the *Cleburne Morning Review* and the *Cleburne Daily Times* were purchased by Southwest Newspapers, Inc., and consolidated to become the *Cleburne Times-Review*. This edition was the largest ever produced. The *Times-Review* continues to be the only daily paper in the county. (Courtesy of Layland Museum.)

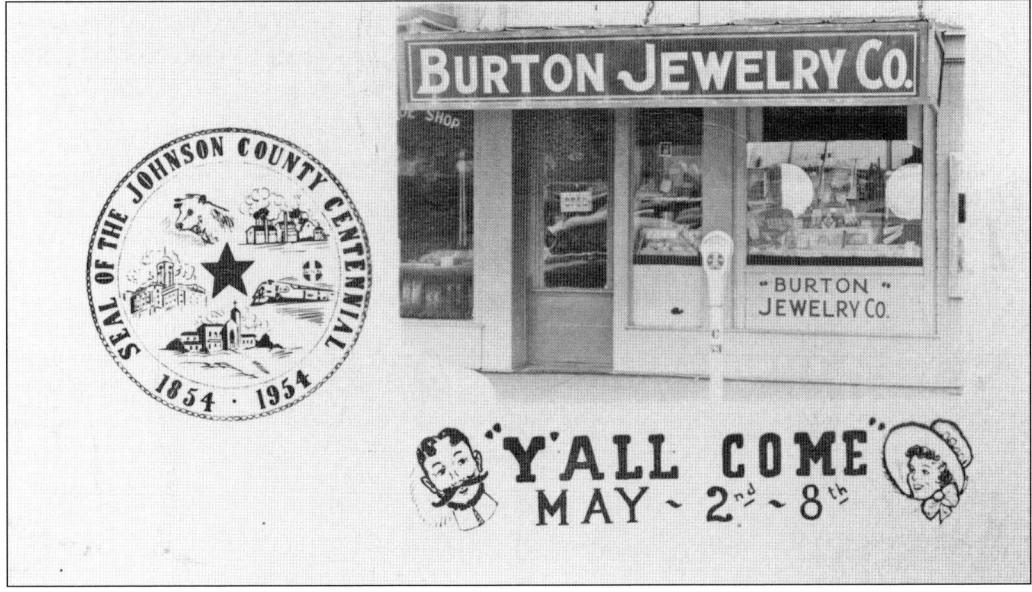

Reaching 100 years old is something to celebrate, and Johnson County did just that for its centennial. There was a beard-growing contest, a mock train robbery, and women dressed in period clothing. A parade was held with an estimated crowd of 50,000. Fay Burton, a watchmaker and jeweler for about 45 years, sent this card during the festivities showing the logo. (Courtesy of Layland Museum.)

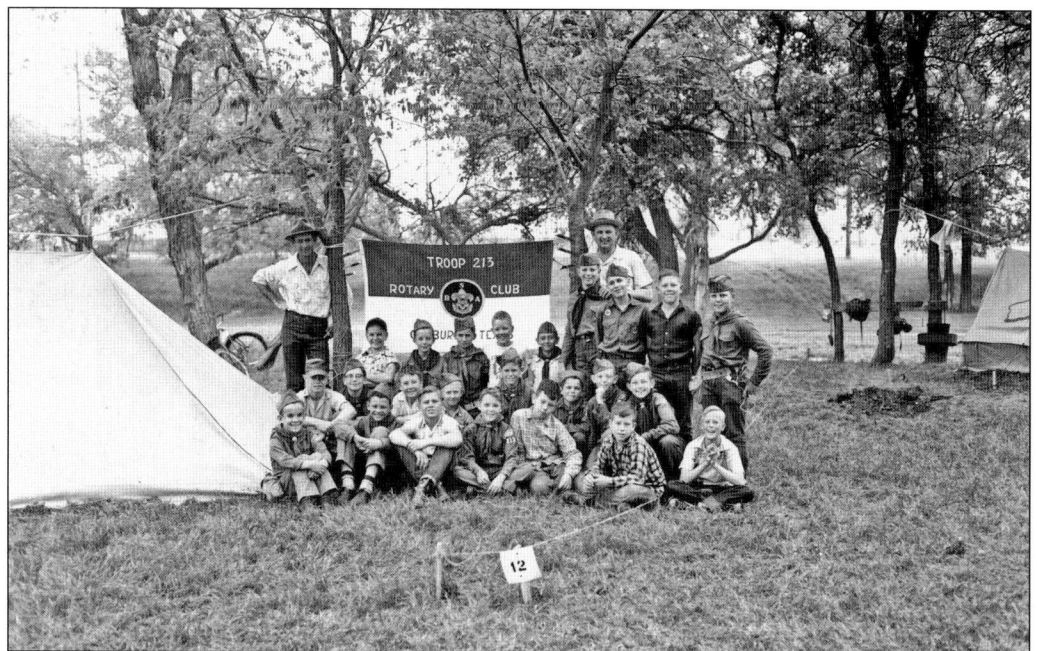

In 1914, a charter was granted to the Cleburne Rotary Club, the first one to organize in a town with a population less than 25,000. The 2009 club serves the community with its American flag program and Goatneck rest stops, and its foundation awards scholarships and financial aid to students. Pictured is Boy Scout Troop 213, which the Rotary Club sponsored for many years. (Courtesy of Layland Museum.)

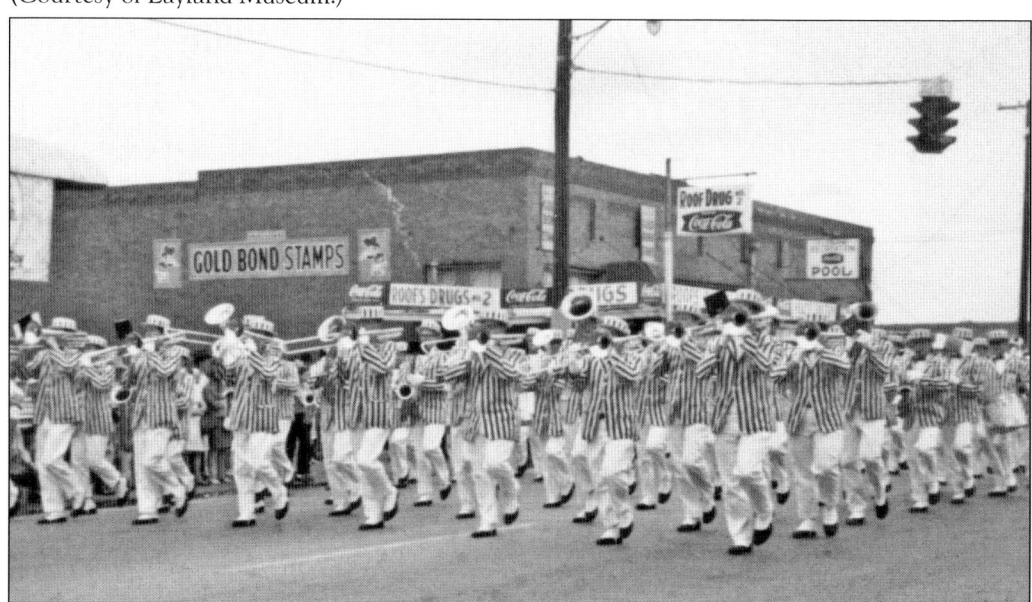

Roof Drug was know for many things, but being open a few hours on Sunday afternoon to fill prescriptions helped many families. This was before chain stores arrived and opened all weekend. Nick Roof Sr. and sons Nick and Glen had three locations: 211 North Anglin Street; Cleburne Shopping Center on North Main Street, which included a soda fountain; and South Main Street, pictured during a homecoming parade. (Courtesy of the author.)

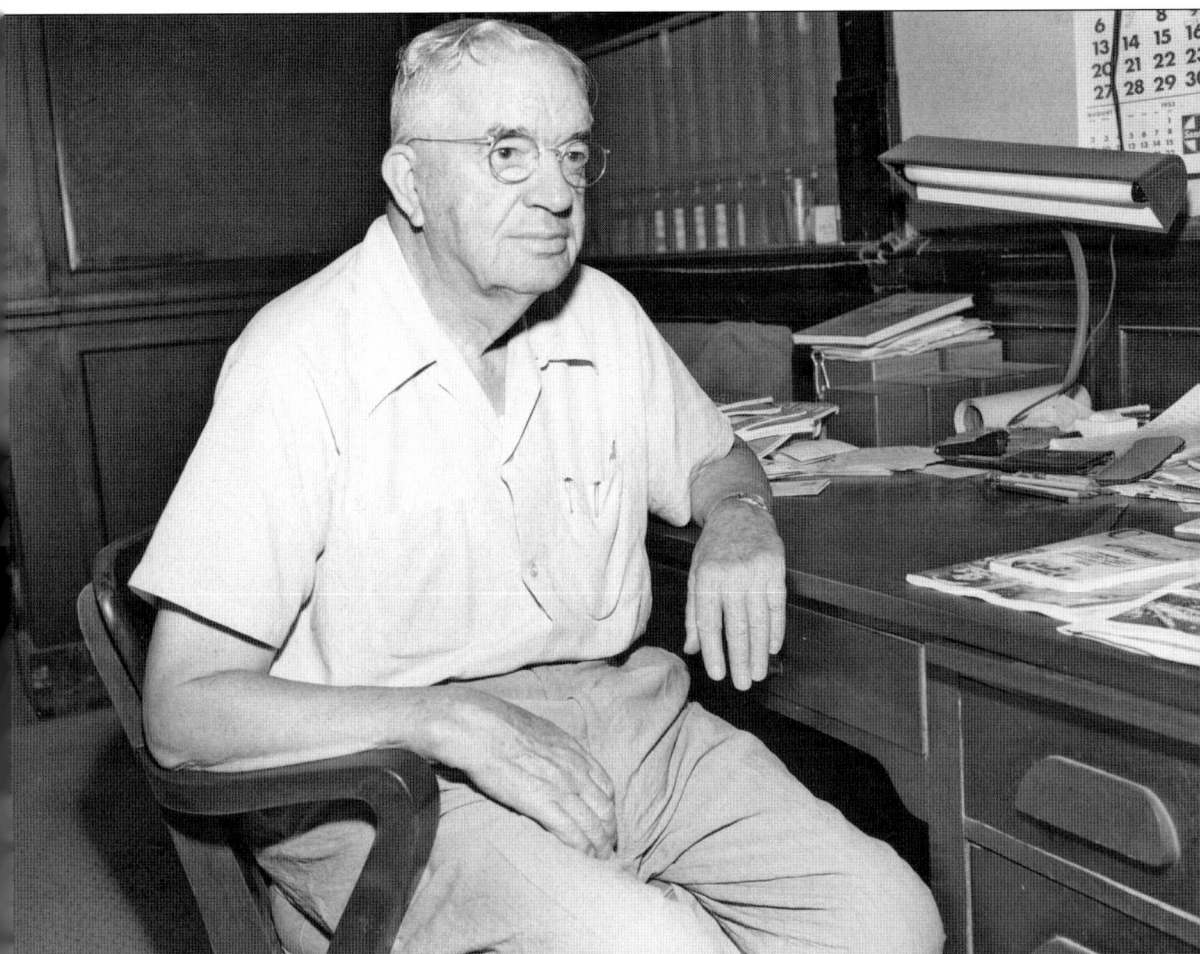

In 1955, Emmett Brown was honored with the first Chamber of Commerce Outstanding Citizen's Award. Brown organized the first Cleburne football team, served as the first coach, and taught math and history. He became principal in 1907 and in 1913 became superintendent, a job he held for 33 years. After Jinks Lee raised a Jersey cow and called it Miss Cleburne, Brown spearheaded the Rural Youth Dairy Program, encouraging businesses to sponsor starter animals so that youth could learn the dairy business. The Cleburne Rotary Club was instrumental in promoting this program. Brown used the motto "The Jersey Isle of Texas" at a Jersey Cattle Club banquet, and the wording stuck, forever linking Cleburne with the Jersey cow. Under his watch, Cleburne High School; Irving, Long, Adams, and Santa Fe Schools; Yellow Jacket Stadium; and Brown Gymnasium were built. He was the first agricultural agent here and helped organize the statewide athletic group that became the Interscholastic League. (Courtesy of Layland Museum.)

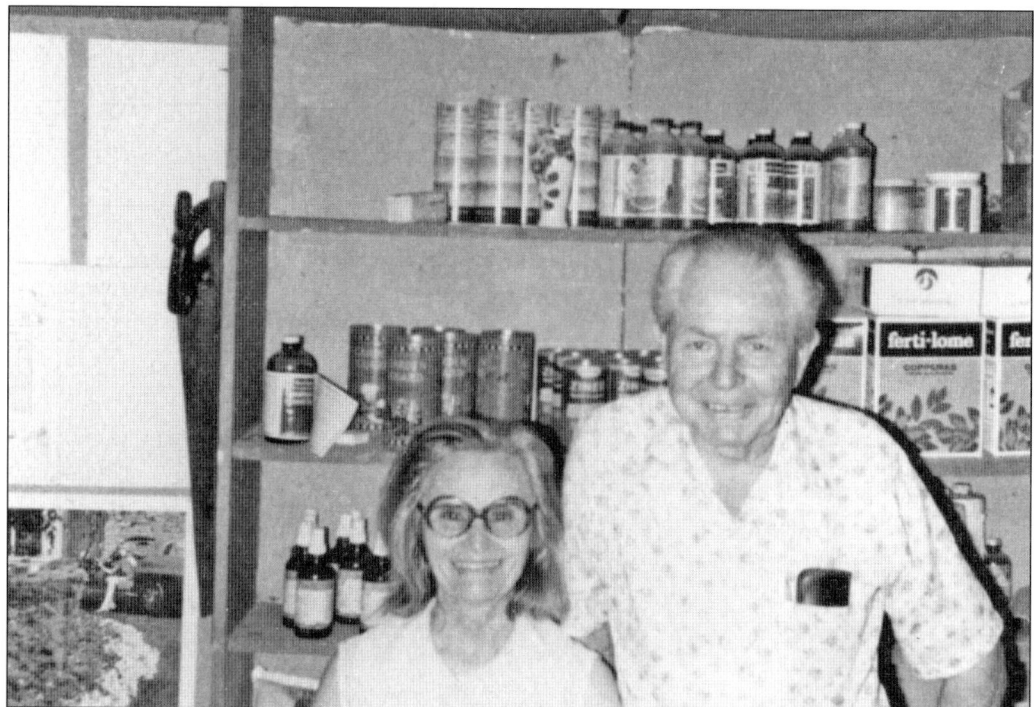

Myers Plant Company, home of 50,000 plants on Erie Street, opened for business the same year the owners married, 1936. This 1950s photograph shows Gladys Myers and Edgar Myers in the office where customers paid for their purchases until the business closed in 2008. They tended to four children, eight greenhouses, and repeat customers, running the business the old-fashioned way and never open on Sunday. (Courtesy of Linda Myers Point.)

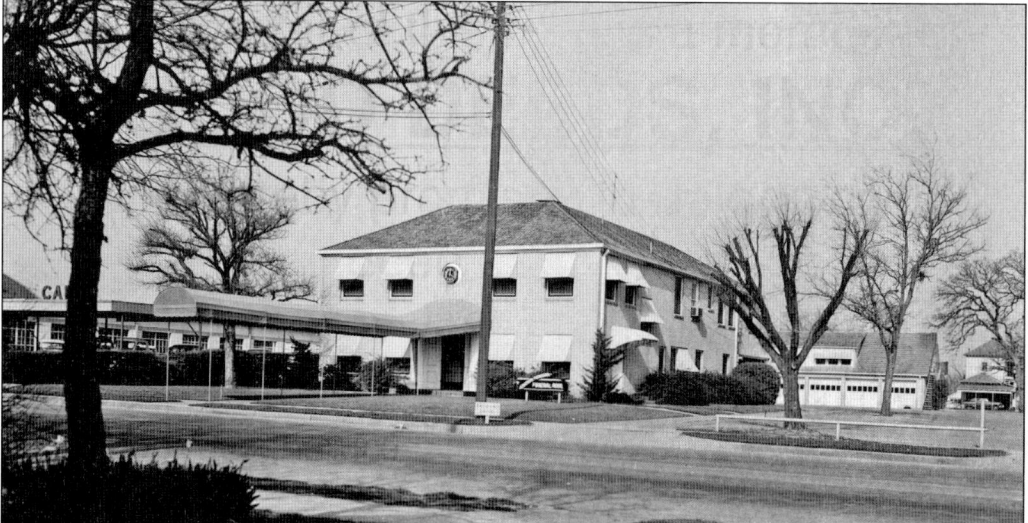

With their business growing, Byron Crosier and Hunter Pearson built a formal chapel on the south side of Crosier-Pearson Funeral Home in 1957, offering a drastic change to the funeral industry in Cleburne. Up to that time, most funerals were in churches, homes, or at graveside. Jimmy Wray joined the firm as a high school part-time helper, remaining there 28 years before joining Martin's Funeral Home. (Courtesy of Layland Museum.)

Wilma Reed (right) won the 1958 Mrs. America contest for the Fort Worth division. The prize was a new gas range, which she gave to her neighbor because she used electric. The original contest was not considered a beauty pageant but a competition of homemaking skills, including table setting, arrangements, laundry, bed making and cooking, as well as managing the family budget, personality, hairstyle, make-up, and formal dress. Jo Dodson won the 1956 Miss Texas USA contest and was the fourth runner-up to Miss USA. Below, she is posed on the front of a Santa Fe Chief engine. (Both, courtesy of Layland Museum.)

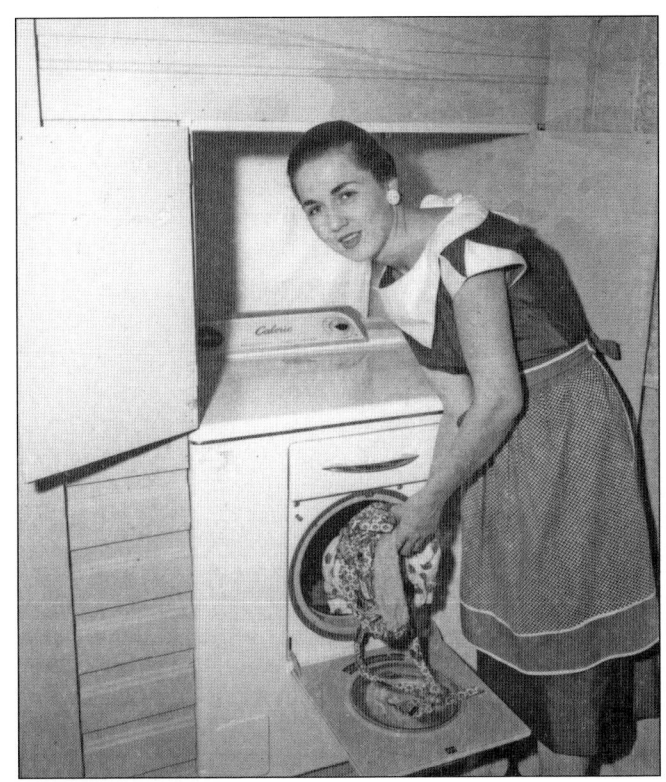

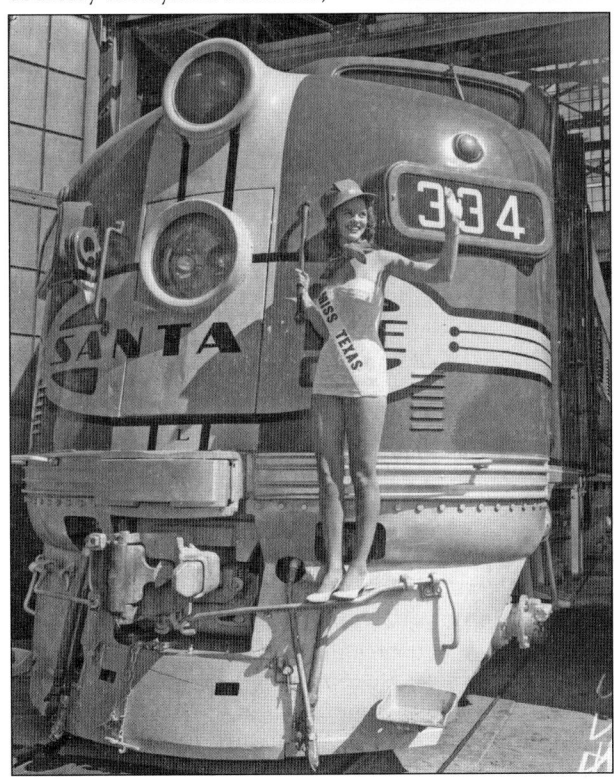

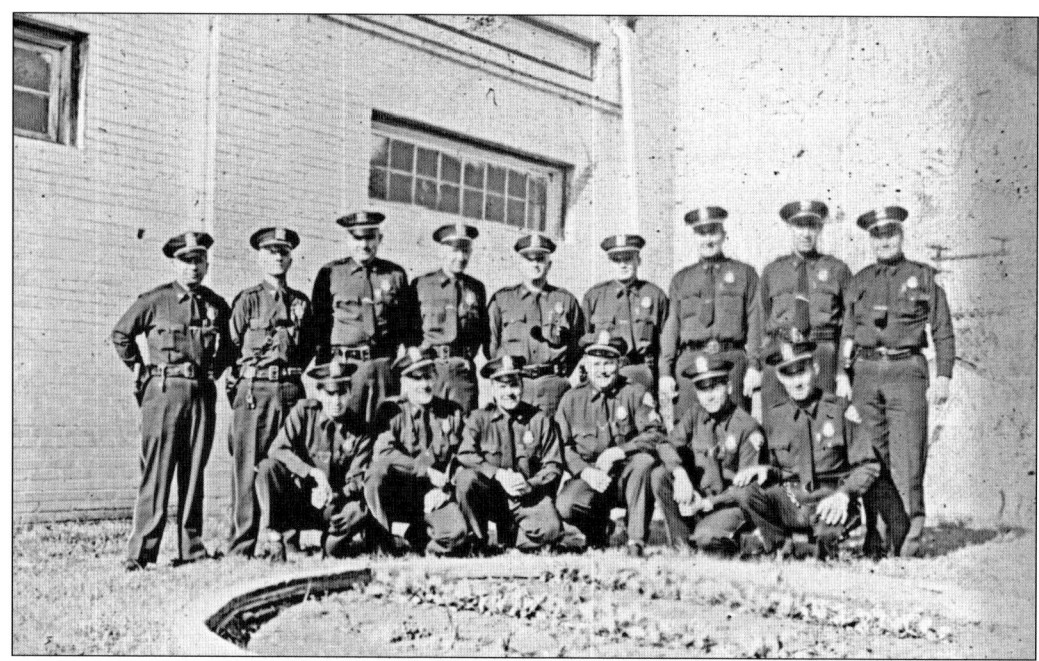

Pictured is the 1958 Cleburne Police Department. From left to right are (first row) ? Pierce, Martin Griffith Sr., Melvin Thompson, Jasper Peugh, Tritus Birdwell, and Tom Kirkpatrick; (second row) Lonnie Hill, J. W. Barton, Ivan Groening, ? Carmichael, James Walker, Bill Sides, ? Averette, Herman Derden, and Floyd Wood. (Courtesy of Layland Museum.)

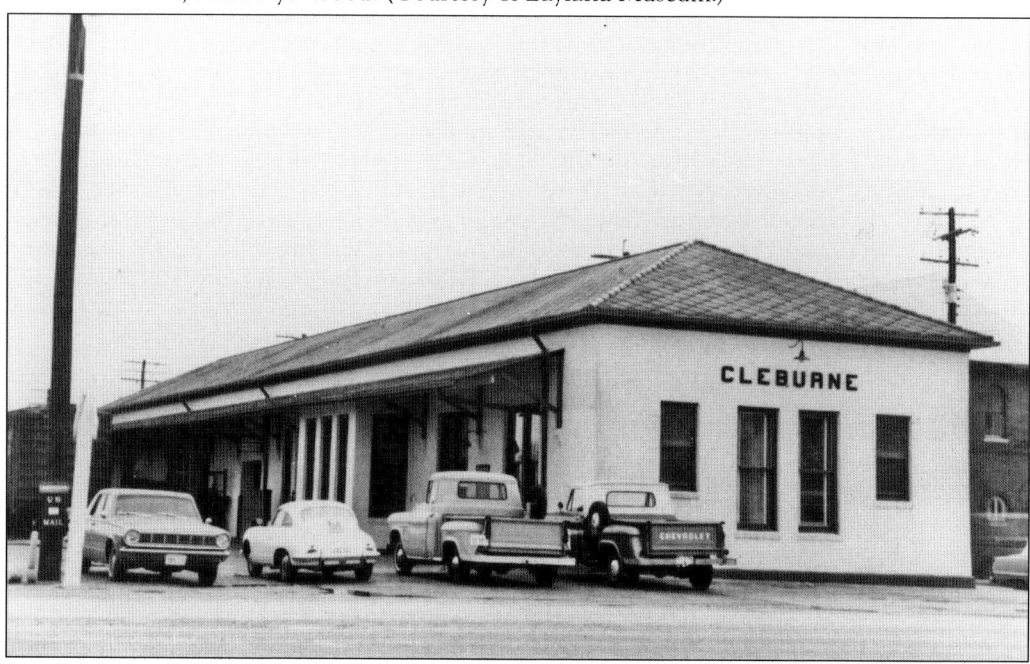

The Santa Fe depot was renovated in 1942 and torn down in 1994 to make way for a needed overpass on East Henderson Street. The City of Cleburne built an intermodal transportation station where riders can board Amtrak twice a day or utilize the local bus service. (Courtesy of Layland Museum.)

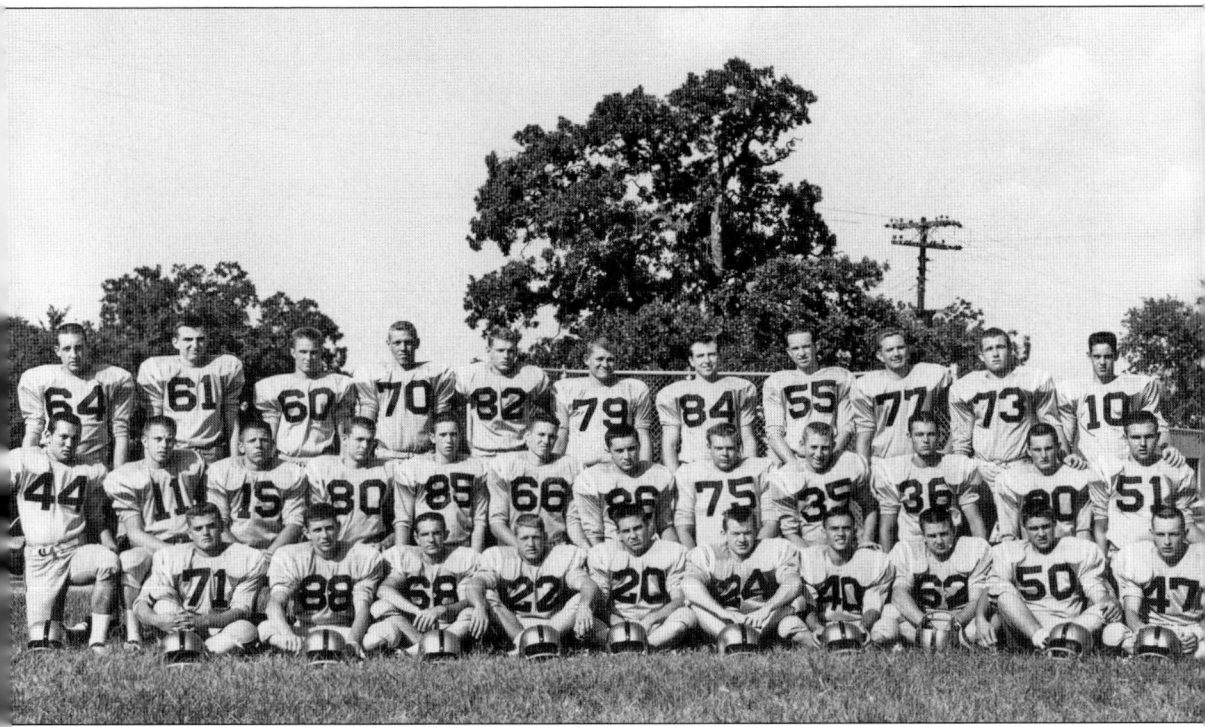

The 1958 Yellow Jacket football team had five players who went on to play in the Southwest Conference. Pat Culpepper, David McWilliams, and Timmy Doerr played for the University of Texas; Lynn Morrison played at Texas Christian University; and Paul Knott played for Southern Methodist University. The following year, 1959, the Fightin' Cleburne Yellow Jackets made it to the state football finals and came away cochampions. The 3A team tied Breckenridge 20-20. Team members were, from left to right, (first row) Pat Lutrick, Ronnie Reece, Ronnie Boyer, Buck McCall, Albert Archer, Cecil Evans, Jimmy Parker, Bill Early, David McWilliams, and Doug Shouse; (second row) Billy Cohen, Ron Yeary, Timmy Doerr, Dan Mason, Robert Parks, Danny Underwood, Johnny Love, Robert Benson, Bill Ewing, John Ed King, Steve Younger, and Charles Chapman; (third row) Robert Finklea, Horace McCowen, David Parnell, Harold Brawner, Jerry Smith, Jimmy Reed, Stephen Lee, Ronald Wallace, Richard Ottinger, Tommy Bentley, and Bill Parks. Their coach, Brooks Conover, was inducted into the Texas High School Coaches Hall of Honor in 1989. Doyle Weldon was the assistant coach. (Courtesy of Robert Finklea.)

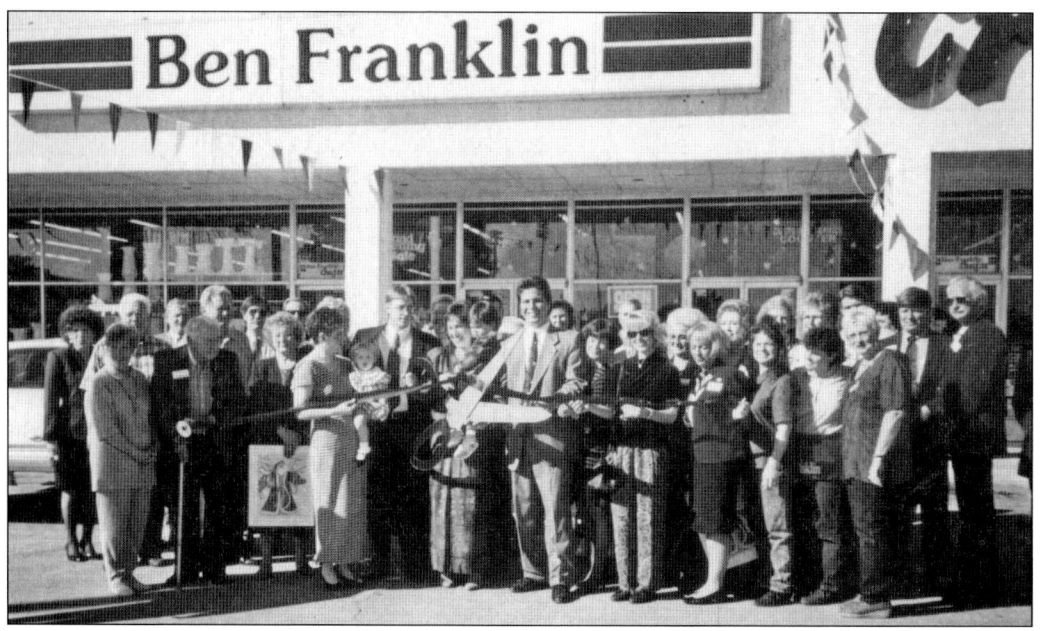

Ben Franklin's opened in the Cleburne Shopping Center in 1960 as a five-and-dime store, but soon owners Bob and Shirley Kandt began to expand. In 1995, they sold to Robert and Rebecca Roe and Jeff Kandt, who moved the operation to West Henderson Street, where a framing and floral department, a full line of seasonal supplies, and a selection of craft items filled 18,000 square feet until closing in 2003. (Courtesy of Kandt and Roe family.)

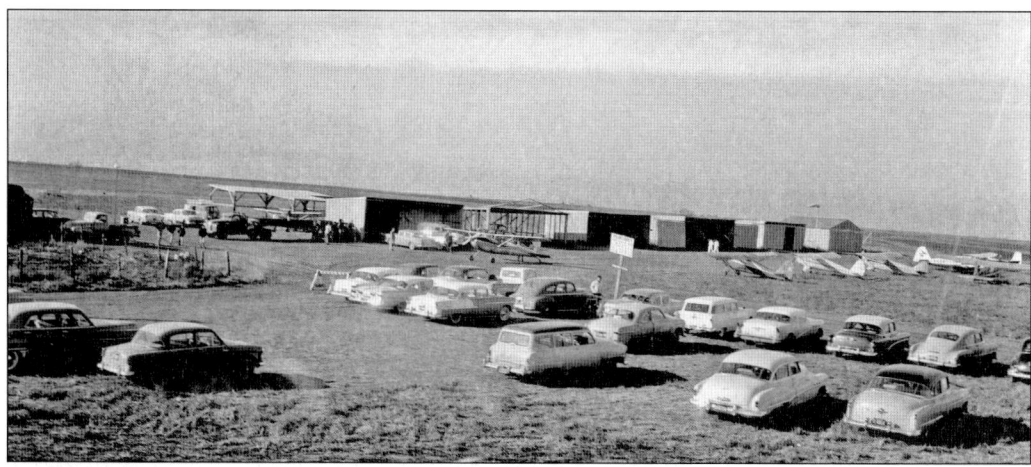

The first airport in Cleburne was Cooke Airport. Located on the present site of Cooke School, it opened shortly after World War II. Land was soon leased east of the present airport for a new location in the mid-1950s. The 1,600-foot-long landing strip was comprised of grass. An old Santa Fe boxcar was first used for an office, metal T-hangars were built, and smudge pots were used for runway lights. Today Cleburne Municipal Airport has a runway 5,700 feet long and 100 feet wide, and pilots and passengers enjoy the terminal and Hazlewood Field, named for former mayor Tom Hazlewood. (Courtesy of Layland Museum.)

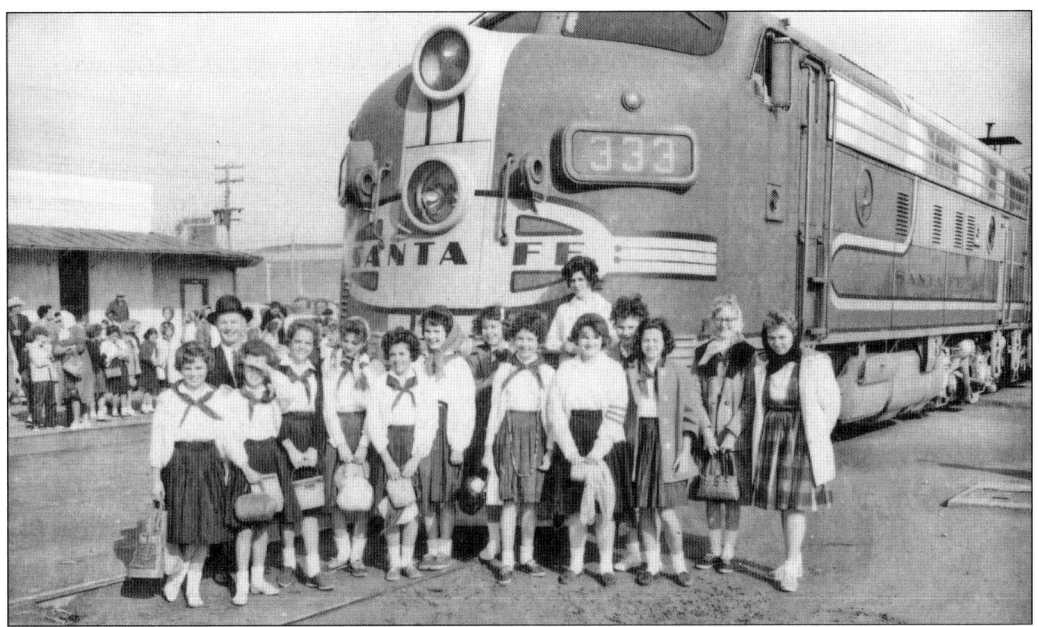

Tesuya Council of Camp Fire began in 1936. During the 1950s and 1960s, groups boarded the Santa Fe Chief to destinations like Turner Falls or Dallas, including this group led by Bessie Wright. Pictured are, from left to right, Mary Virginia Wright, Jan Bratcher, Charwynne Bass, Pam Shiflett, Lynn Wall, Sally White, Melinda Liser, Christy Chafin, Jamie Miles, Joyce Sullivan, Sherry Marshall, Kathy Beckham, Sandi Steadman, and Vicki Murry. The Cleburne Santa Fe traveling passenger agent pictured is R. M. Martin. Other groups toured companies like the Coca-Cola Bottling Company, which was established in Cleburne by W. T. George and operated from a warehouse on South Wilhite Street. Ben George managed the firm, which stopped bottling but continued to warehouse and ship six types of drinks. (Both, courtesy of Layland Museum.)

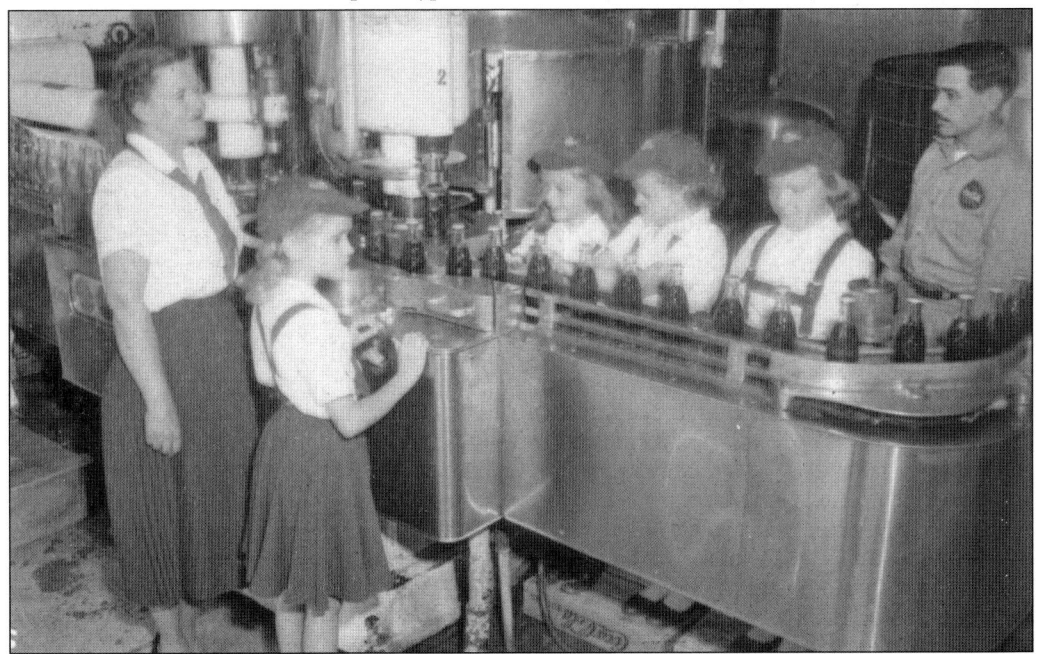

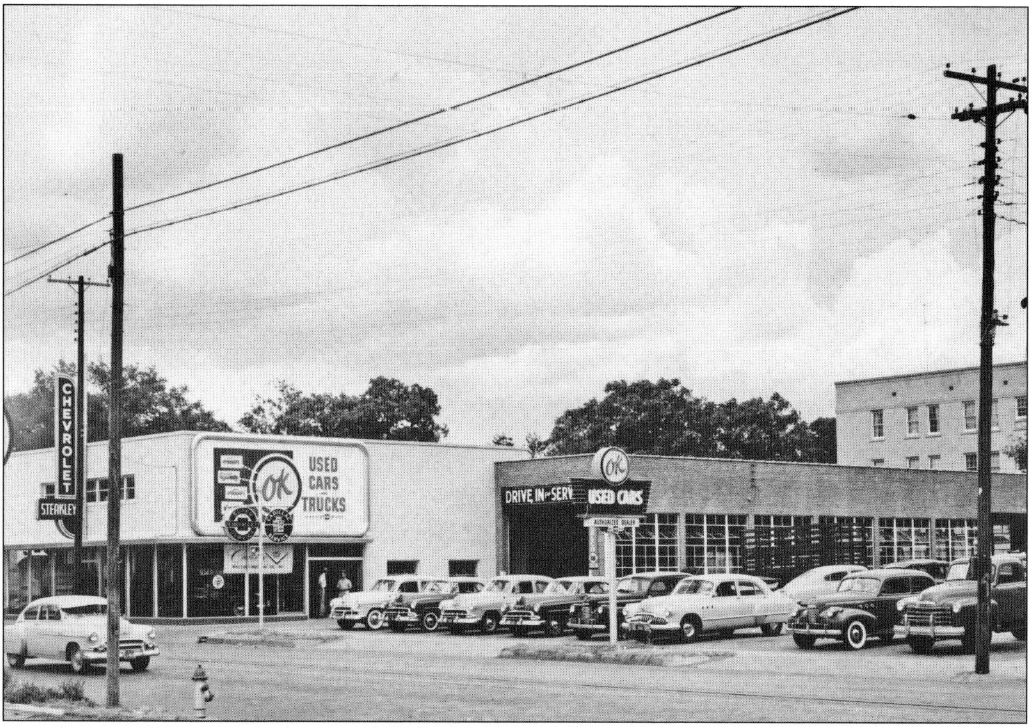

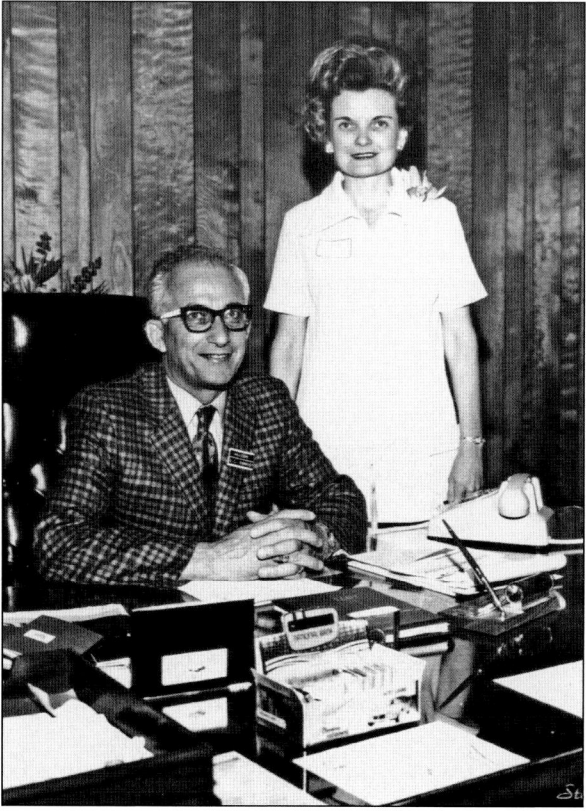

O. C. Forrest began selling cars in 1949 for Steakley Chevrolet at 400 North Main Street and became general manager. Forrest purchased the business in 1961 and changed the name to Forrest Chevrolet-Cadillac in 1965. By 1971, it had outgrown the facility and moved into new buildings at 2400 North Main Street. In 1990, the Forrest family purchased the Pontiac-Buick dealership and the following year bought out the Oldsmobile-GMC dealer. Forrest died in 1997, and his wife, Martha Clarke Forrest, became acting president with assistance from sons Clint and Michael. Clint retired in 2001. A new facility was added adjacent to the company in 2005, which brought all vehicles to the same side of the street. (Above, courtesy of Layland Museum; left, courtesy of Martha Forrest.)

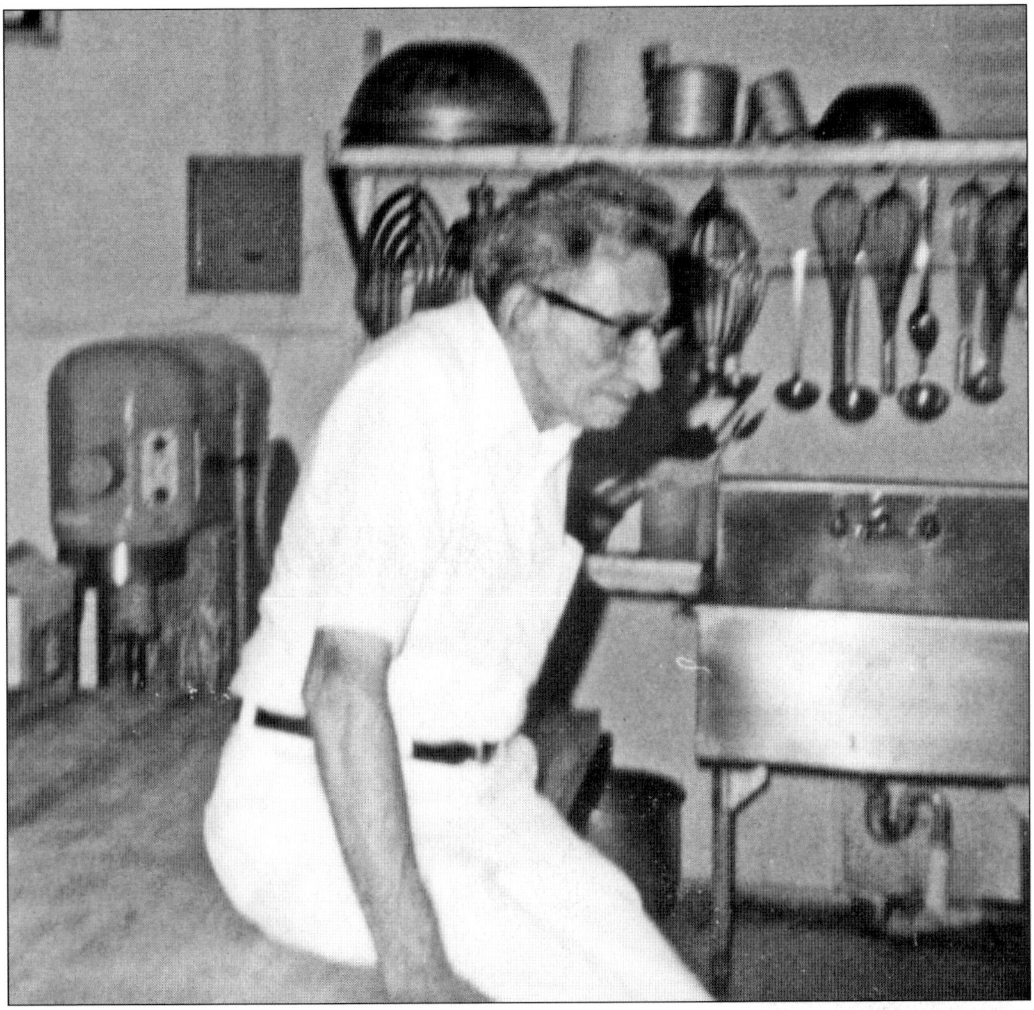

Joseph "Bill" and Sarah Kitchens began working for the family bakery in 1956. Sweet smells filled the air behind the post office from Kitchens' Bakery on East Henderson Street. Dorothy Williams purchased the business in 1979 and closed it to make way for the overpass. Pictured is Bill Kitchens. The Schepps family bakery at 317 East Henderson Street is remembered for its Yellow Jacket Bread, wrapped in waxed paper. Pictured at right is an image showing the bread advertised in a 1929 *Cleburne Times-Review* newspaper. Tyson E. Payne Sr. assumed ownership of the store, changing the name to Payne Bakery and moving it to North Anglin Street. Jessie Ballew and Henry Kohler were bakers, with the help of Joe Ballew and Horace Clack. Doc Wright made the deliveries. (Above, courtesy of the Kitchens family; right, courtesy of Layland Museum.)

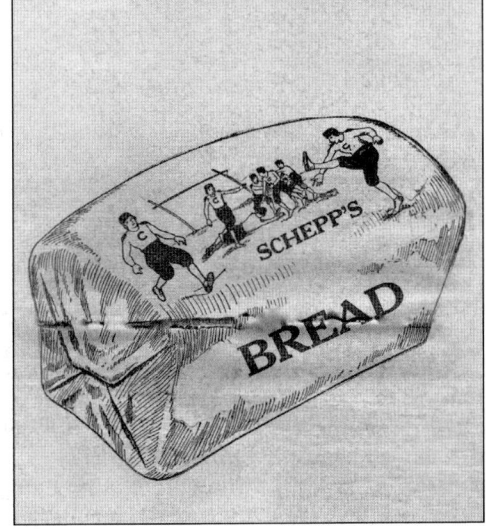

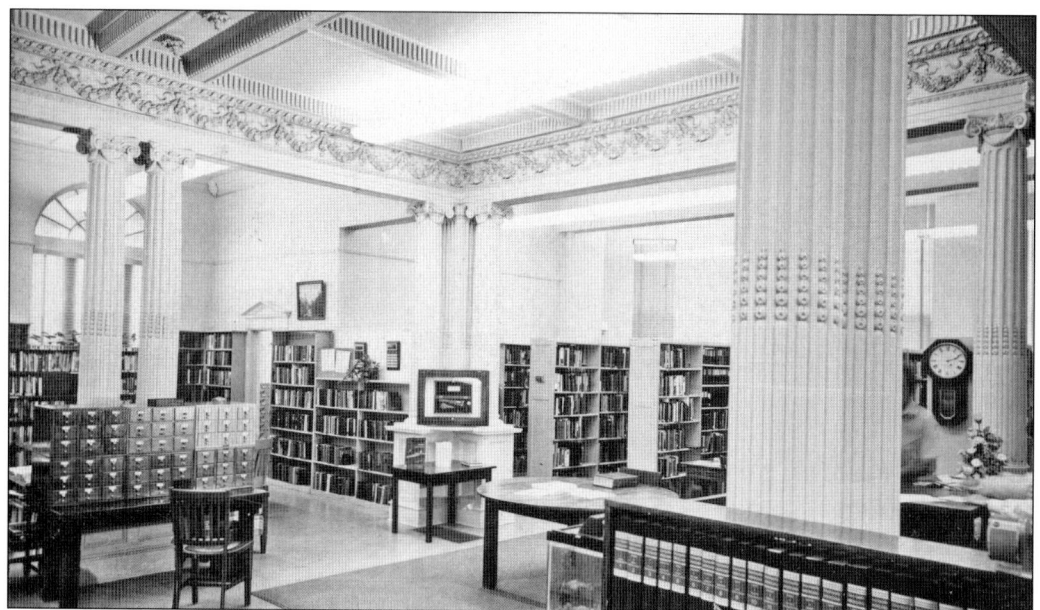

Layland Museum opened on the second floor of the Carnegie Library with a collection donated by businessman W. J. Layland. When the library moved in 1978 to its present location, the museum expanded its collections to include home and life exhibits plus temporary and traveling exhibits. Programming includes educational and cultural events. There have only been two directors, Mildred Padon and Julie Baker, now assisted by collections curator Ben Hammons. (Courtesy of Layland Museum.)

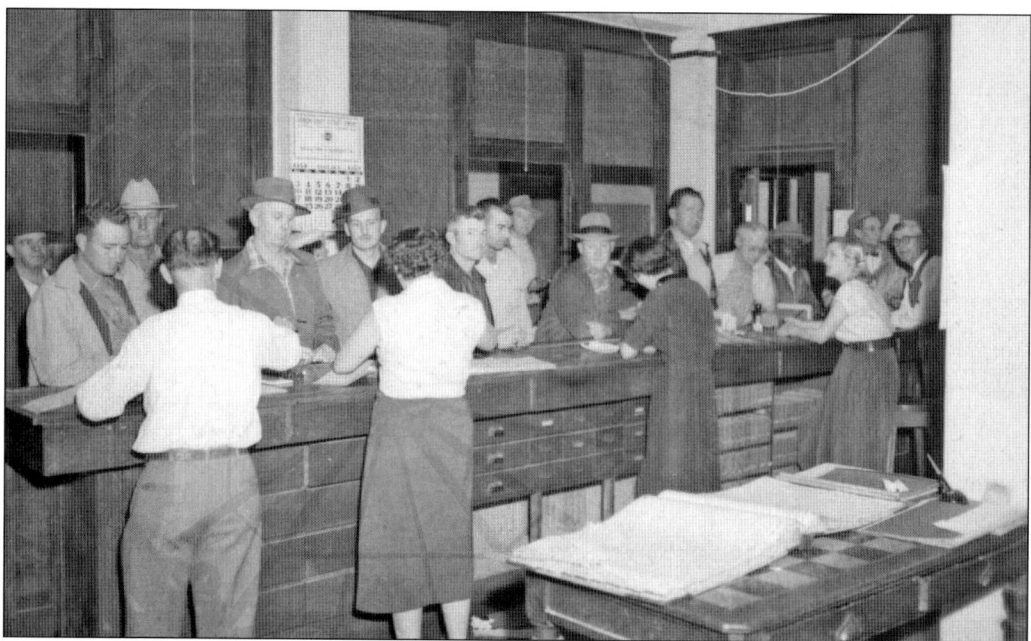

From 1903 until the elections of 1964, residents paid a poll tax before being allowed to cast a vote. Pictured are residents lined up to pay their tax in the Johnson County Courthouse. The poll tax was abolished by the 24th Amendment to the U.S. Constitution as a requirement for voting for federal offices. (Courtesy of Layland Museum.)

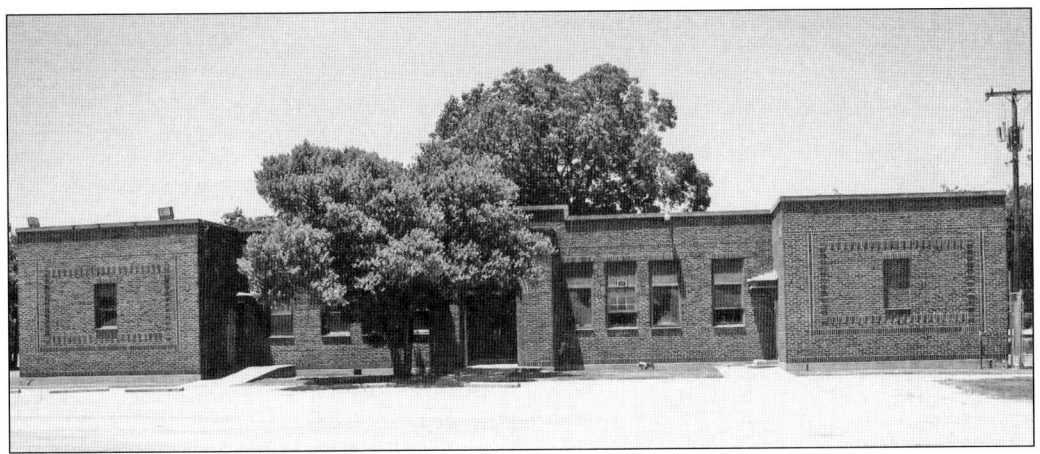

The first Booker T. Washington School was a frame building. After burning, it was replaced in 1926 using insurance money and $4,000 donated by Julius Rosenwald. The larger brick structure, including a gym, was used by black students for all grades until the fall of 1965, when Cleburne schools were desegregated. (Courtesy of John Warren.)

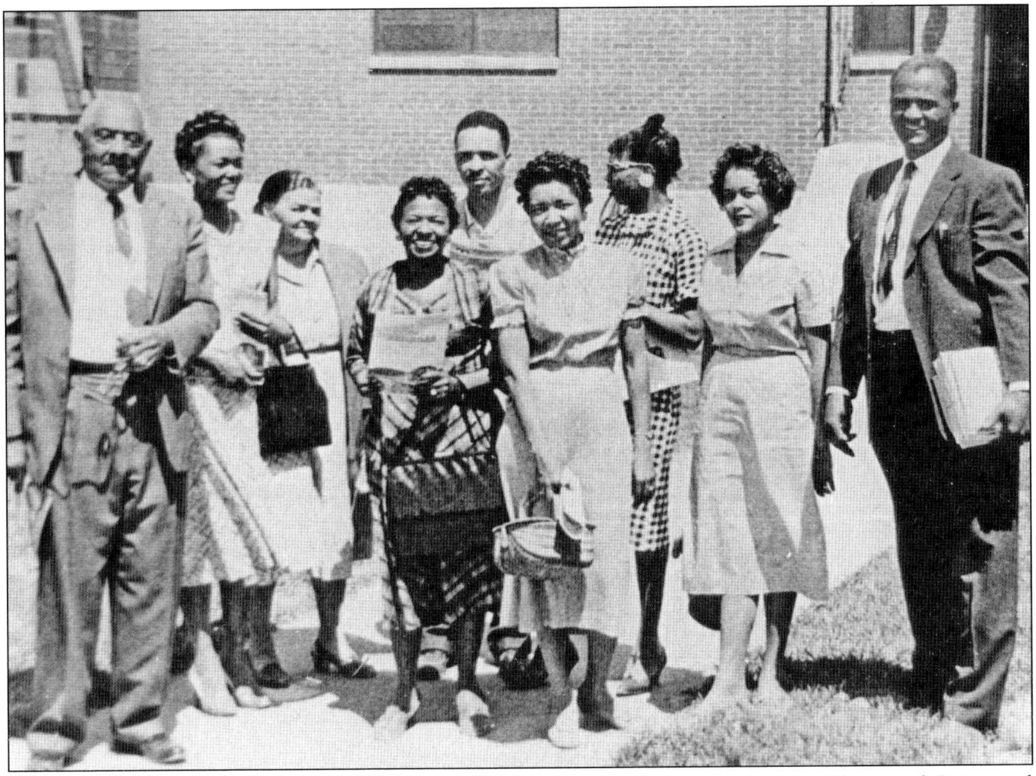

Staff members of Booker T. Washington School included, from left to right, (first row) Principal Files Fred Douglas Kelly, Agusta Sue Robinson, Avis Dorine Corzine, Dorothy Matthews, Shirley Anderson, and assistant principal Joseph Matthews; (second row) Charlie Matthews, Rod Ell Cotton, and Marie Crane. (Courtesy of John Warren.)

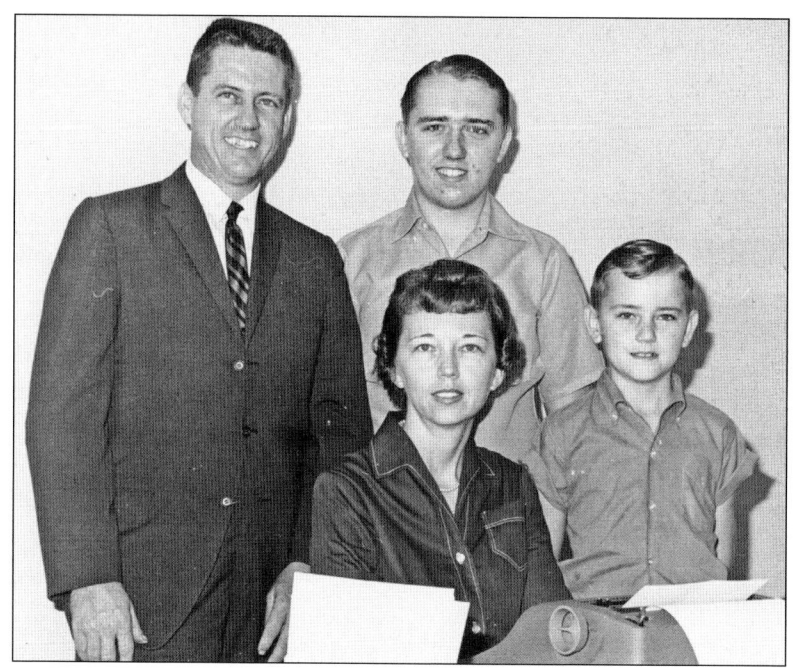

Fred and Peggy Bennett moved to Cleburne in 1965 to open a print shop. Pictured with their first typesetting machine, an IBM Selectric typewriter, are, from left to right, (seated) Peggy and Mark Bennett; (standing) Fred and Gary Bennett. Gary Bennett and his wife, Melissa, now oversee several locations. (Courtesy of Bennett Printing and Office Supply/Gary and Melissa Bennett.)

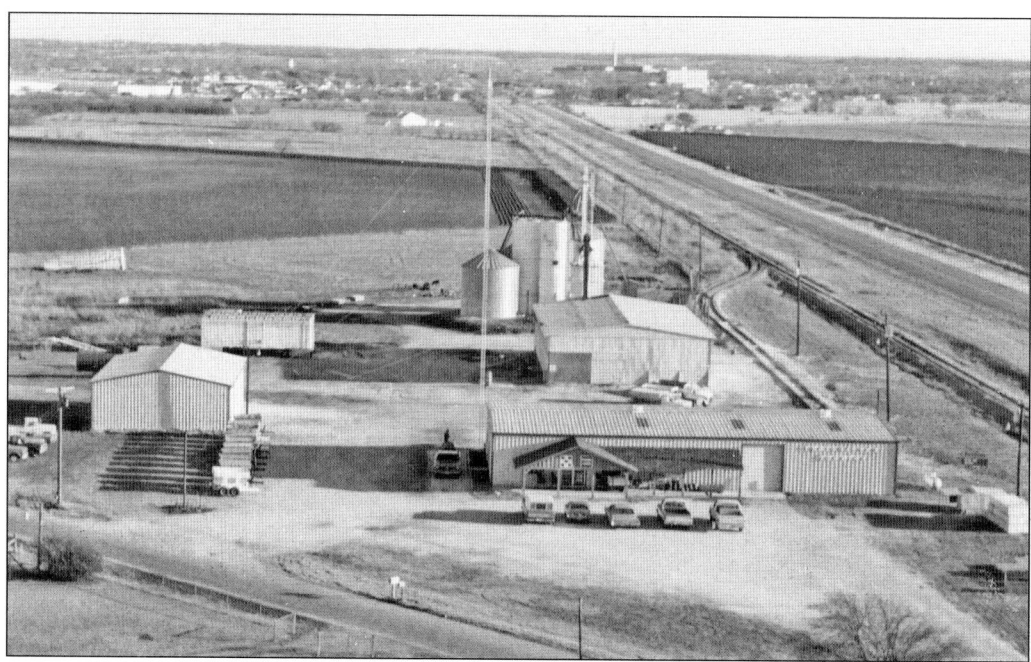

Opened in 1965 on Woodard Avenue, Mann Ag Service was family owned by Sam and Dorothy Mann for almost 40 years before they retired in 2007. They had the first fertilizer spreader truck in the county and delivered seeds and animal feed. The family expanded the business and moved it to the present location on Highway 171 in 1969, providing fertilizer, seeds, Western clothing, and housewares. (Courtesy of Dorothy and Sam Mann.)

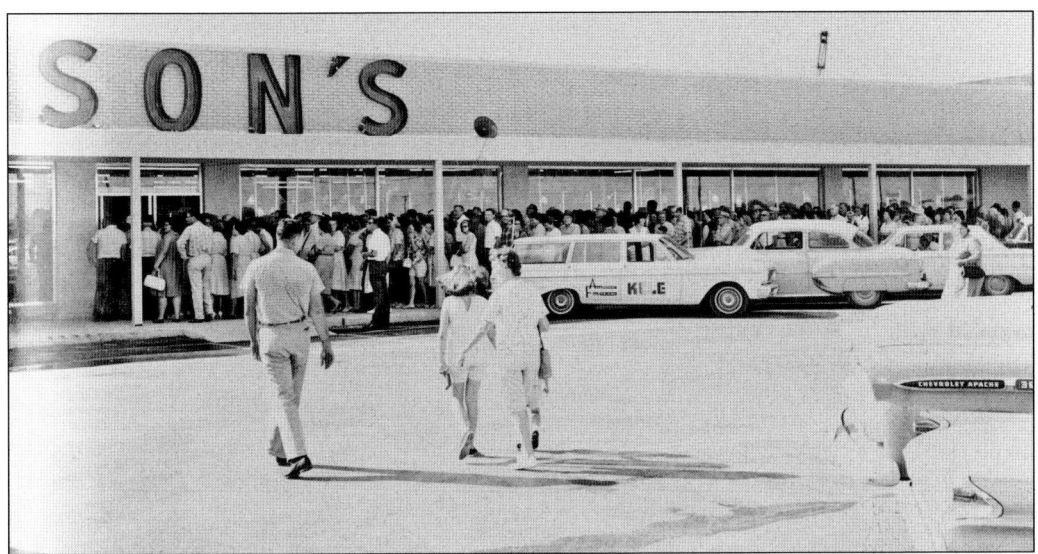

Opening day of Gibson's drew over 12,000 people to the large department store on West Henderson Street. Dick Alsup was the general manager, August Koehne Jr. ran the pharmacy, and Curtis Boese created the advertising for many years. Cars filled the parking lot and the field across the street, then shoppers lined up for hours to get inside. Due to crowding, only a few were allowed inside at a time. The store enlarged in 1970 to expand the grocery department. Until it closed in 1988, Gibson's held many events, including penny hunts, fireworks, car and television giveaways, and costume contests. Tony Douglas and the Shrimpers played a parking lot dance in 1974. The aerial view shows the National Guard armory on the right, which became the civic center. (Both, courtesy of Sylvia Boese.)

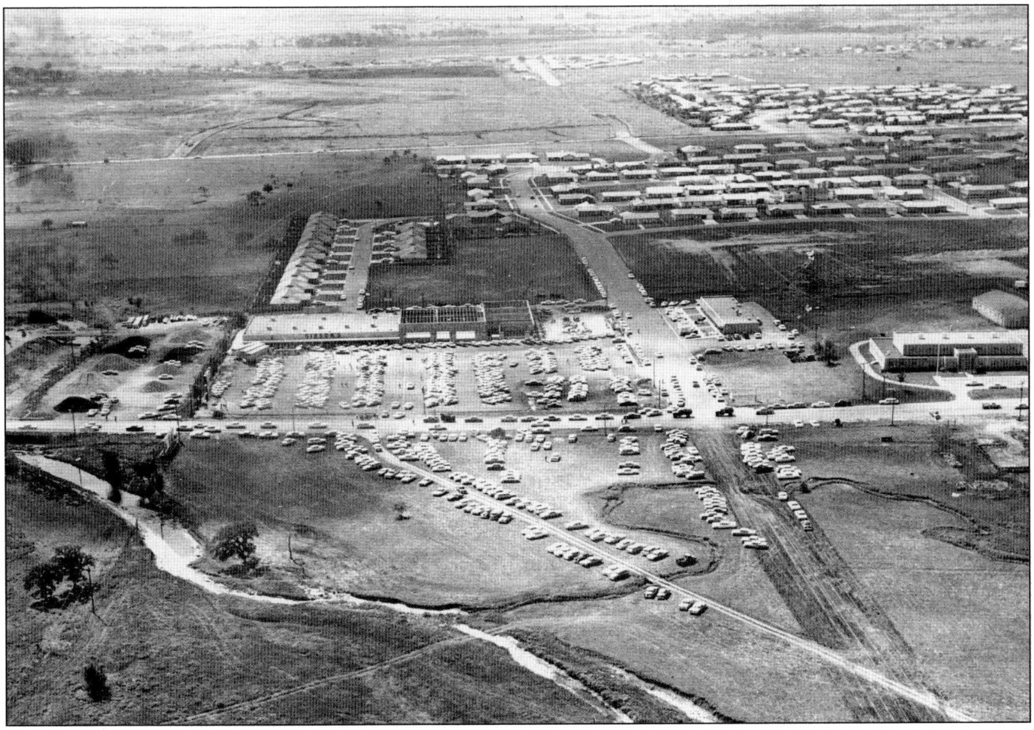

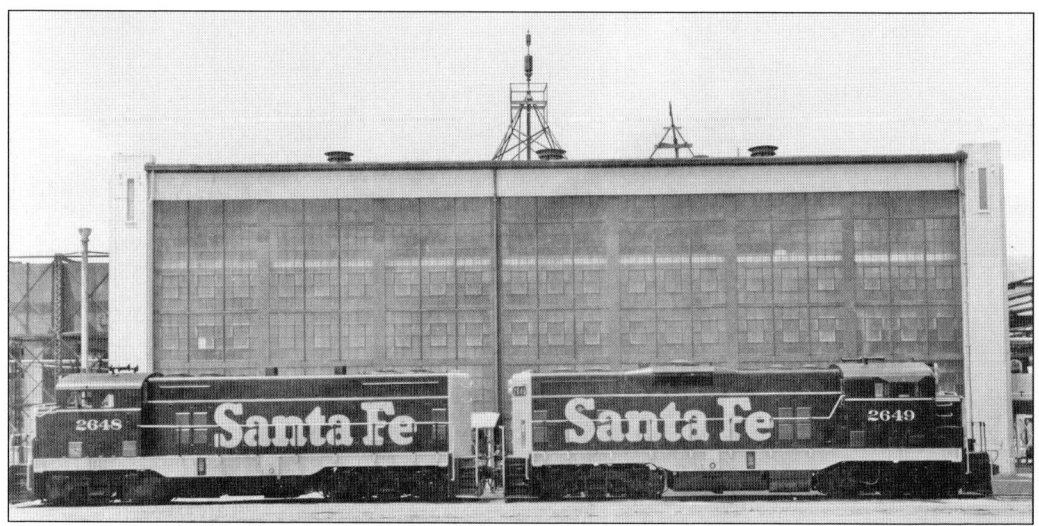

Skilled Santa Fe employees economically transformed the worn out 20 to 30 year old F3, F7, and F9 diesels into versatile dual-purpose CF7s. During this eight-year 1970s program, 233 units were converted and painted bright yellow and blue. This photograph shows two of the first units completed. (Courtesy of Sonny Burt.)

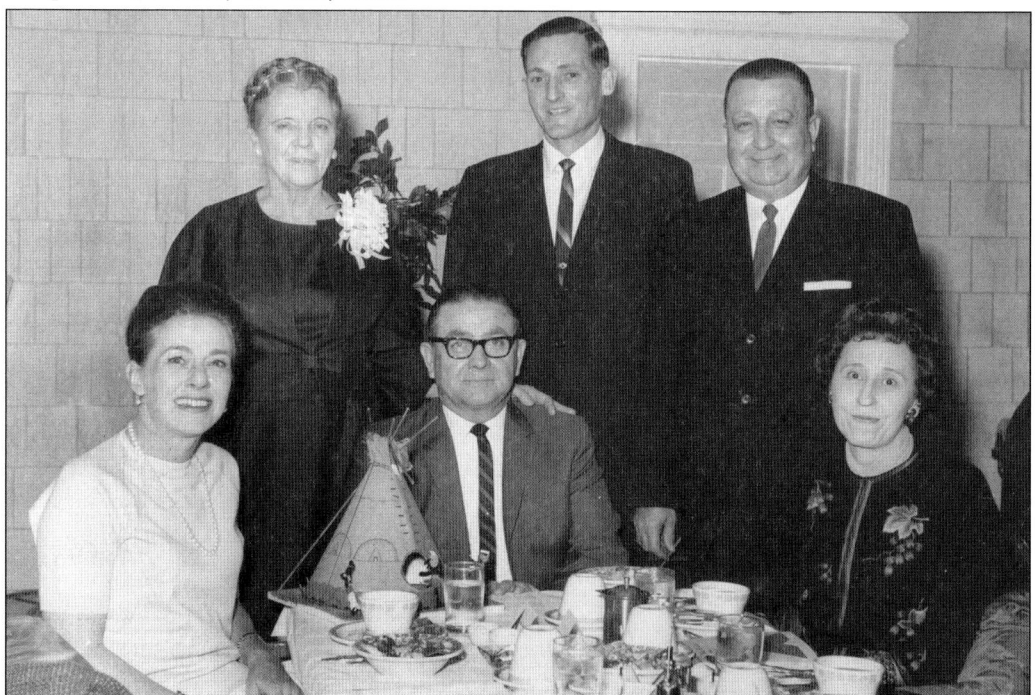

Heritage and preserving it has always been on the minds of some Cleburne people. Pictured at this 1966 Blue Bird-Horizon Club dinner were some of those people. From left to right are (seated) Tommie Kimbro (founder of the Heritage Assembly), Shirley Clark (postmaster), and Willie Dell Culpepper (charter member of the local Daughters of the American Revolution); (standing) Vera Mangum (Tesuya Council of Camp Fire executive director), Ralph Garrett (Camp Fire and Boy Scouts volunteer), and Duke Bennett (mayor). Another organization that remains active is the Kings Daughters, whose local union is the largest in Texas. (Courtesy of Layland Museum.)

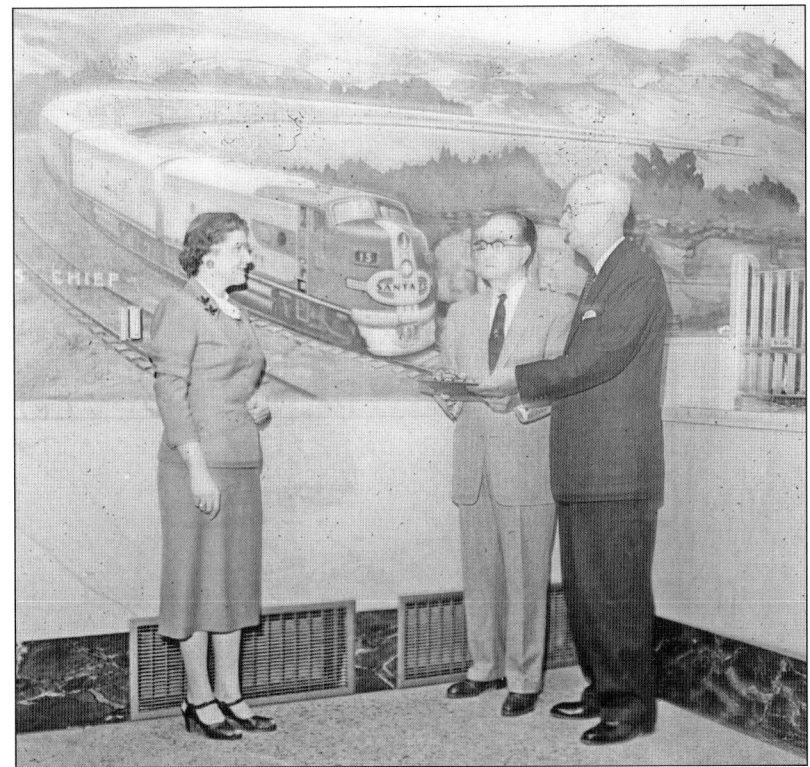

Cleburne National Bank, on the southwest corner of the square, was remodeled in 1951, when this mural was added. A new building was constructed in 1976. Pictured are, from left to right, Lorraine Barnes, bank president Tim Aubrey, and unidentified. It became Interfirst Bank in 1984, and currently Bank of America is located there. (Courtesy of Layland Museum.)

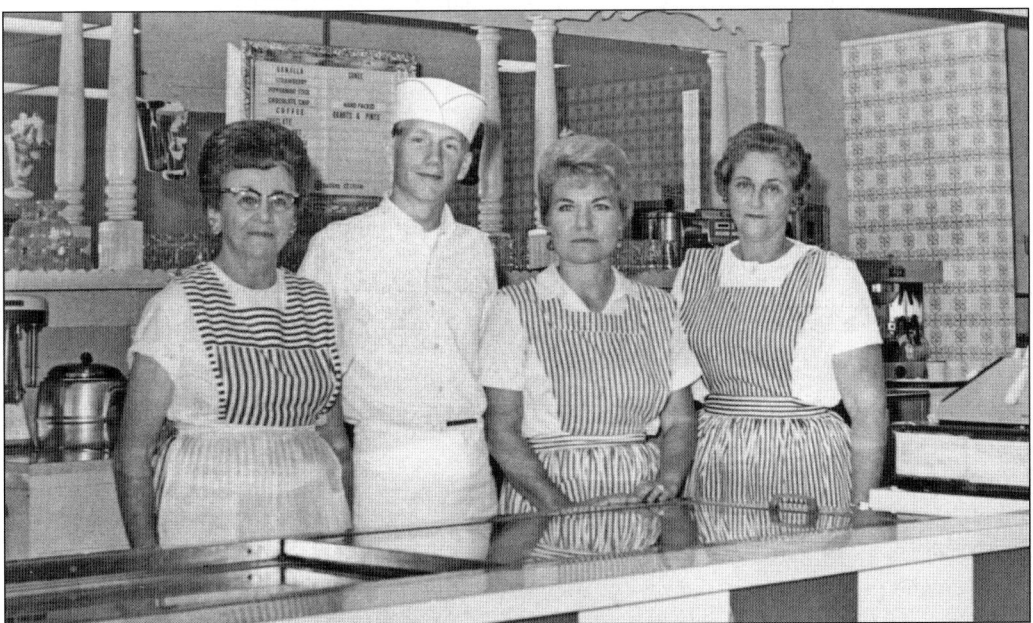

Gay 90's, the first restaurant in town to serve pizza, was located in the shopping center on Ridgeway Drive. Opened by Rudy Doty and Dick Powell, it soon became a popular hangout for teenagers and family outings, serving Frisco burgers for 60¢ and banana splits for 45¢. Employees pictured are, from left to right, Ida Williams, Rick John, and two unidentified. (Courtesy of Beverly Holden.)

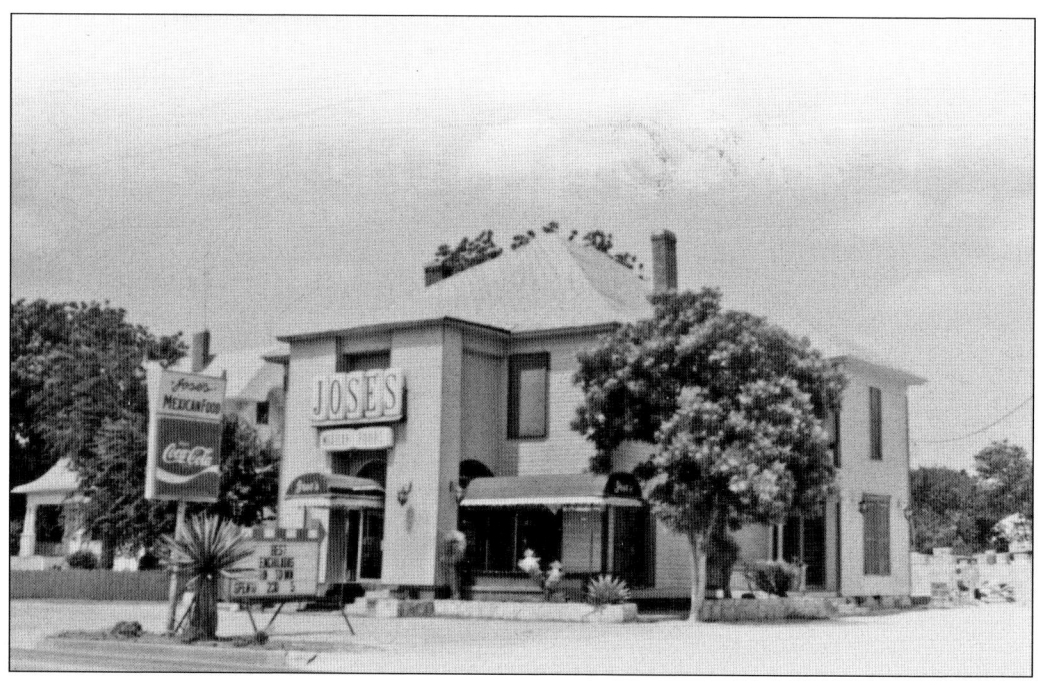

Jose's Mexican Restaurant opened in a two-story house on North Main Street in 1972 and thrived until the new building was constructed next door a few years later. The cooks slept upstairs. This was the first Mexican food establishment in town, and its buffet was a hit from the beginning. Cleburne saw an economic boom due to the building of Comanche Peak's nuclear power plants in Glen Rose during the first years of Jose's. Pictured below are, from left to right, Raymond Vasquez, Joe Vasquez, and their father, Jose Vasquez, in the kitchen of the restaurant a few years before closing. (Above, courtesy of Loma Pritchard; below, courtesy of the author.)

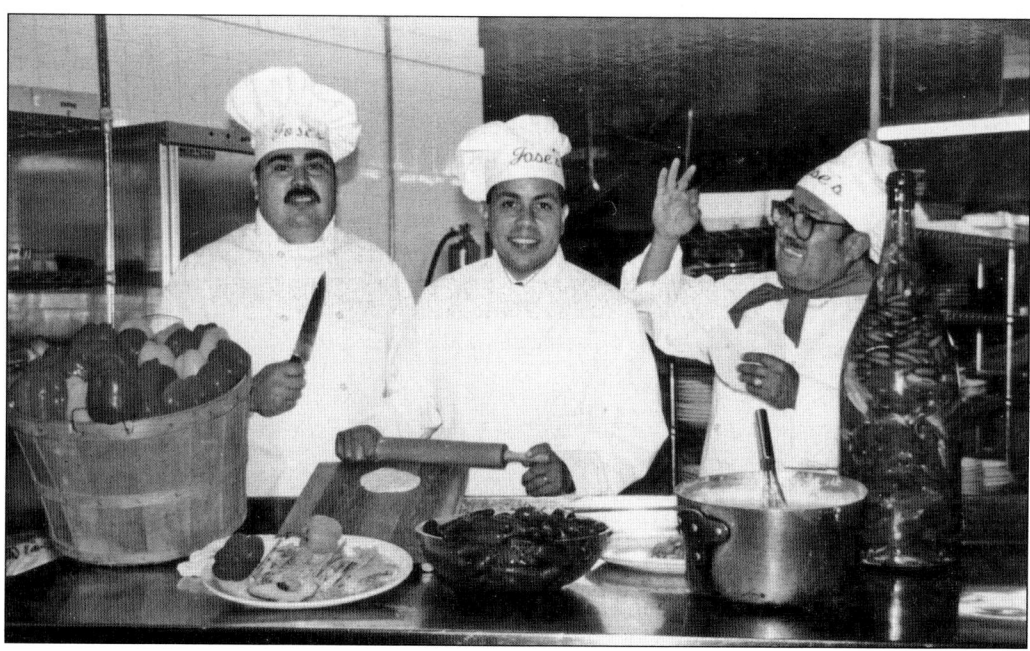

# Five
# 1976–2000

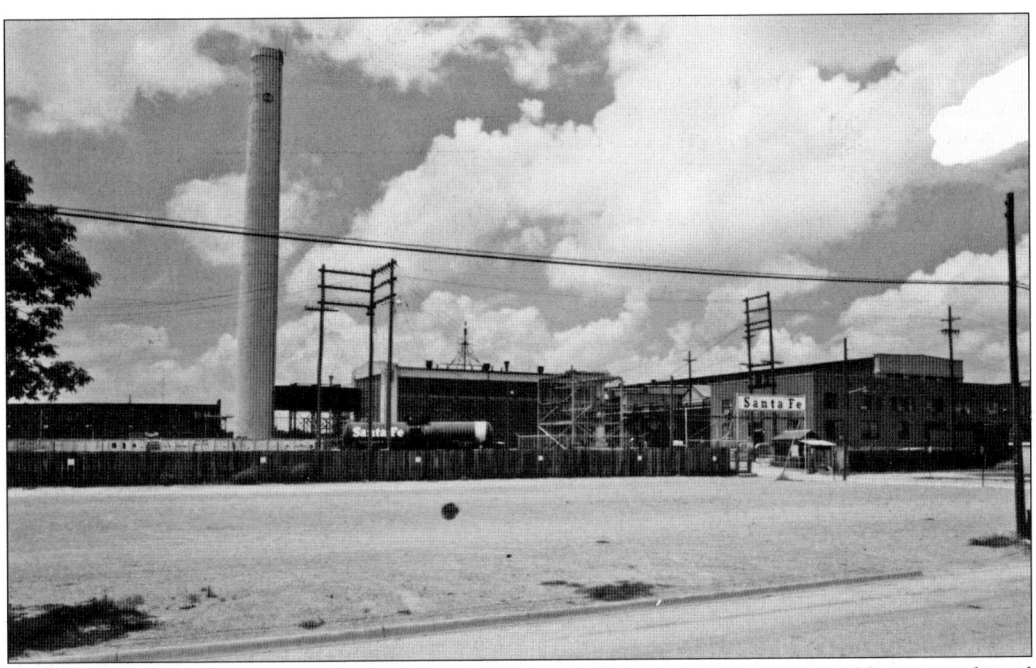

Santa Fe Railroad closed the Cleburne facility in 1989. Most machinery was sold or moved, and many lost their jobs. Others moved or commuted to Santa Fe facilities for continued employment. The shops are currently occupied by Greenbrier Rail Services, where rebuilding and repairing is done for several railroads. In 1989, a refurbished Santa Fe caboose was relocated to the grounds of the Layland Museum. (Courtesy of Layland Museum.)

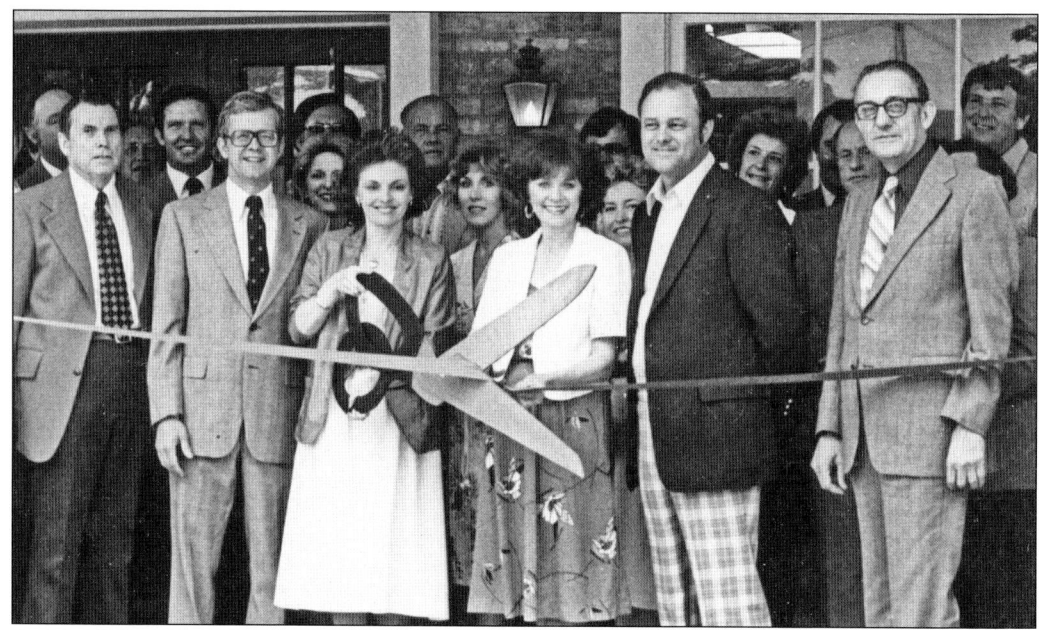

Castle Collection moved to a larger location in 1978 on Ridgeway Drive, where this photograph was taken. Pictured on the front row at the ribbon cutting are Earl Senter, Dr. James Johnson, co-owners Nancy Johnson and Mary King, John Ed King, and Mayor George Marti. Two years later, Nolan River Mall opened with K-Mart, Bealls, J. C. Penney, Zales Jewelers, Peanut Shack, and Regis Hairstylist. (Courtesy of Mary King and Nancy Johnson.)

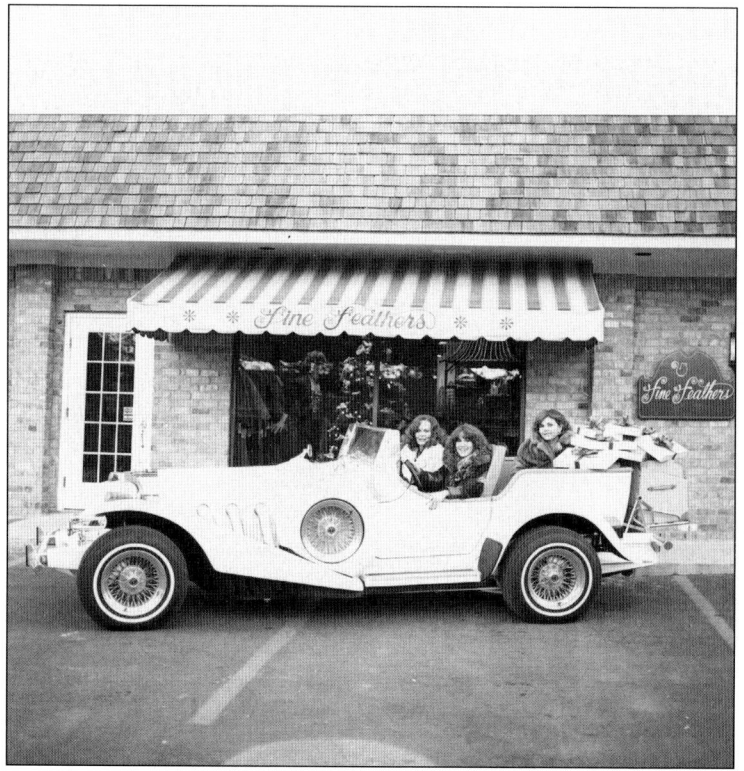

Miss Lake Whitney 1957 LuLane Ward used her knowledge as a former model and employee at Lintz Department Store to open Fine Feathers in 1978 with two friends. Pictured from left to right are owners Jan Turner Murski, Ellen Noble, and LuLane Ward in front of the boutique on Pendell Street. It was open for 10 years. Neighboring stores included Mommies Favorites, Montains, and Fancy Stitches. (Courtesy of Layland Museum.)

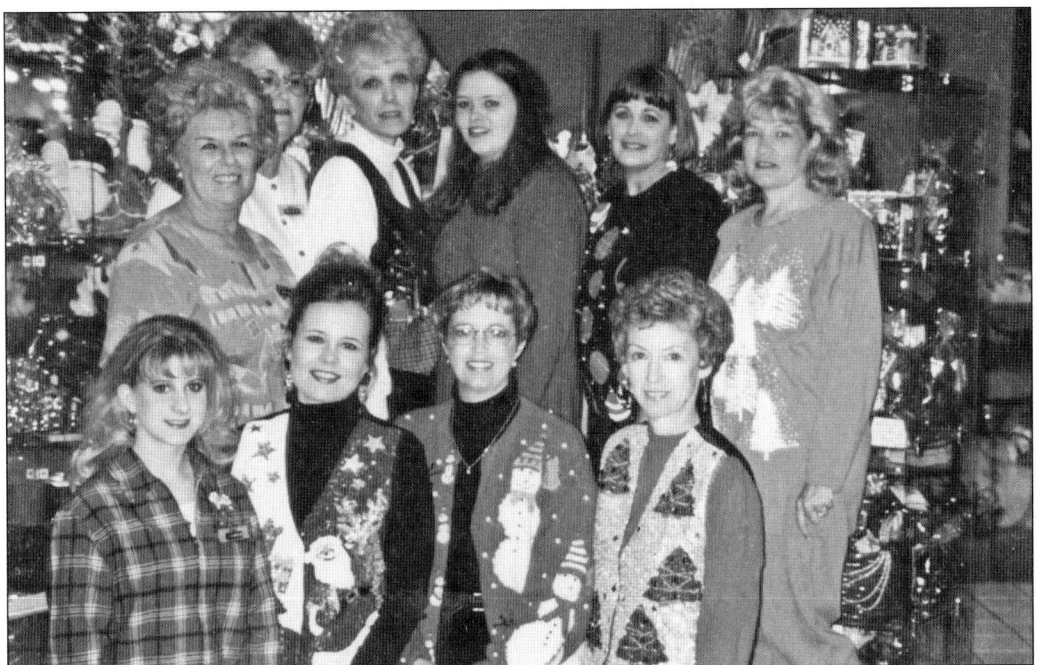

Owner Betsy Harty has grown Accents from a small store on North Main Street to a warehouse on Mill Street in 1981 to a destination for shopping at Nolan River Mall in 1986. Pictured are employees at the annual holiday open house in 1998. From left to right are (first row) Lauren Tribble, Jeanie Burris, Jamie Evans, and Betsy Harty; (second row) Beverly Reagen, Barbara Lane, Susan Turner, Stacy Lowe, Bonnie Thomas, and Debbie Farber. (Courtesy of Betsy Harty.)

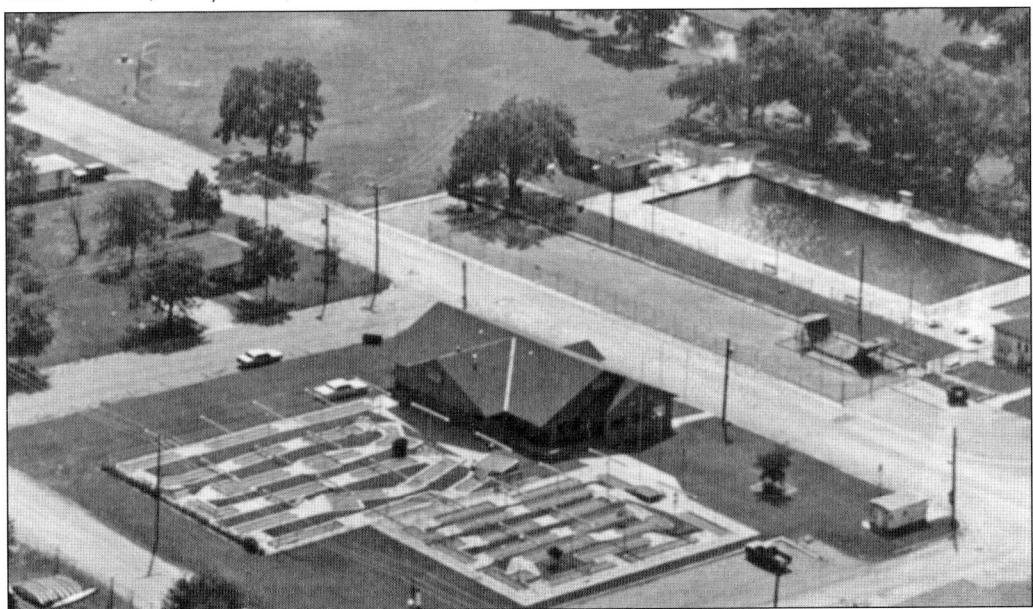

During the 1970s, Bill and Margaret Schick purchased the golf course and game room across the street from Hulen Park. In 1982, partners Bill and Adele Reece and son Ronnie Reece were added to the business. They built a second putt-putt golf course and a 4,000-square-foot game room, as seen in this photograph. (Courtesy of the Reese family.)

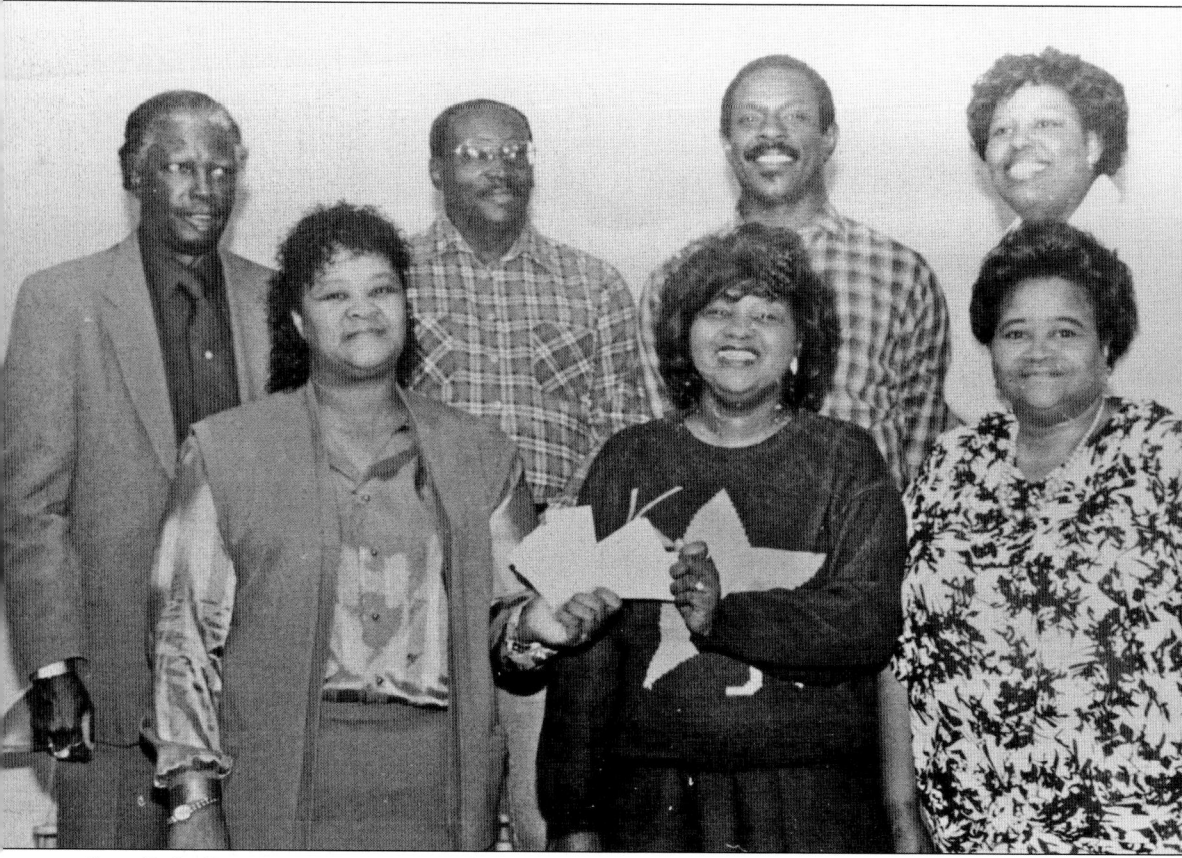

Rev. D. L. Barrett was instrumental in creating and organizing the East Cleburne Community Center. A renovated grocery store was used for programming before it moved into the Booker T. Washington School. Board members in 1989 included, from left to right, (front row) Mattie Barrett, Jean Pickett, and Jessie Fantroy; (second row) D. L. Barrett, John Warren, Michael Fuller, and Pauline Lauderdale. Others charter members were Kirklin Cross and Herbie Stone. Jessie Fantroy also helped found the Johnson County Crisis Center and the County Child Welfare Board, she was a deaconess at Mount Zion Baptist Church and president of League of Women's Voters, and she served on the board of the local NAACP. Hired by Sen. Lyndon B. Johnson in 1953 to work in his district office, Jessie continued to work for him when he was vice president and president, including 16 years as a cook at their lake house near Marble Falls. She also worked 21 years as a cook and hostess at the Cowpasture Bank in Rio Vista. When she retired, the bank established a scholarship fund for graduating black students in her honor. (Courtesy of John Warren.)

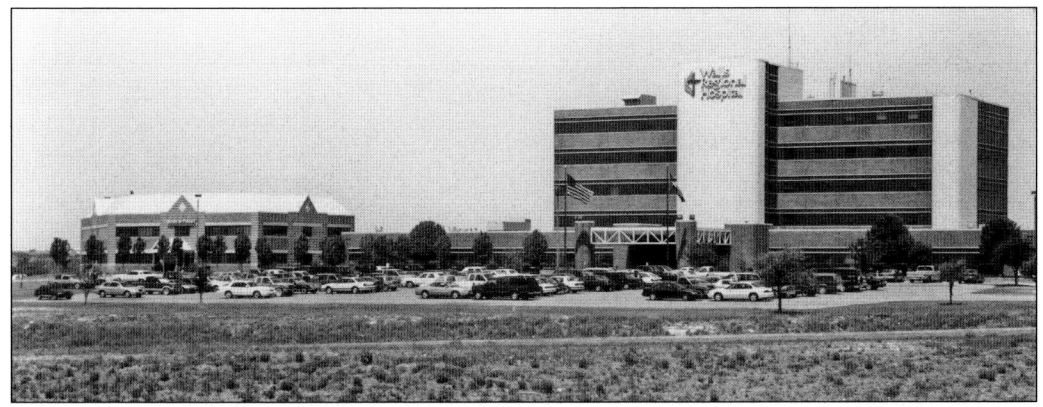

Johnson County Memorial Hospital was purchased in 1983 by Harris Methodist Affiliated Hospitals. Harris Methodist Walls Regional Hospital opened in July 1986 on land just east of Lake Pat Cleburne donated by George Walls and his family. The Physicians Office Building opened in 1993. The name changed in 2009 to Texas Health Harris Methodist Hospital Cleburne. In 1993, Kay Walls founded the volunteer organization that hosts the annual Black and White Gala. This successful event raises funding for health-related causes, including Mammograms Are a Must and Shots for Tots. (Courtesy of Bob Force.)

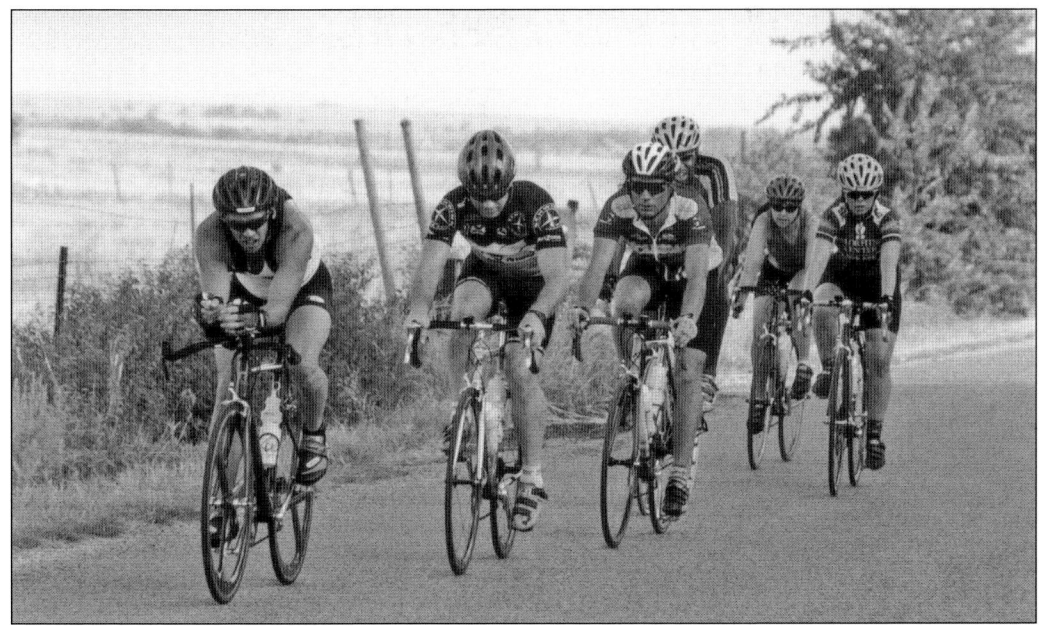

Over 2,500 riders from across the country compete in the annual Goatneck Bike Race, organized by the Cleburne Jaycees. Since 1987, racers compete in the 10-mile, 27-mile, 41-mile or 100-kilometer legs of the race beginning at Cleburne High School. Local organizations provide water and rest stops along the bike path. (Courtesy of Bob Force.)

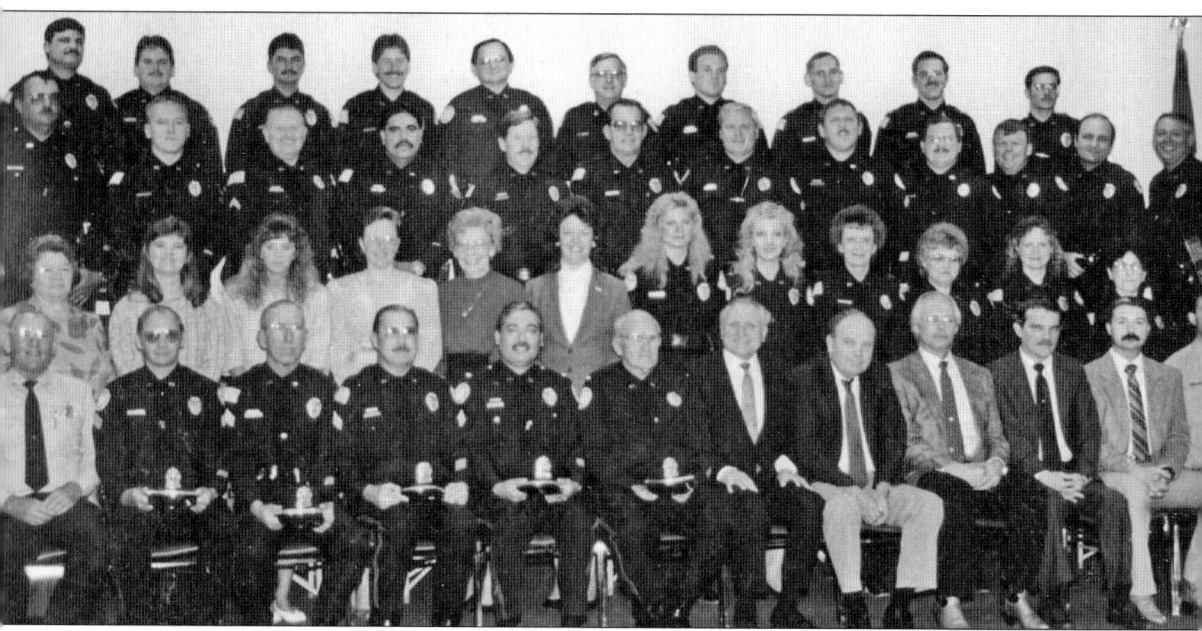

The Cleburne Police Department in 1989 was, from left to right, (first row) Fred Langston, Sgt. James Morton, Sgt. Al Stone, Sgt. Ronnie Martin, Lt. Tony Vidaurri, Lt. Bill Hudson, Chief Claude Zachry, Lt. N. H. Laseman, Sgt. Tom Hargrave, Cpl. Paul Haley, Cpl. Terry Powell, and Jerry Dean; (second row) Signe Harrell, Karmen Bootz, Leslie Johnson, Cheryl Cappers, Bernice Proffitt, Maureen Goebner, Cathy Kinney, Nila Plwers, Judy Davis, Karen Lusk, Tammy Cockerham, and Pam Gallop; (third row) Cpl. Steve Aston, Bob Redding, Cpl. Ron Miller, Robert Vidaurri, Steve Grady, Bob Killinger, Cpl. Jack Rosiere, Cpl. Martin Griffith Jr., Bill Black, Kent Grover, Richard Powers, and Cpl. Jerry Scott; (fourth row) John Bell, Mark Malcom, Tom Moore, Russell Payne, Steve Carter, Rick Goon, Danny Rogers, Chris Moody, Kenneth Meador, and Michael Irwin. Deputy Chief N. H. Laseman joined the Cleburne Police Department in 1964 and is the most senior officer in the department. He has been the commander of the Criminal Investigations Division since 1976. In 2009, the police department had 55 officers and 22 civilian support personnel. (Courtesy of Deputy Chief Tony Vidaurri.)

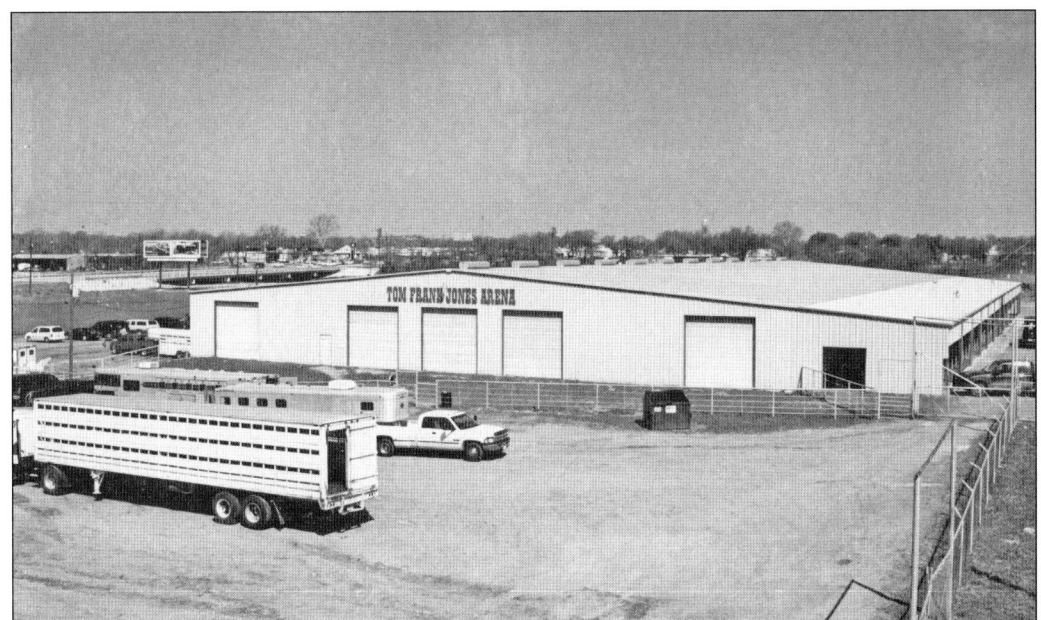

Johnson County Sheriff's Posse purchased 33 acres on South Main Street in 1962. The arena was built in 1963 complete with restrooms and six rows of bleachers. The Blue Barn was built in 1964 as well as additional bleachers plus 59 box seats. An indoor arena was constructed in 1988 on the grounds and was later named to honor volunteer Tom Frank Jones. By 1995, seating capacity reached 5,000. (Courtesy of Sandra Davis Jones.)

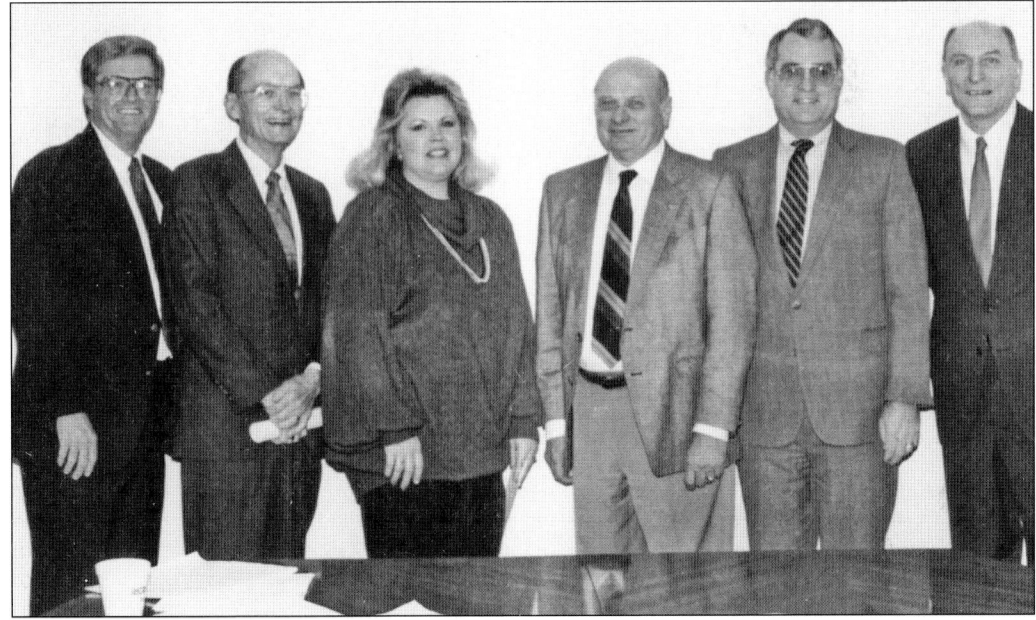

Cleburne Economic Development Foundation began in 1963 and partners with the chamber of commerce, Cleburne Independent School District, city and county officials, and others to attract industries to the area. In 1989, the board officers were, from left to right, Eddie Saylors, Bill Anderson, Diane Bryant, Dr. Larry Willis, Jerry Wheatley, and Lowell Smith. Over 40 industries currently provide jobs. (Courtesy of Layland Museum.)

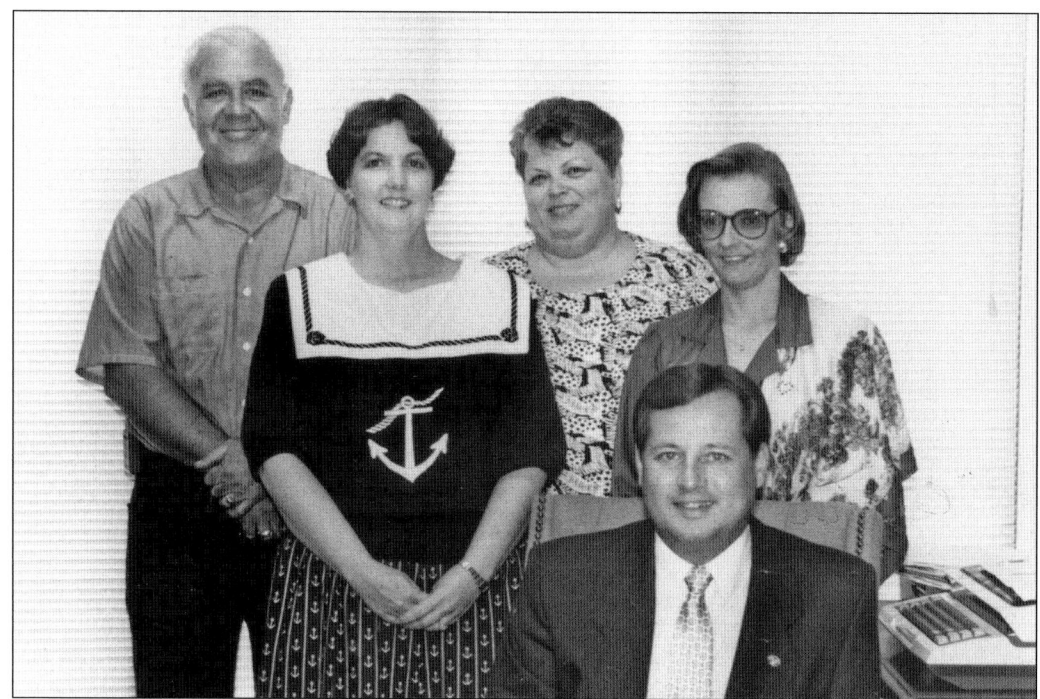

The Cleburne Ex-Students Association works with the school district to organize the annual homecoming parade and select the Coming Home Queen and Wall of Fame award winner. Association dues benefit the Alumni Scholarship Fund. The interest from this $1 million trust provides scholarships to graduating seniors. The 1990 officers pictured are, from left to right, Gary Lillard, Sheryl Hudzieth, Virginia Prine, Carol Whitworth, and Mike Lehrmann (seated). Jack Burton was the first president. (Courtesy of Layland Museum.)

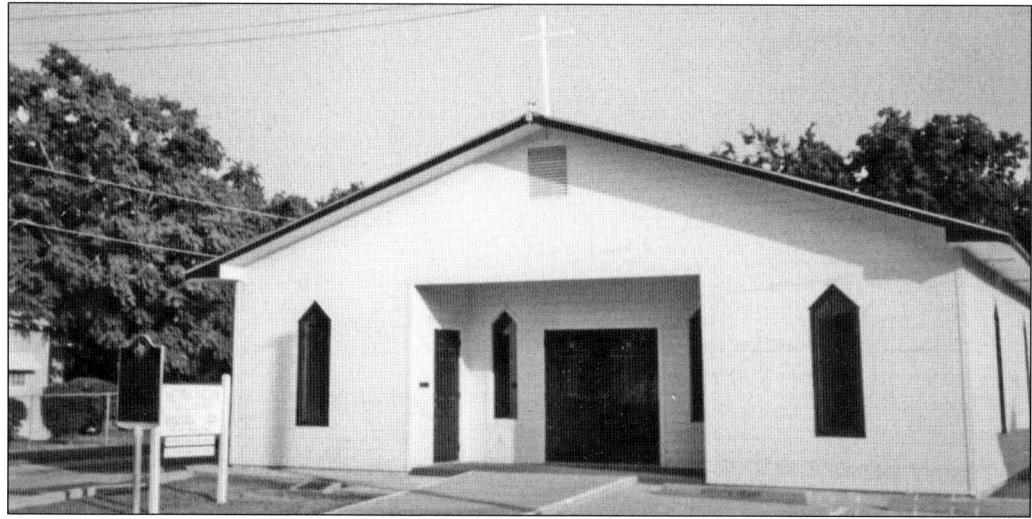

Rev. John Warren became pastor of Bethel Salter Chapel African Methodist Episcopal Church in 1992. That same year, the aging building at 106 Olive Street was replaced with the help of community volunteers. First established in Cleburne in 1887, this church and another community church in Oak Hill merged to form one congregation. A historical marker was dedicated in 1997. (Courtesy of John Warren.)

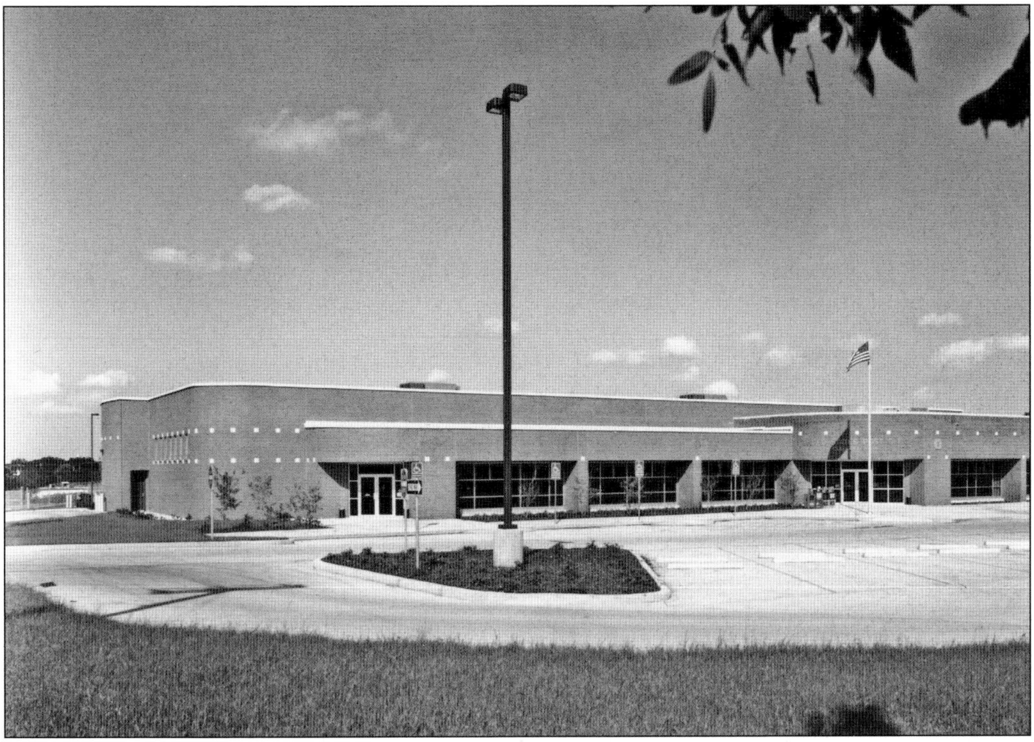

The 1912 federal post office was renovated and became home to Cleburne City Hall as a Main Street Project under the Texas Historical Commission for the Preservation of Historic Structures. The population of Cleburne was over 22,000 by 1990, and a new facility was necessary. Pictured is the new post office, which opened on Faircrest Drive in 1991. (Courtesy of Bob Force.)

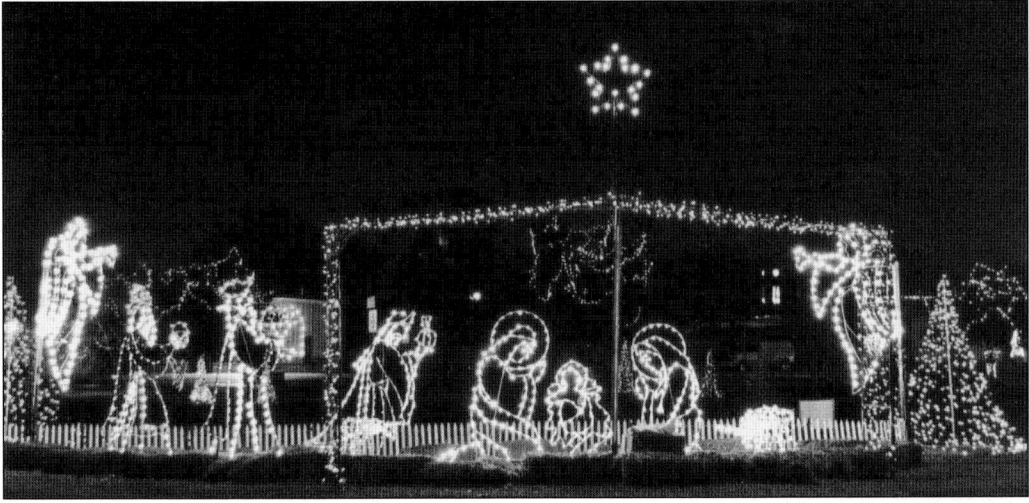

Since 1996, Hulen Park glows with over three million lights during the holidays for Whistle Stop Christmas. Rebecca and Robert Roe were instrumental in organizing this annual event. Always popular is the steam engine 3417, which was relocated to the park in 1954. Volunteers, including Bob Force and Nell and Troy Dixon, help assemble the displays, coordinated by the City of Cleburne, the chamber of commerce, and the Johnson County Sheriff's Department. (Courtesy of Bob Force.)

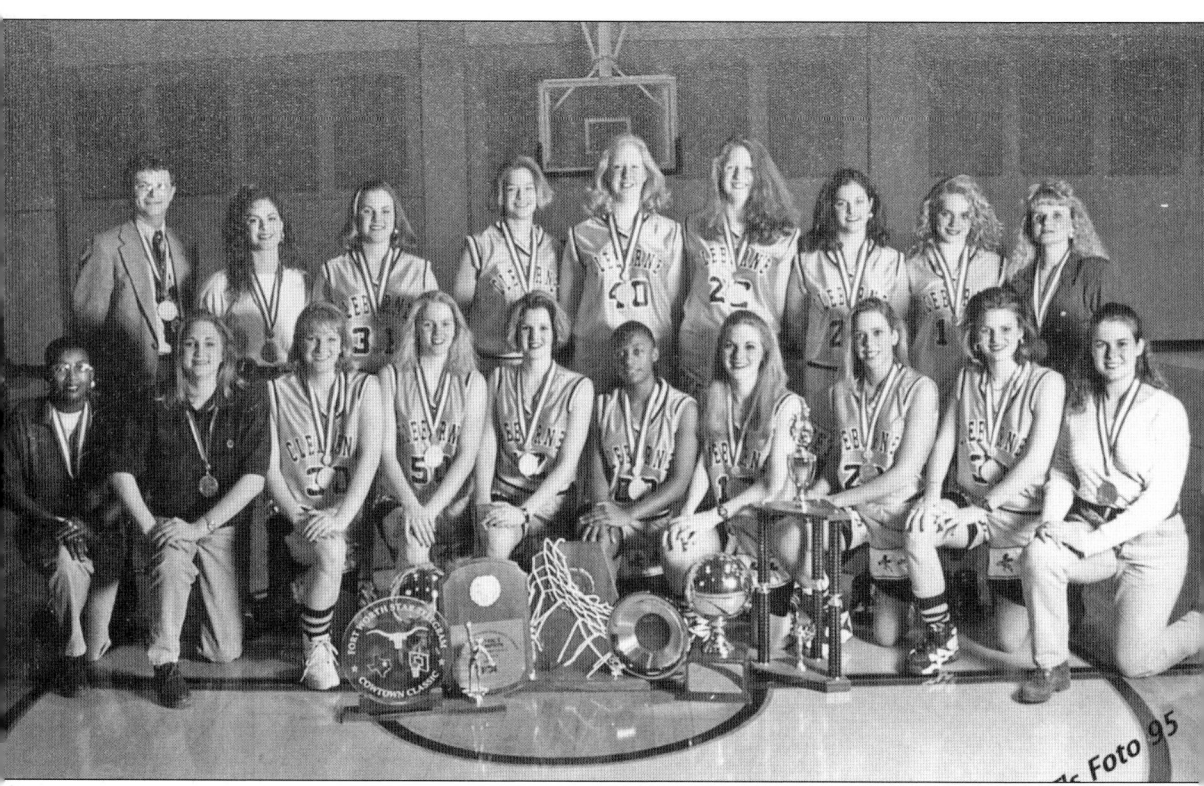

The Cleburne High School girls' basketball team beat Silsbee 55-50 in 1995 to win the state title. A town-wide reception and parade was held to honor the team and coaching staff headed by Judy Brown. Pictured are, from left to right, (first row) Effony Wooldridge, Brandi LaCombe, Brei Silvia, Megan Parker, DeAnne Fagan, Mary Rochelle, Kalani Ross, Wendy Bullard, Kim Lummus, and Ande Kelso; (second row) assistant coach Bill Rehl, freshman coach Paige Younger, Melanie Oppel, Kristin Shewmaker, Lily Glick, Amy Lavender, Amy Yeats, Kelli Tull, and coach Judy Brown. During her senior year, team leader Kim Lummus made every all-state team and was the 4A Player of the Year as well as Most Valuable Player of the state tournament, where she scored 34 points, including 10 three-pointers. Lummus went on to play at the University of Texas and to coach at the University of California–Irvine, and she was inducted into the Texas High School Hall of Fame in 2003. (Courtesy of Chuck Lummus.)

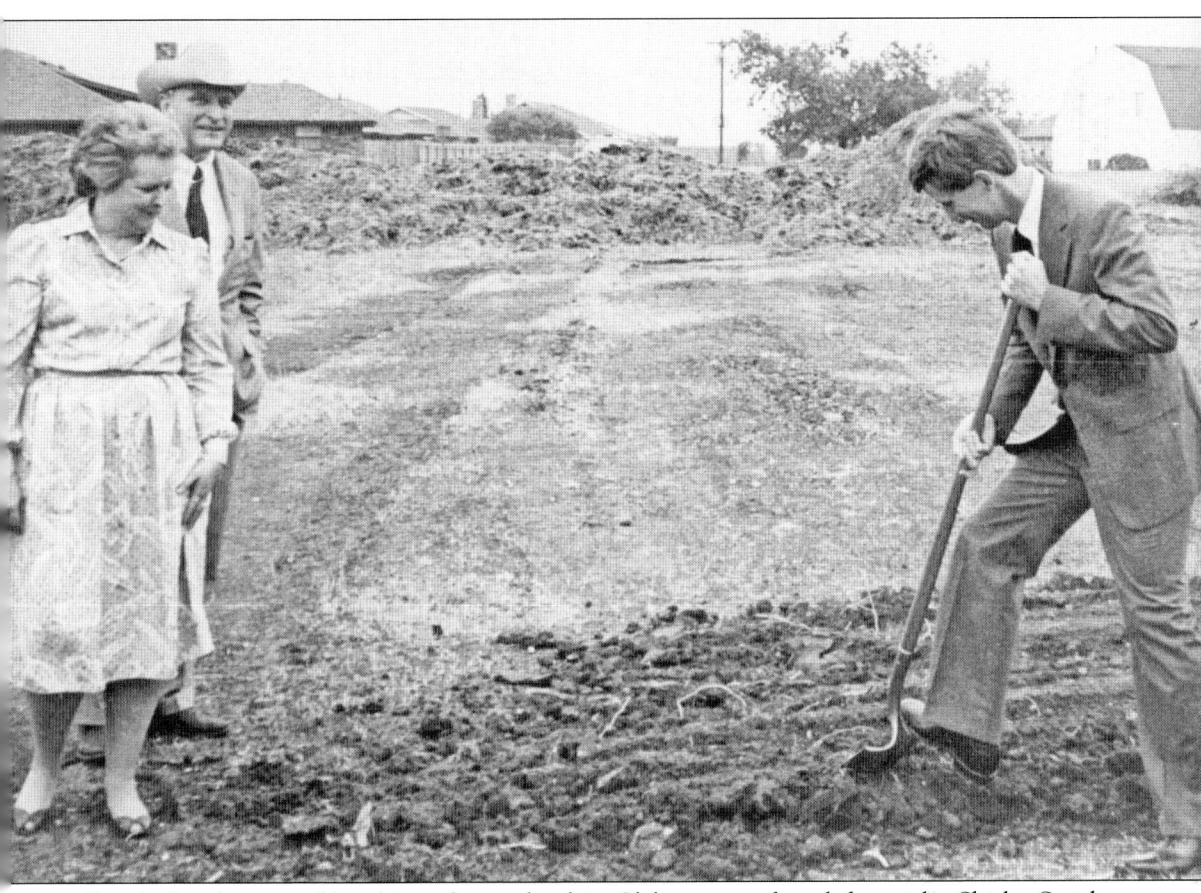

Pictured at the ground breaking of a new bank in Cleburne are, from left to right, Shirley Smith, Lowell Smith, and Larry Parker, who oversaw the construction of the bank and was the president when the facility opened in 1985 as Johnson County Bank, N.A. After a law regarding branch banking changed, it merged with the Cowpasture Bank in Rio Vista and the name changed. Lowell Smith was chief executive officer and chairman of the board of the legendary Cowpasture Bank, also known as the First State Bank of Rio Vista. He is an active member of the Cleburne Rotary Club and was instrumental in starting the vocational and technical scholarships awarded each year. He received the Chamber of Commerce Lifetime Achievement Award in 2006 and was recognized for 50 years in banking by the American Bankers Association. Lowell Smith Jr. Middle School in Cleburne, where he and Shirley volunteer each week, is named in his honor. One of the first freestanding ATMs in the area was opened by Lowell Smith about 1980 on the corner of Ridgeway Drive and West Henderson Street. (Courtesy of Smith family archives.)

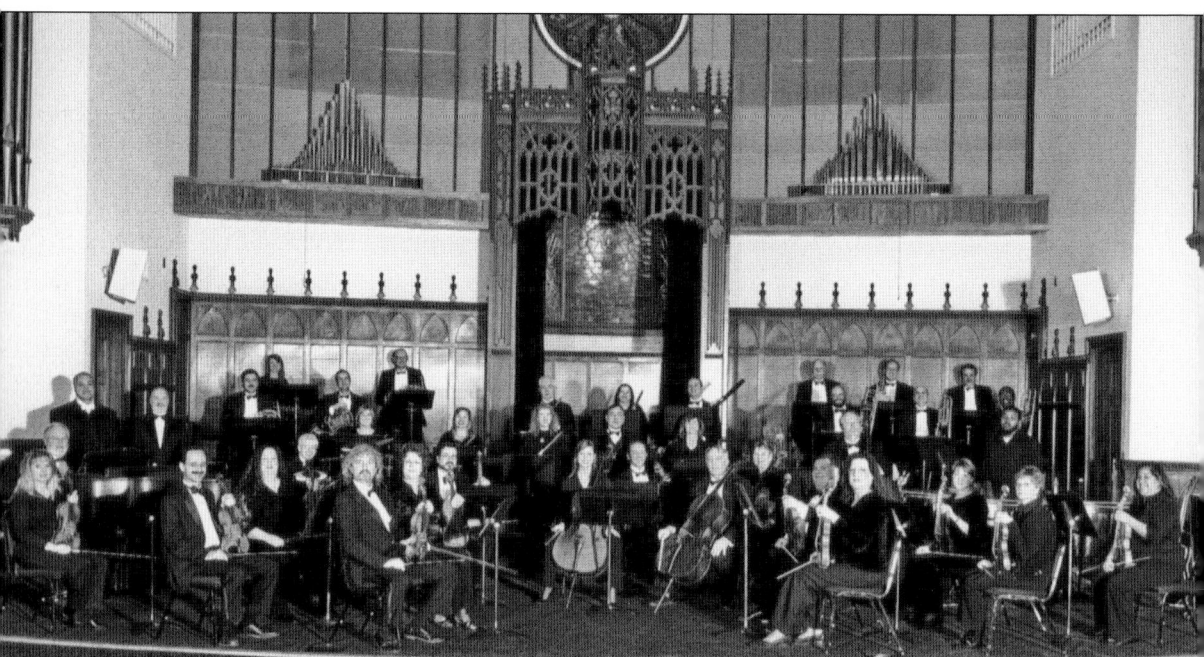

The Brazos Chamber Orchestra, founded in 1998, brings symphony music to Cleburne and the county several times a year. The orchestra is made up of 45 wind, string, brass, and percussion musicians from this area and the metroplex. Programming consists of a cross section of music from the classical repertoire and popular music from all time frames of the 20th century, including music from Broadway, the movies, and popular music. Members include Susan McGinnis, Melvin Harrison, concertmaster Kurt Sprenger, Sharon Hawkins, Kristi Harrison, Megan Spivey, John Boyd, Dawn Davis, Shilloy Garman, Michael Stringer, Kim Payne, conductor David Anavitarte, Bill Whitworth, Darrell Spooner, Brett Hawkins, Simone Garman, Todd Evans, Jeffrey Raymond, Mary Maneikis, Bob Gracey, Taylor Brooks, Jen Frederick, Debra Midkiff, Catherine Duncan, Jon Shipley, Karen Victor, Charles Renfro, Randal Senter, John Stone, Terrie Bayless, Ryan Beaty, Shane Johnson, Randy Jones, Tyrone Block, Emily May, David Clarke, Ron Poarch, Jimmy Tullos, and Ramon Dinsdale. (Courtesy of Brazos Chamber Orchestra.)

# Six

# 2001–2009

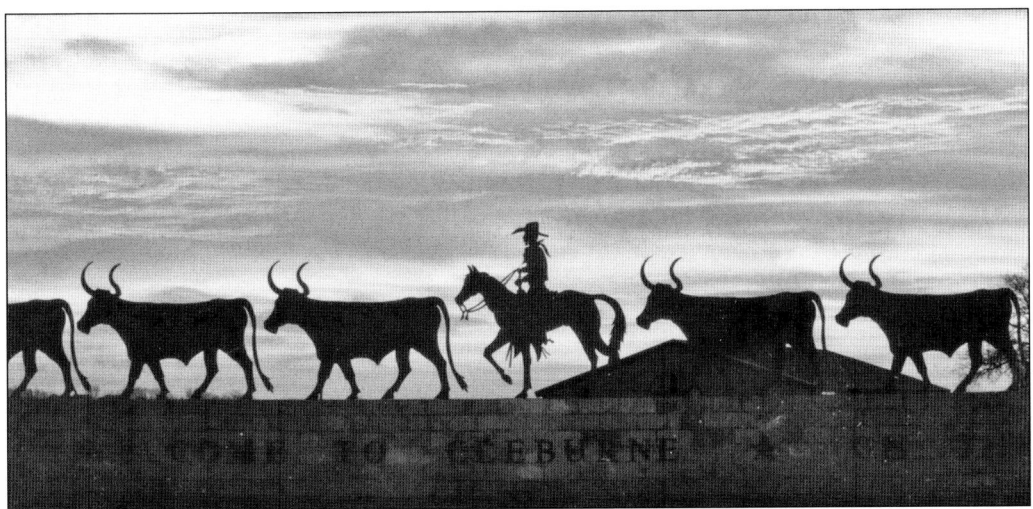

Cleburne merchants once welcomed cowboys who made a living driving herds of cattle on the dusty Chisholm Trail. This sunrise image features a silhouetted cattle drive welcoming travelers to town at the Chisholm Trail Outdoor Museum on the west bank of Lake Pat Cleburne. The museum opened in 2005. The log courthouse, built in 1854, was used when Wardville was the county seat and is now restored and back in the place of its origin at this site. (Courtesy of Max Robertson.)

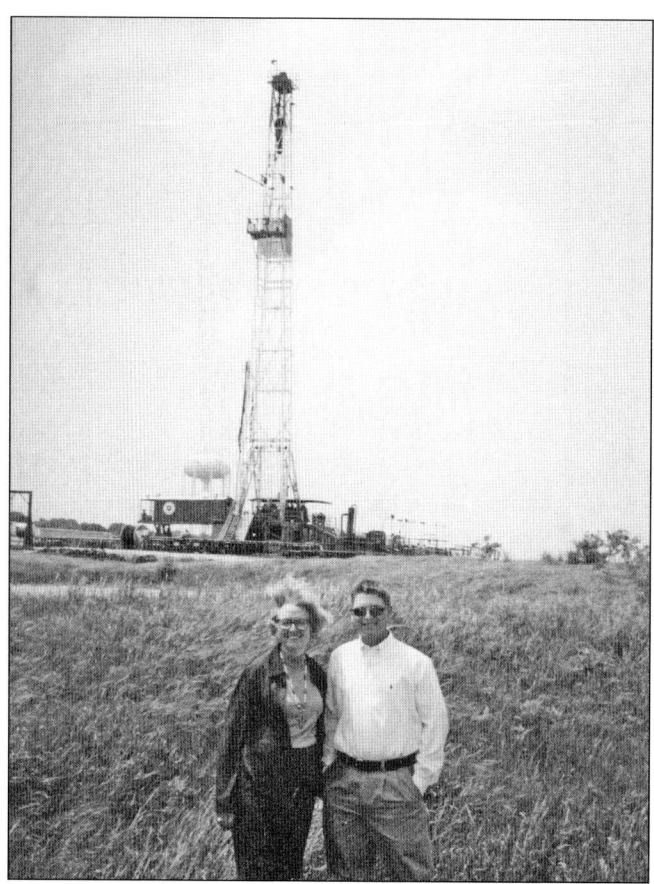

The Barnett Shale is located deep beneath the farms and homes of generations of pioneers and modern-day settlers in Cleburne. Now drilling rigs, water trucks, pipelines, and royalty checks flow throughout the city. Motels and restaurants were packed during the heaviest drilling years. Over 150 energy-related companies have come to the area since 2001. Hallwood Energy Corporation drilled the first gas well in Cleburne—S. Mann No. 1, owned by Dorothy and Sam Mann—in 2002 near Industrial Boulevard and Highway 171. This was also the first producing well in the county. Pictured are Dorothy Mann and grandson Adam Mann. Fracking of the well, pictured below, is the process of injecting water, sand, and chemicals into the wells, loosening the rock, which maximizes the flow of gas to the surface. (Both, courtesy of Dorothy and Sam Mann.)

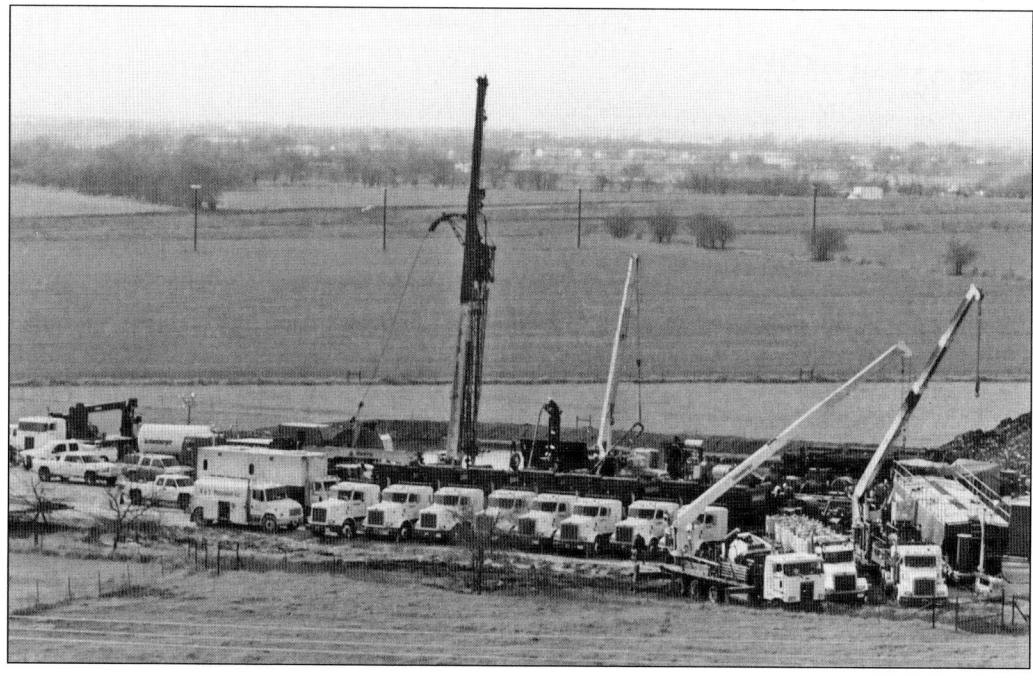

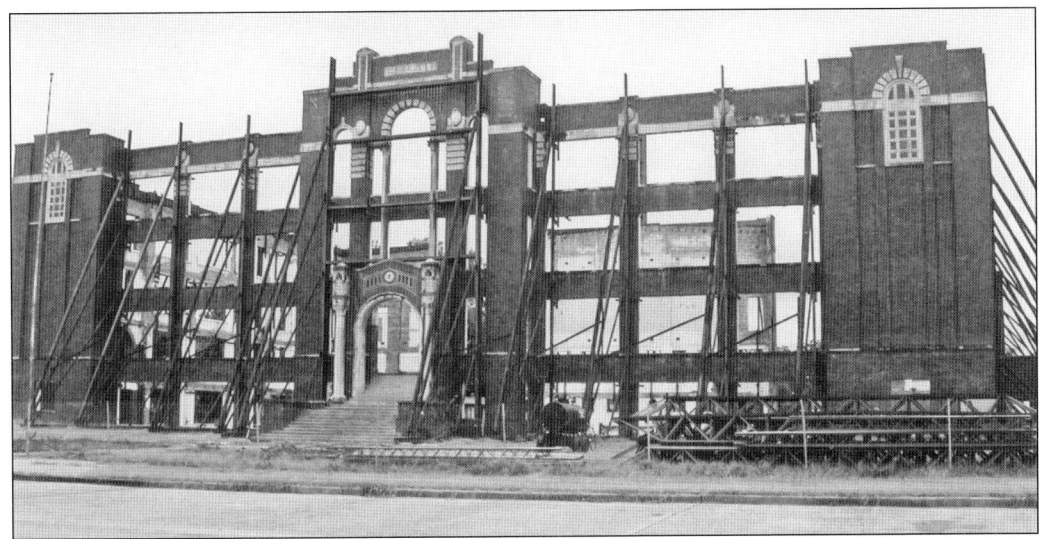

The Johnson County Guinn Justice Center dedication ceremony was held in November 2004 after a two-year complete renovation project of the original Cleburne High School by the county. The 106,000-square-foot historic building now houses three district courts, two county court-at-law, and offices for the district clerk, county clerk, district attorney, county attorney, and probation officers. It was named to honor former school superintendent Ernest Guinn. (Courtesy of the author.)

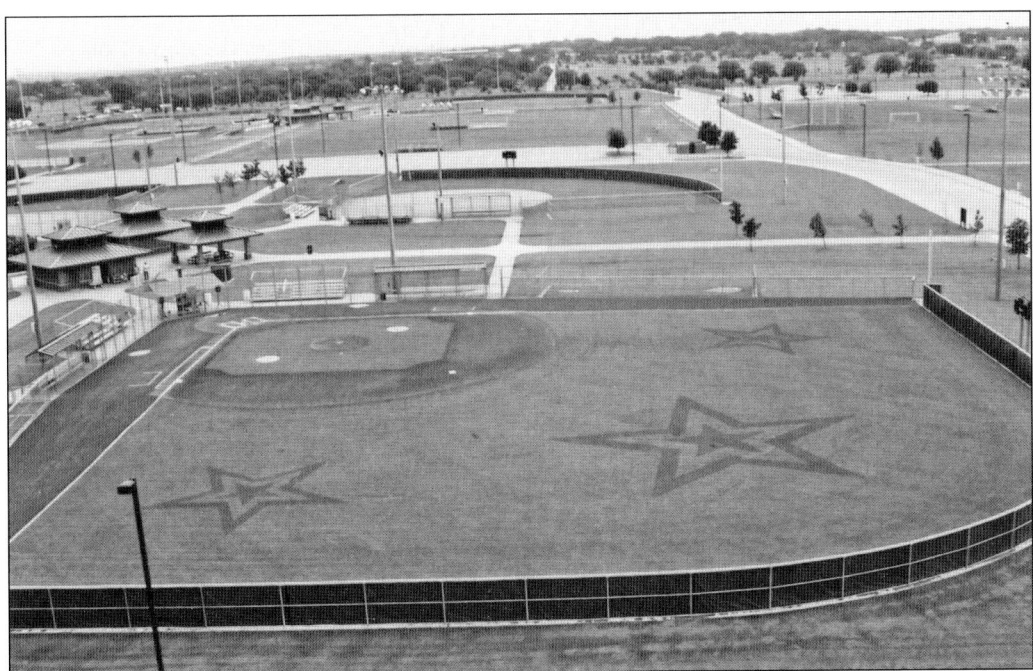

The youth sports complex is set on 90 acres in southeast Cleburne and was completed in 2005. With seven baseball/softball fields, 20 soccer fields, and two football fields, there is more than enough space for competition. Added attractions include two playgrounds, batting cages, four pavilions, and scoreboards. Funding for this project came from 4B sales tax. (Courtesy of Max Robertson.)

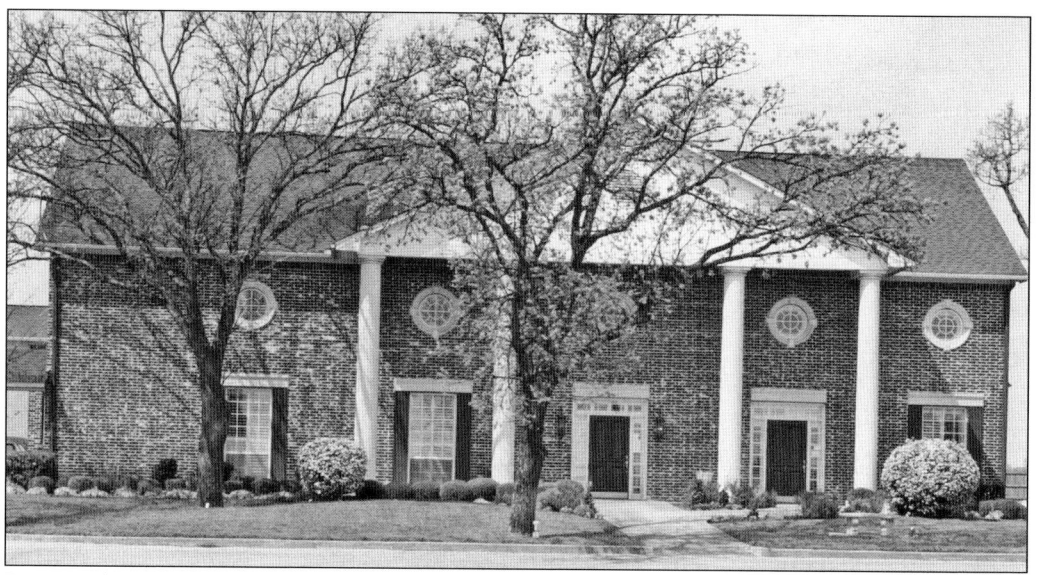

Perry and Mindi Rosser opened Rosser Funeral Home in 2001 after purchasing Martin Funeral Home. That same year, Crosier-Pearson-Mayfield Funeral Home celebrated 135 years in business. Bob Mayfield and Hunter Pearson bought the Crosier interest in the firm in 1975. In 1986, Mayfield became the owner. By 2006, Jimmy and Carol Wray expanded Cleburne Funeral Home, merging with Crosier-Pearson-Mayfield at a new location on Ridgeway Drive. (Courtesy of the author.)

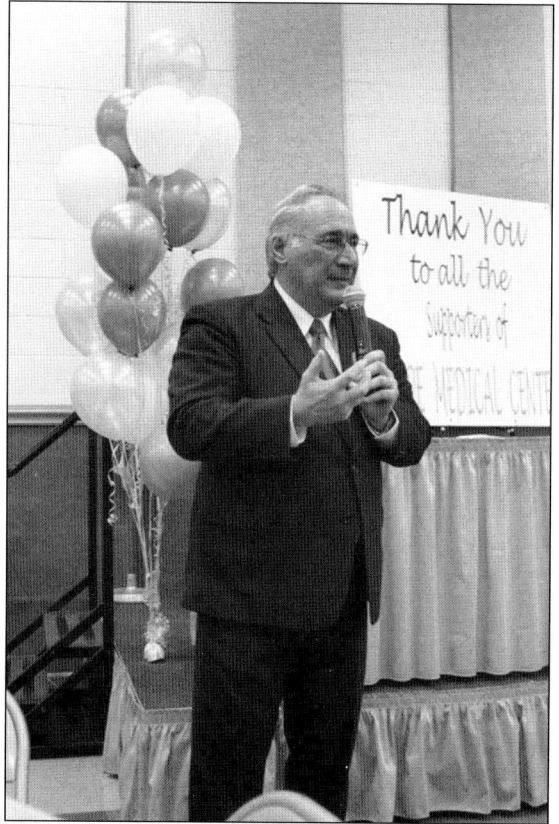

By early 2009, the staff at HOPE Clinic had already seen over 3,000 people, just two years after opening. Dr. Tony Torres—missionary, pastor, physician, and founder of the free health clinic—oversees the medical and dental volunteers who work several days a week with patients without health insurance. This image was taken at an annual anniversary volunteer event. (Courtesy of Monica Green.)

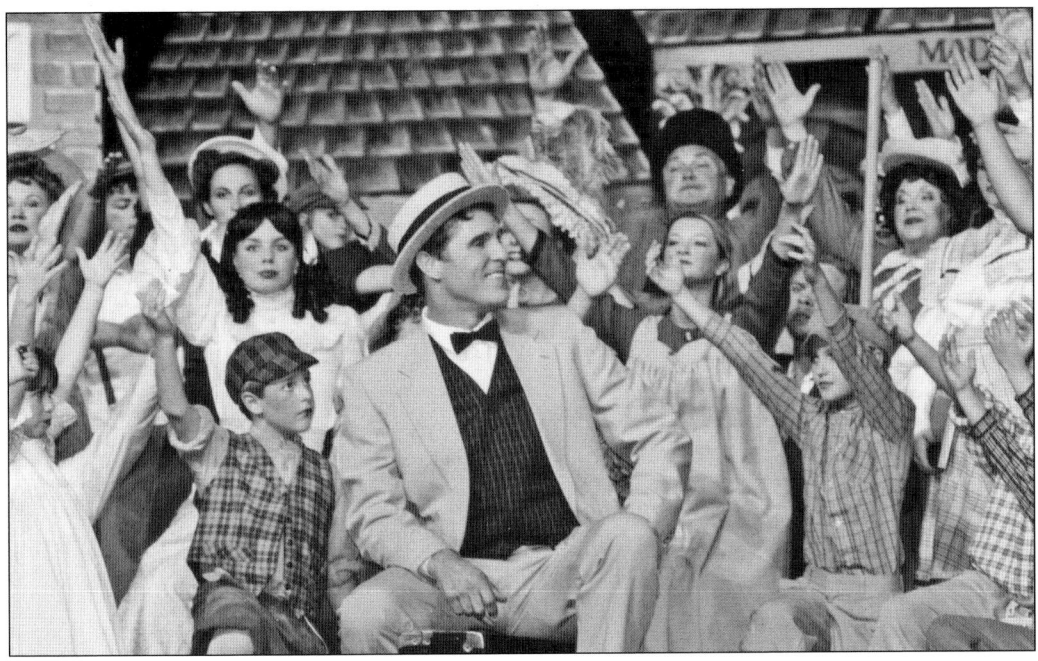

Cleburne has many cultural opportunities, including two theater groups. The Greater Cleburne Carnegie Players began their nonprofit theater group in 1980. After a two-year renovation of the second floor of the Carnegie building, they began producing live plays, and they continue with four shows a year. Pictured is Hillard Cochran (center) as Harold Hill surrounded by actors portraying townspeople of River City from the 2006 production of *Music Man*. Presenting live performances every week of the year, the Plaza Theatre Company is located just south of the courthouse on South Main Street. The building housed Cleburne Hardware for many years. Just south of this is the Wright Building, a historical mural, and several thriving businesses. (Above, courtesy of Ginny Rodgers Photography; below, courtesy of the author.)

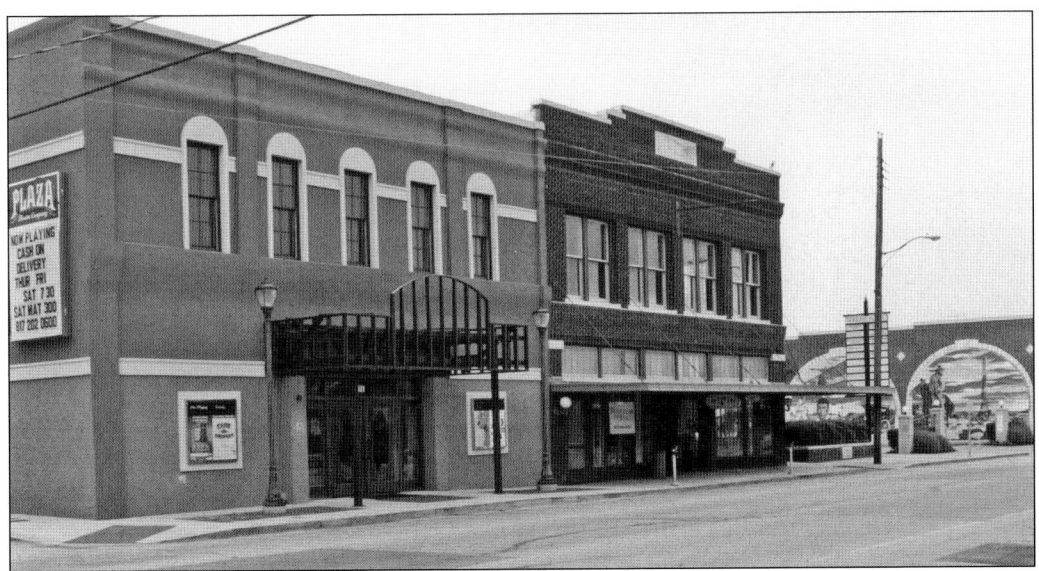

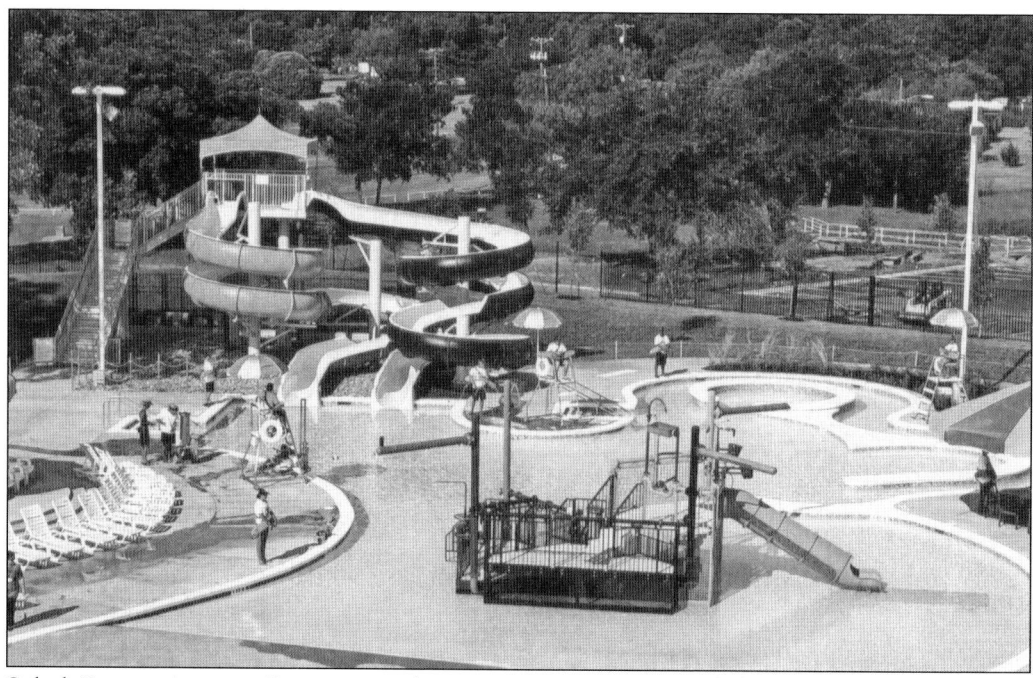

Splash Station Aquatics Center opened in 2004 in Hulen Park on the site of the aging public pool. Funding for the zero-entry leisure pool, slides, vortex pool, spray pad, and eight-lane competition pool was from the city 4B sales tax. During winter months, the large pool is covered with an air dome, providing year-round swimming. (Courtesy of Max Robertson.)

The bearer of this card is a member of
## GOOD DEEDS, INC.
and hereby promises to do one good deed each day

Member's signature

A. D. Wheat, Founder

A. D. Wheat served as Cleburne High School's agribusiness teacher for much of his 36-year career. The agricultural facility is named in his honor. He was also known for being an Aggie, for visiting residents in nursing homes, for being Citizen of the Year, and for donating toward the hospital emergency room expansion. He handed out red Good Deed Club cards, encouraging the bearer to do a daily good deed. (Courtesy of the author.)

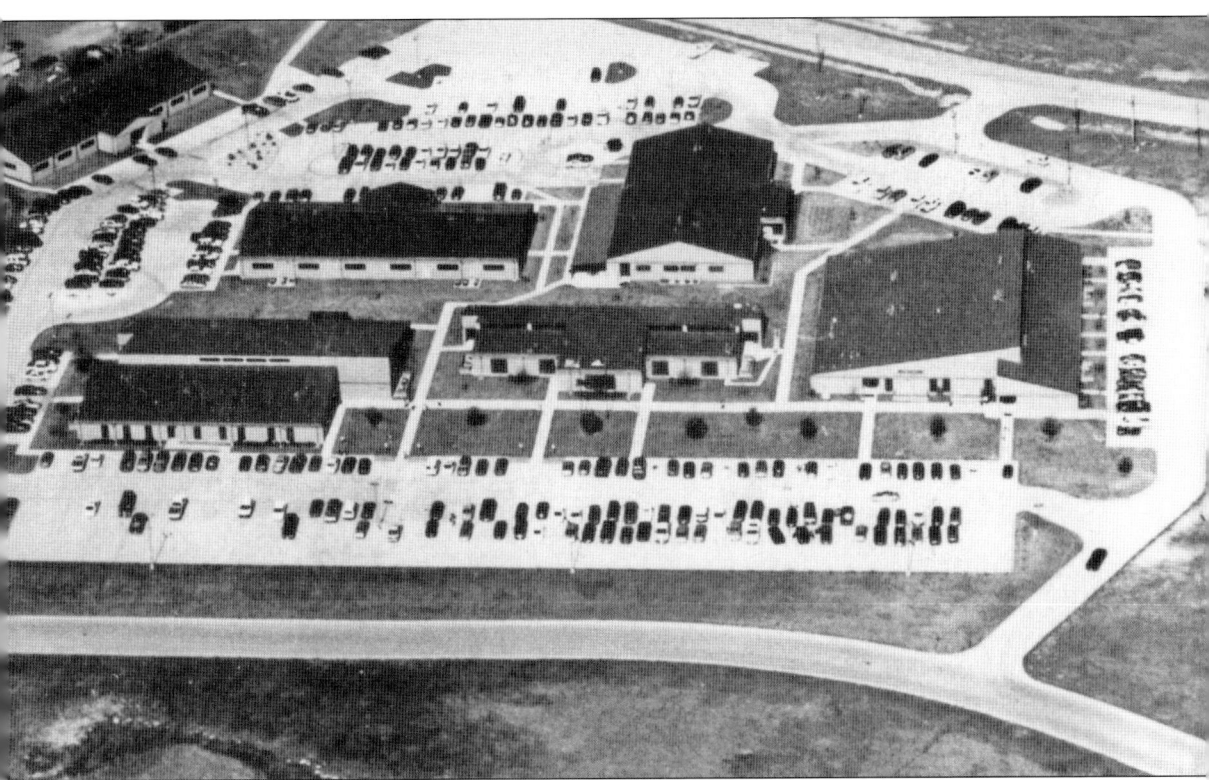

Hill College Johnson County Campus had its beginning in Cleburne from 1968 to 1974, when night classes were held in the National Guard armory (later the civic center). Prior to that time, students caught a bus to attend classes in Hillsboro. The following year, the Hill College Extension Center offered day and night classes and had 150 students. By 1976, it moved into the former fairground buildings. In 1990, college enrollment expanded, and the campus was moved to the former Cleburne High School building and the Marti buildings on Westhill Drive. With the leadership of Ed Carroll, Tom Hazlewood, Dewey James, and Eddie Saylors, a Hill College maintenance tax passed in several school districts across the county. Tolbert and Margaret Mayfield donated land overlooking Lake Pat Cleburne on Highway 67 for a campus. The first three buildings were completed in 2001, and three more were added in 2003. A. D. and Alta Mae Wheat donated funds to construct a health/science classroom building named in honor of their daughter, Margie Faye Wheat Kennon. (Courtesy of Sheryl Kappus, Ph.D.)

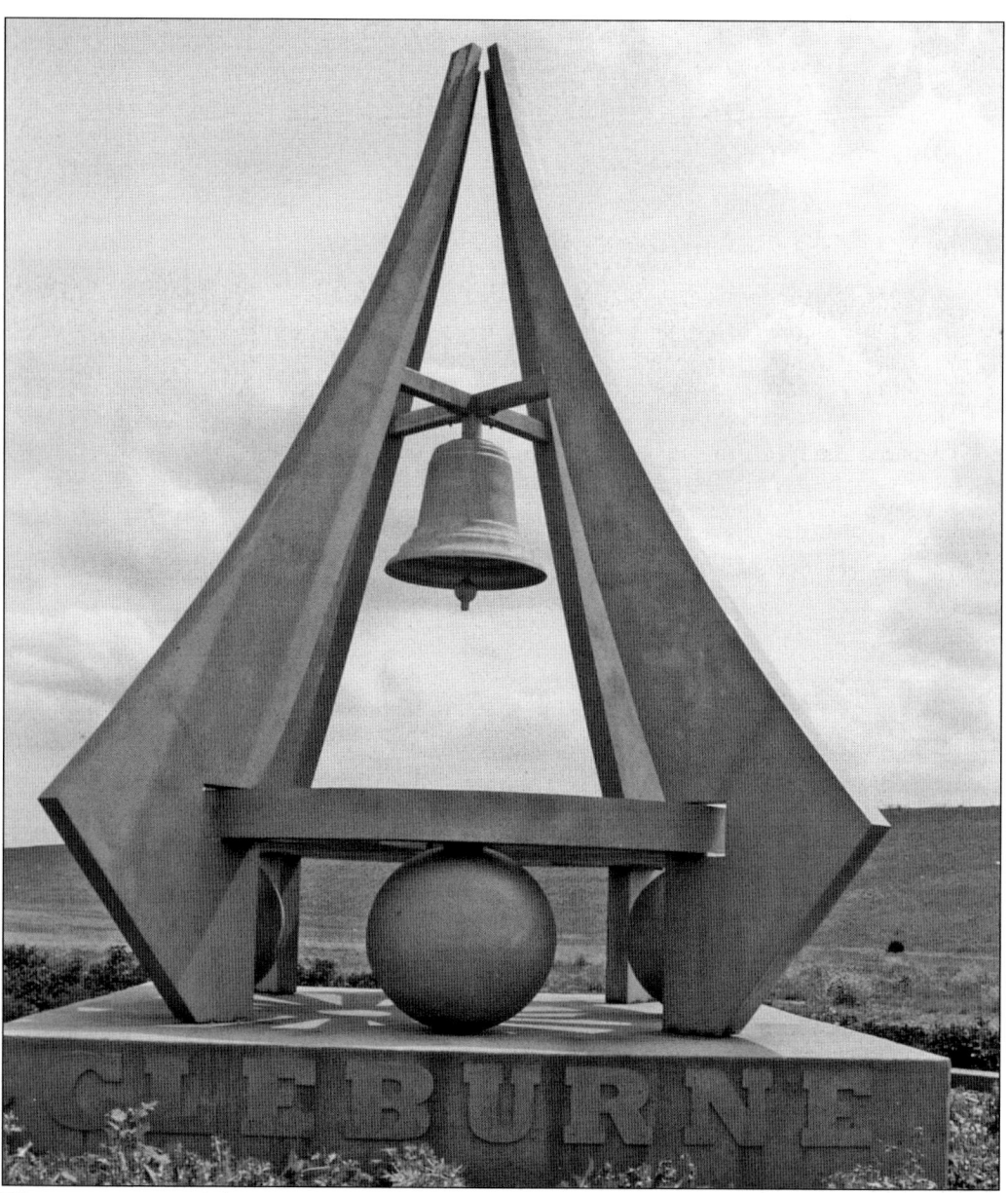

The components of the Heritage Monument symbolize diversity, progress, tradition, and honor. Designed by artist Yuri Trushin, the bell represents a voice for everyone and liberty for all. The cannonball honors Civil War commander Patrick Cleburne and also symbolizes the bearings that turn the wheels of progress. The wagon wheel, horizontal above the cannonball, represents the pioneers who moved here, the more modern wheels of the railroad industry, and continuing progress. The flame can be interpreted as a tepee representing Native American predecessors or as a gas flame honoring the Barnett Shale exploration. The four parts that make up the flame serve as a reminder that Cleburne was and still is being settled by diverse ethnicities from all directions. The stainless steel monument was built by Supreme Corporation, funded with private donations, and placed just north of the Highway 67 bypass at Highway 174 in 2007. (Courtesy of the author.)

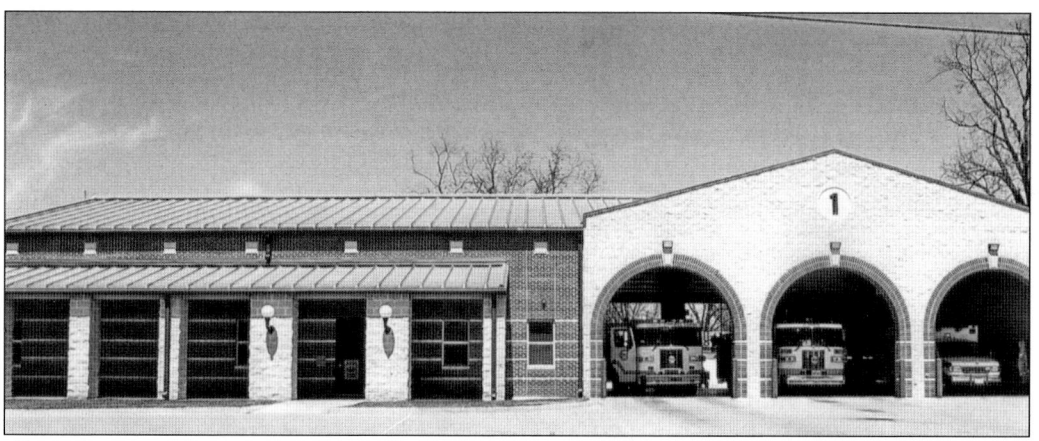

The Cleburne Fire Department operates and maintains three neighborhood fire stations like the one pictured. The fire administration offices are located in a downtown building. In 2009, the department had 55 employees and 10 pieces of equipment, including three fire engines, a Quint (a combination fire engine and ladder truck), a rescue unit, two ambulances, two brush trucks, and a boat. (Courtesy of Cleburne Fire Department.)

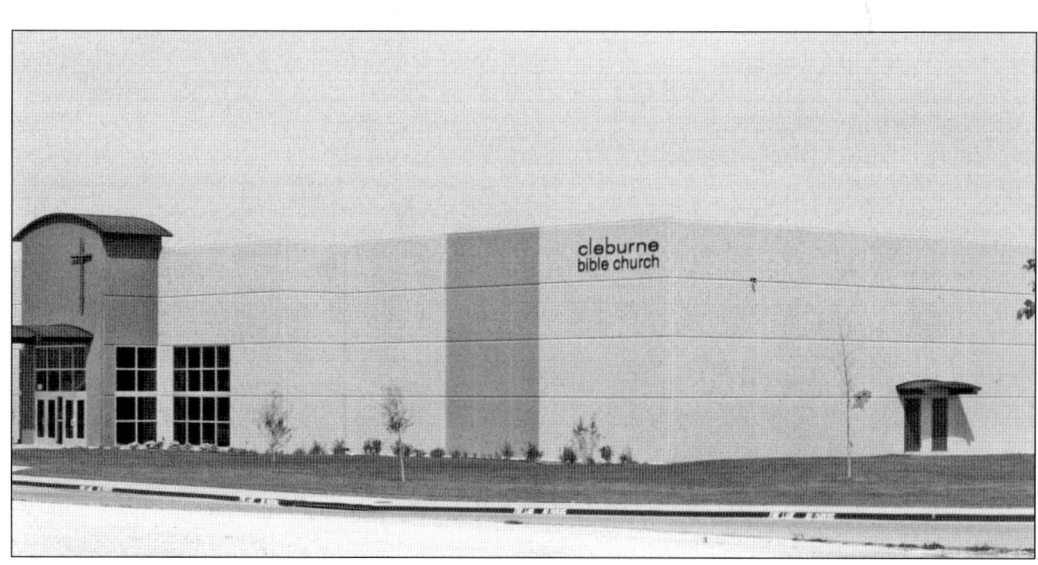

Cleburne Bible Church had its beginning in 1980 as a Bible study group and grew into a mission. By late 2008, the congregation had moved into a contemporary 33,000-square-foot worship center on Nolan River Road. The foyer is almost as large as the auditorium and is a comfortable space with leather couches, tall artistic tables and stools, and fresh coffee. (Courtesy of the author.)

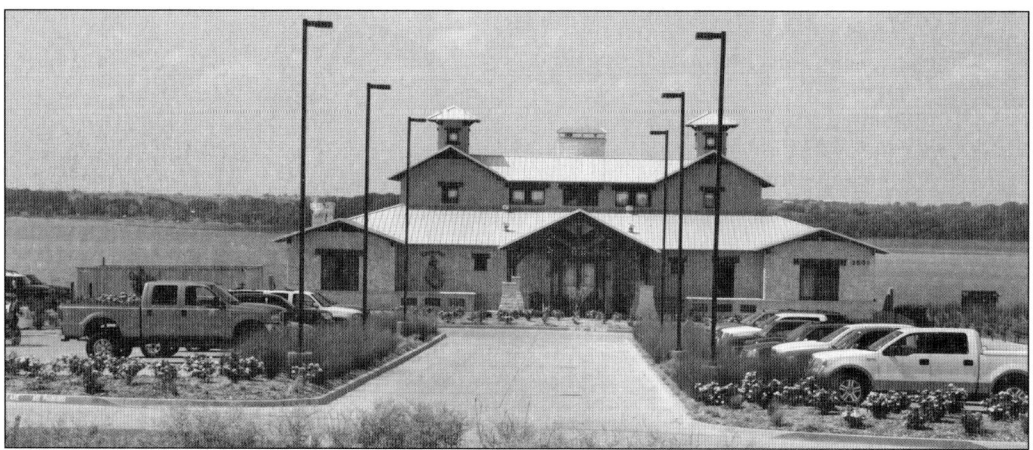

Cleburne Links Golf Course opened in the summer of 2009. Each of the 18 holes has a view of Lake Pat Cleburne. There is a large clubhouse complete with a pro shop, café, and deck overlooking the lake, making tournaments much easier to organize and produce than in the past. (Courtesy of Max Robertson.)

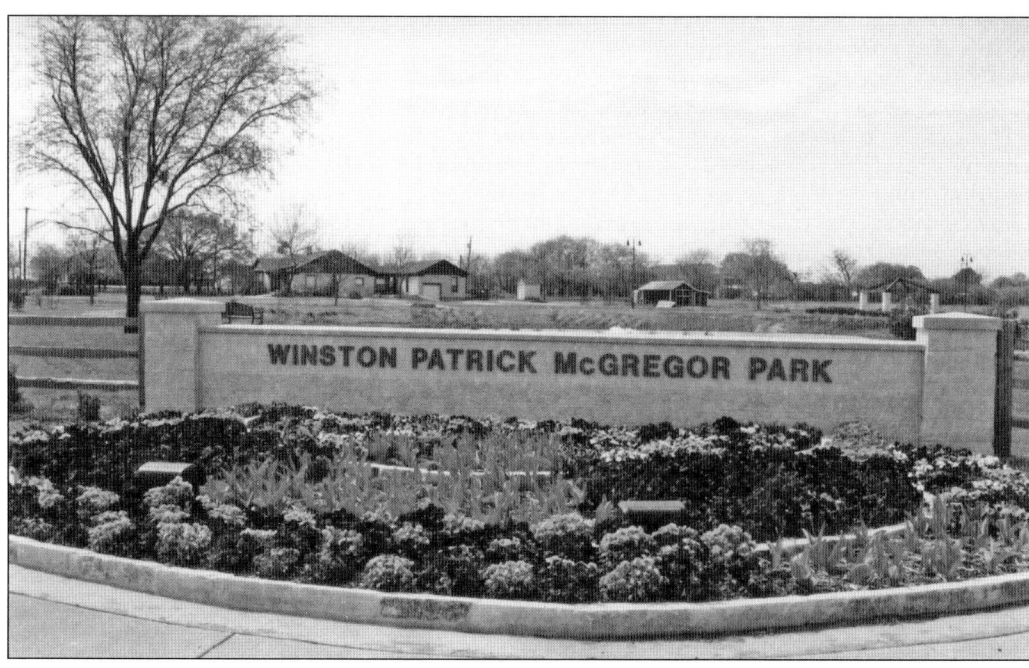

Located on the corner of West Henderson Street and Colonial Drive, Winston Patrick McGregor Park is a 10-acre botanical park with walking paths, native plants, a children's garden, and a pond with a fountain. M. Frank Scott donated the land and his home to the city of Cleburne for the purpose of creating this type of park. The remodeled house is available for gatherings. (Courtesy of the author.)

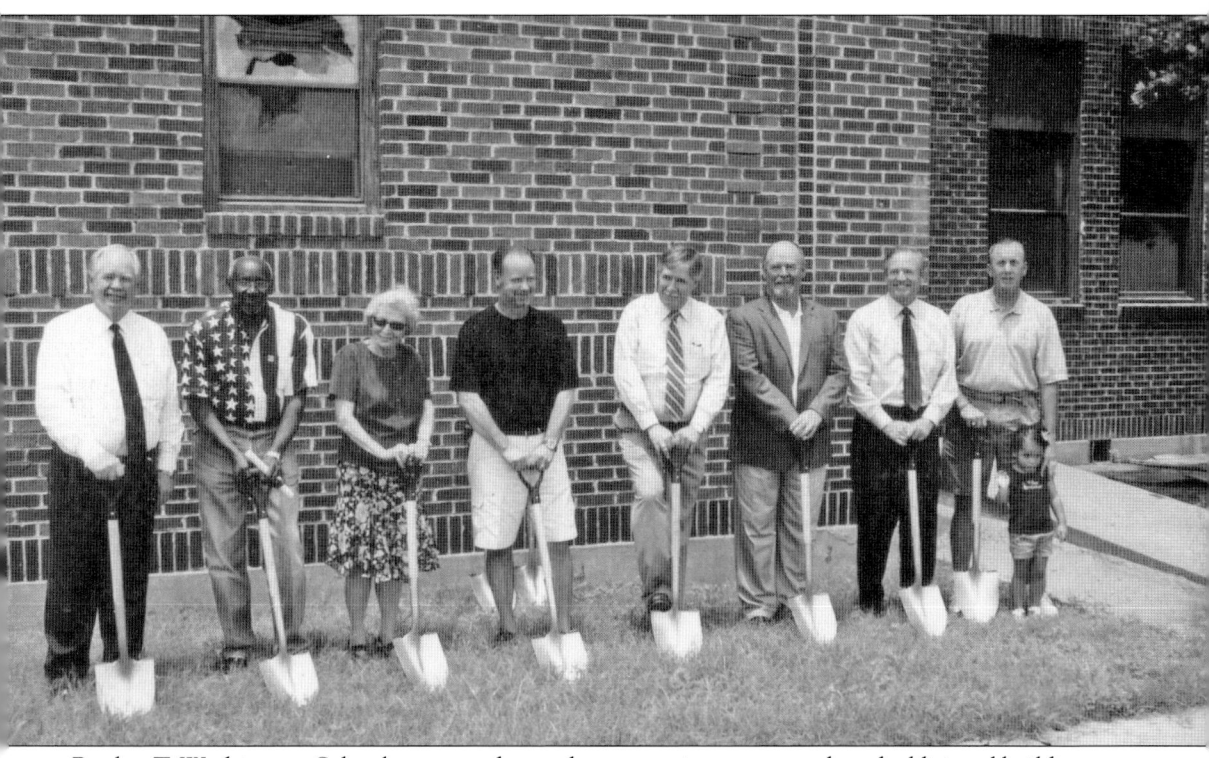

Booker T. Washington School was torn down, the gymnasium renovated, and additional buildings added. The 14,000-square-foot Booker T. Washington Community and Recreation Center opened in 2009. The facility sports a multiuse gymnasium, exercise room, commercial kitchen, computer room, and meeting rooms. A display case houses memorabilia from the former school. This was a 4B sales tax project. Pictured at the ground breaking are, from left to right, Chester Nolen, city manager; John Warren, city councilman; Ruth Ann Hill, 4B board member; Jeff Dugger, 4B board member; Dale Hannah, president of the 4B board; Ted Reynolds, mayor; Congressman Chet Edwards; Mark Banton, 4B board member; and Aynsli Lawson. (Courtesy of Cleburne Chamber of Commerce.)

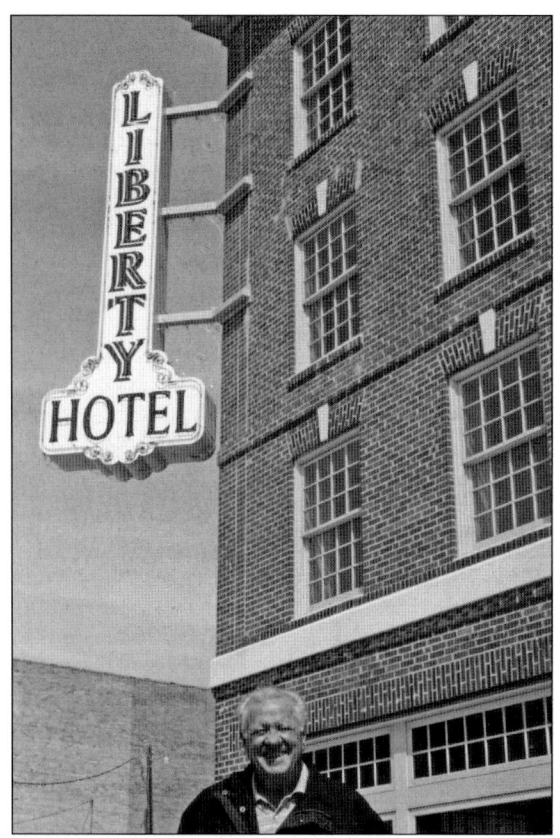

Howard Dudley, the owner of Technical Chemical Company and a progressive businessman, has been instrumental in revitalizing downtown Cleburne during the last 10 years. Dudley purchased the Liberty Hotel in 2002 and has completely renovated the historic building. The hotel, part of the Choice Hotels International franchise, reopened in April 2009 with 50 rooms. The elegant lobby has a custom-made chandelier and the original black and white terrazzo flooring. Other buildings Dudley has built or refurbished include the Wright Building, Caddo Street Grill, and several office and industrial buildings. Commissioned by Dudley, artist Stylle Read showcased the Chisholm Trail in one section of the mural located south of the courthouse. Dudley and wife Sherry also have donated funding toward the expansion of the emergency room at Texas Health Harris Methodist Hospital Cleburne and for Hill College. (Both, courtesy of the author.)

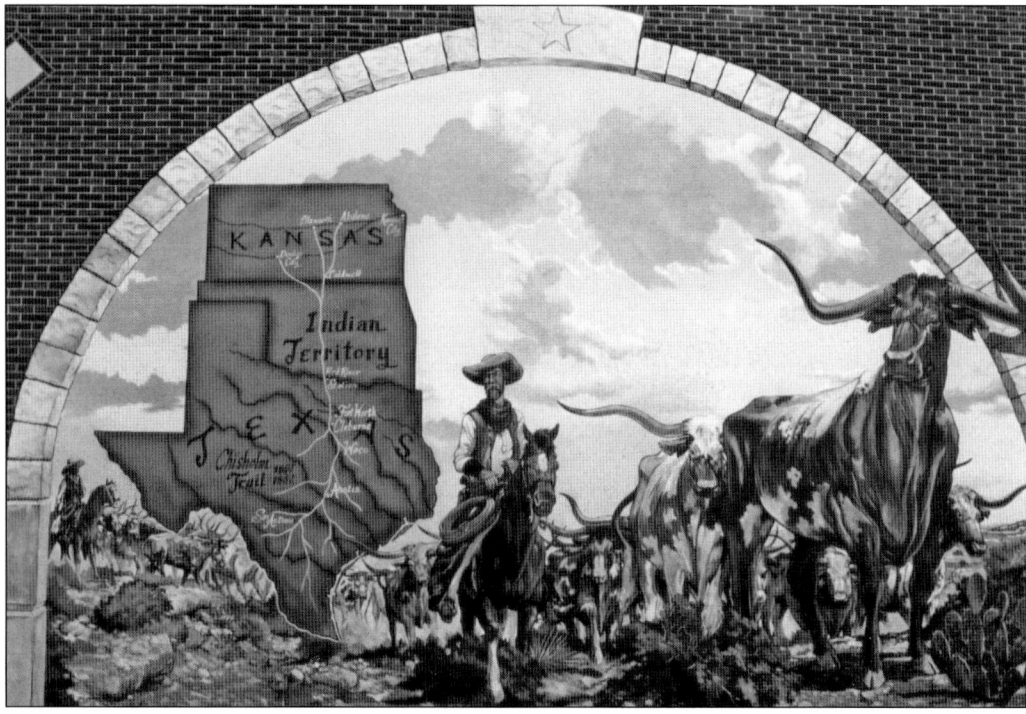

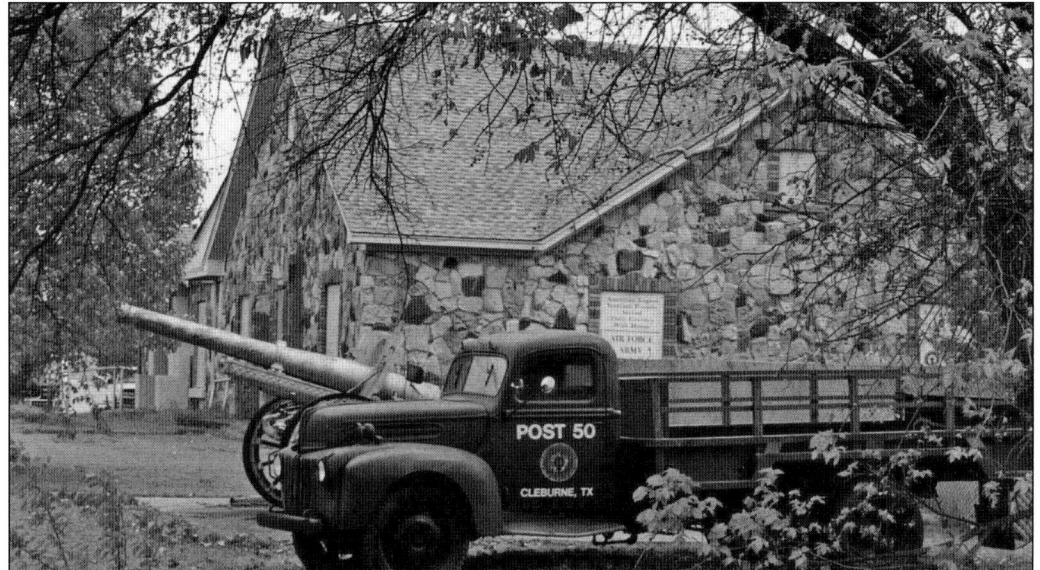

American Legion Post 50 constructed their rock building at 113 East Chambers Street on land that was once known as Biro Park. They celebrated their ninth anniversary in 2009. The park was a cooperative effort between the Cleburne Bible Club and the Cleburne Rotary Club. An active legion and auxiliary continues. (Courtesy of the author.)

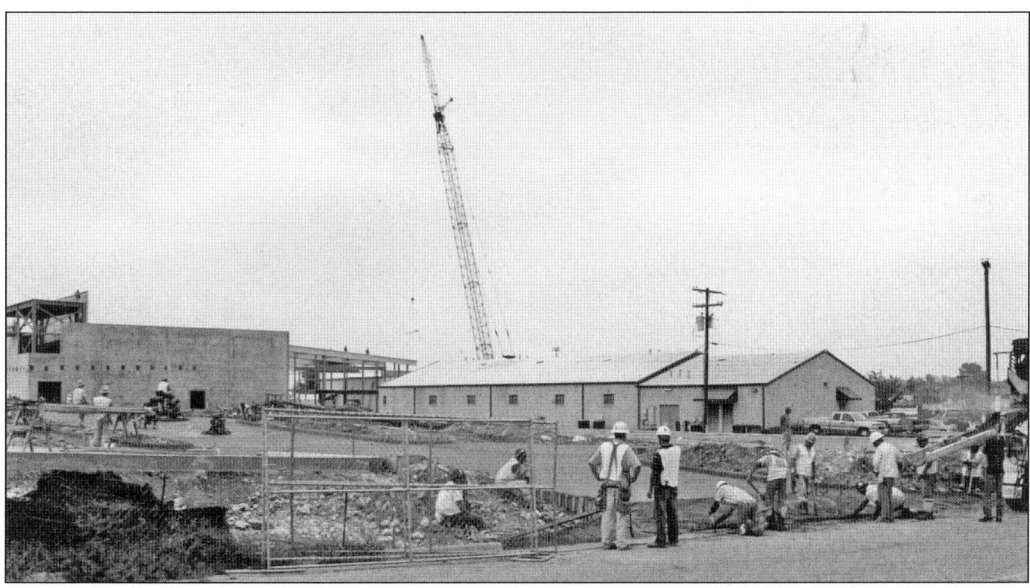

Funded by 4B sales tax, the civic center is undergoing a complete remodeling and the addition of a new building. The 45,000-square-foot Cleburne Conference Center will be ready in 2010. The Cleburne Chamber of Commerce began in 1918, and two of the original companies are still operated by family members, Patrick's Cleburne Floral and Zimmerman's Auto Supply. A new chamber facility is being planned. (Courtesy of Larry Mims.)

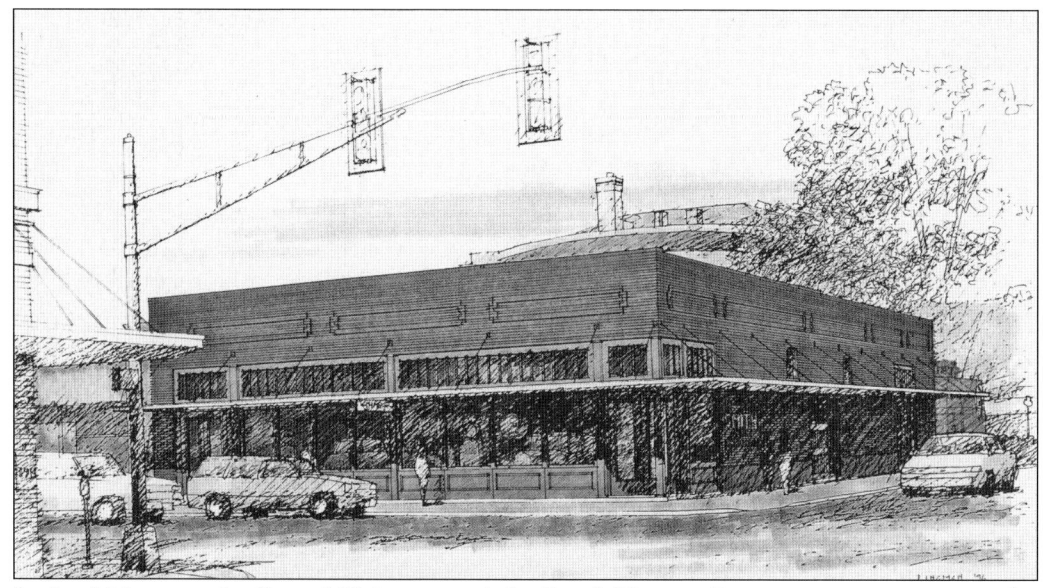

Layland Museum, the City of Cleburne, and the Smith History Center project team are in the process of rehabilitating a historic 1915 structure at 200 North Main Street. The Lowell Smith Sr. History Center will include an education center, curatorial center, artifact preservation vault, demonstration kitchen, and a 24-hour street-side automobile history exhibit. (Courtesy of Layland Museum.)

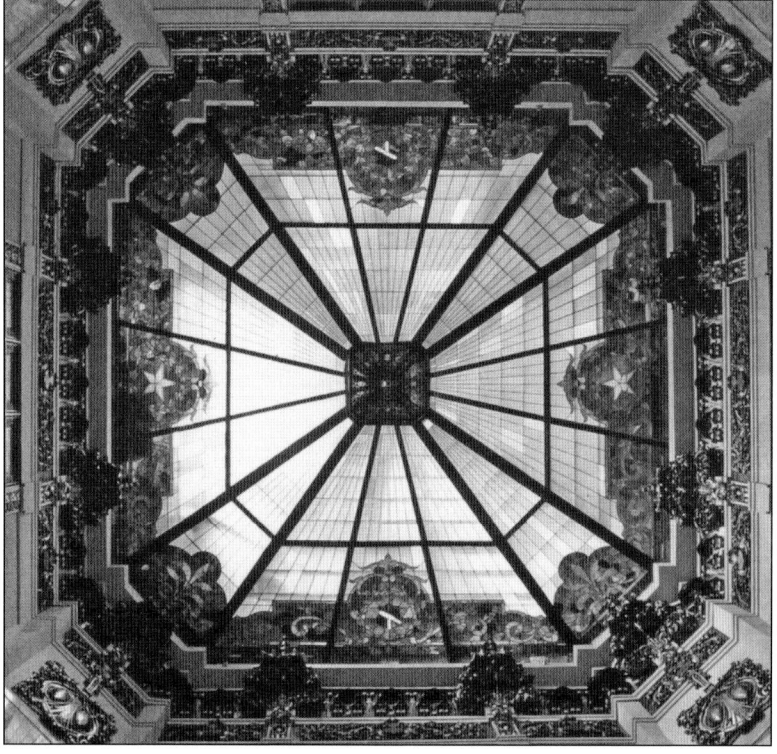

The Johnson County Courthouse is one of the most architecturally significant early-20th-century courthouses in North Texas. The atrium soars six stories, is flanked by staircases on two sides, and features Sullivanesque foliated detailing, marble walls, and an exceptional art glass dome. The 1913 building is on the National Register of Historic Places. (Courtesy of the author.)

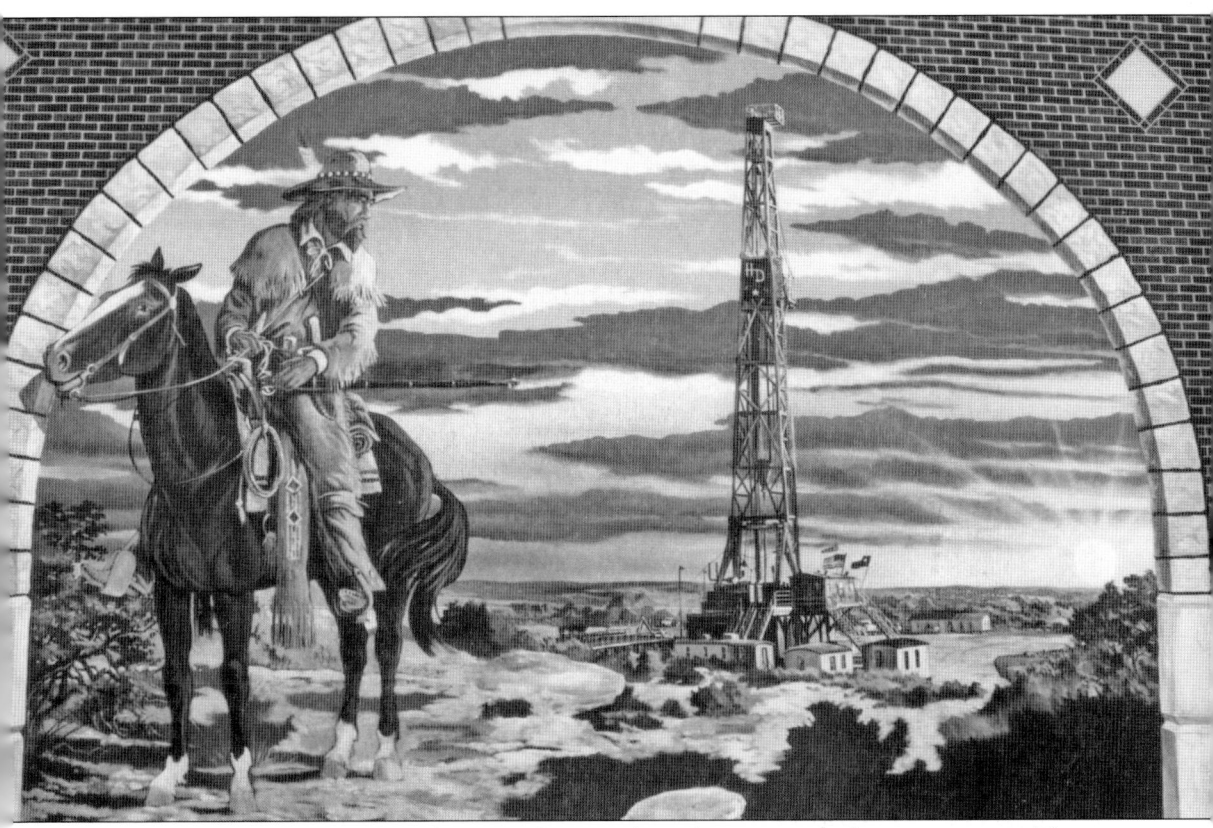

In 1900, most people worked on their own farms and ranches or operated a store in town. There were wagons circling the courthouse and at market square. The area has changed from mostly rural to a growing industrial-based community. The major industrial employers in 2008 were Wal-Mart Distribution, Pumpco Service, Johns-Manville Corporation, Rangaire Corporation, Slumberger, Ltd., Greenbriar Rail Services, Key Energy, James Hardie Building Products, Supreme Corporation, Devon Energy, Walls Industries, Technical Chemical Company, and Chesapeake Energy. This photograph, part of the historical mural commissioned by Howard Dudley and painted by Stylle Read, depicts a cowboy of the past looking forward into the 21st century. The century began with a gas-drilling boom and growth. Along with it came challenges, including preserving the historic past so future generations can understand how the community changed with the times. (Courtesy of the author.)

# www.arcadiapublishing.com

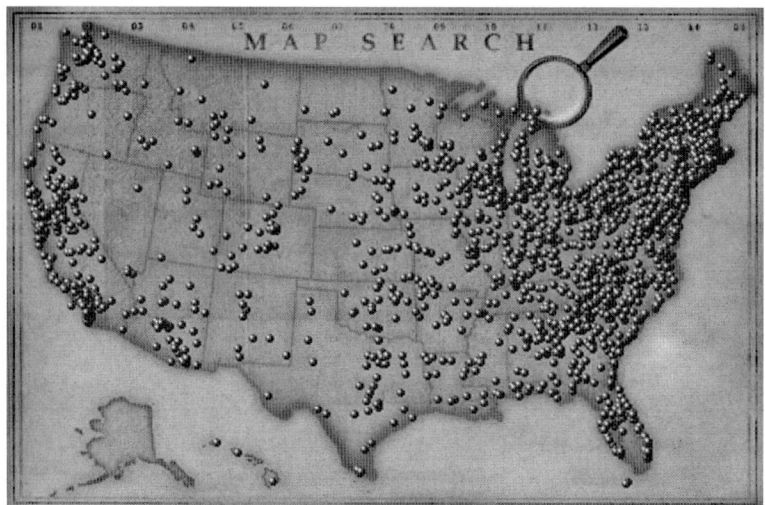

Discover books about the town where you grew up, the cities where your friends and families live, the town where your parents met, or even that retirement spot you've been dreaming about. Our Web site provides history lovers with exclusive deals, advanced notification about new titles, e-mail alerts of author events, and much more.

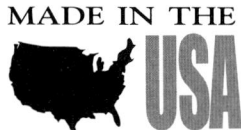

Arcadia Publishing, the leading local history publisher in the United States, is committed to making history accessible and meaningful through publishing books that celebrate and preserve the heritage of America's people and places. Consistent with our mission to preserve history on a local level, this book was printed in South Carolina on American-made paper and manufactured entirely in the United States.

This book carries the accredited Forest Stewardship Council (FSC) label and is printed on 100 percent FSC-certified paper. Products carrying the FSC label are independently certified to assure consumers that they come from forests that are managed to meet the social, economic, and ecological needs of present and future generations.

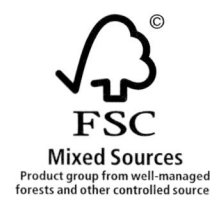

**Mixed Sources**
Product group from well-managed forests and other controlled sources

Cert no. SW-COC-001530
www.fsc.org
© 1996 Forest Stewardship Council

*Find Your Place in History.*